Human Knowledge

Publications of the Archive of Scientific Philosophy
Hillman Library, University of Pittsburgh

Steve Awodey, Editor

Publications of the Archive of Scientific Philosophy
Hillman Library, University of Pittsburgh

Human Knowledge
A Classic Statement of
Logical Empiricism

Eino Kaila

Translated by Anssi Korhonen
Edited by Juha Manninen, Ilkka Niiniluoto, and
George A. Reisch

Open Court
Chicago, Illinois

To order books from Open Court, call toll-free 1-800-815-2280, or visit our website at www.opencourtbooks.com.

Open Court Publishing Company is a division of ePals Corporation.

Designed by John Grandits.

Library of Congress Cataloging-in-Publication Data

Kaila, Eino, 1890-1958.
  [Inhimillinen tieto. English]
  Human knowledge : a classic statement of logical empiricism / Eino Kaila ; translated by Anssi Korhonen ; edited by Juha Manninen, Ilkka Niiniluoto and George A. Reisch.
    pages cm. -- (Publications of the Archive of Scientific Philosophy, Hillman Library, University Of Pittsburgh ; Volume 6)
  Includes bibliographical references and index.
  ISBN 978-0-8126-9848-0 (trade paper : alk. paper) 1. Logical positivism. I. Manninen, Juha, editor of compilation. II. Title.
  B824.6.K3513 2014
  121--dc23   2014003105

Contents

Editors' Introduction

Eino Kaila, Logical Empiricist

by Juha Manninen and Ilkka Niiniluoto

Eino Kaila (1890-1958) was Professor of Theoretical Philosophy at the University of Helsinki. In 1939 he published the book *Inhimillinen tieto: Mitä se on ja mitä se ei ole* (*Human Knowledge: What It Is and What It Is Not*).[1] The same year a Swedish translation appeared, *Den mänskliga kunskapen: vad den är och vad den icke är* (Söderström, Helsingfors; Natur och kultur, Stockholm) by Kaila's student Georg Henrik von Wright. Kaila conceived the book both as a textbook of scientific philosophy for laypersons and university students and as a systematic introduction to logical empiricism for professional philosophers. In the two countries where it could most easily be read, it performed those functions for several decades and paved the way for analytic philosophy to become a dominant trend in the Nordic countries.[2] Still, four decades later, von Wright remarked that Kaila's introduction to logical empiricism "was and still is, I think, the best of its kind"[3]–evidently better than von Wright's own exposition, *Den logiska empirismen* of 1943.

1. Helsinki: Otava, 1939. For Kaila's bibliography, see Juha Manninen and Ilkka Niiniluoto, *The Philosophical Twentieth Century in Finland: Bibliographical Guide*, *Acta Philosophica Fennica* 82 (Helsinki: The Philosophical Society of Finland, 2007).
2. For the background of analytic philosophy in Finland, and the decisive role of Kaila and his students G.H. von Wright (1916-2003), Oiva Ketonen (1913-2000), Erik Stenius (1911-1990), and Jaakko Hintikka (b. 1929), see Leila Haaparanta and Ilkka Niiniluoto, eds., *Analytic Philosophy in Finland* (Amsterdam: Rodopi, 2003).
3. See G.H. von Wright, *Den logiska empirismen: En huvudriktning i modern filosofi* (Helsingfors: Söderströms, 1943) and G.H. von Wright, "Introduction," in Eino Kaila, *Reality and Experience: Four Philosophical Essays*, ed. Robert S. Cohen, *Vienna Circle Collection* 12 (Dordrecht: Reidel, 1979), ix-xlii.

Kaila's old friend Rudolf Carnap (1891-1970) read the book in Swedish, but not without some difficulty. Shortly after he read it, Finland was attacked by the Soviet Union in the wake of the Molotov-Ribbentrop pact between Stalin and Hitler. Carnap wrote to Kaila from Chicago that January of 1940:

> From the moment Finland was dragged into the tragic events in Europe, I have thought of you very much. We follow the events with vivid concern here. The newspapers report the details daily and not only we Europeans but all Americans are united in sympathy for your country. When you wrote your letter of 12 November, you were still in peaceful Helsinki and now I do not know where you are meanwhile. [. . .] When I read the newspaper reports and see pictures of Helsinki in ruins, vivid memories reawaken of the time when I was in your beautiful city, in Wiborg, in Sortavala, on the island of Valamo, at Imatra, and other places in Finland and grew fond of your beautiful country. [. . .] I urgently hope and wish from my heart that in the not distant future a peace is made which secures Finland's independence.[4]

Finland was able to preserve her independence and democracy without ever being occupied by any of the national forces that rushed into war—but not without losing territory to its enormous neighbor to the east, including some of the areas mentioned by Carnap as he recalled his travels (one of which, Terijoki, was a popular holiday resort near St. Petersburg, where Carnap went in the early 1920s in connection with a conference dedicated to Esperanto). Most of Carnap's comments, however, concerned Kaila's book and some critical observations about it. Responding to a letter from Kaila (now lost), Carnap wrote:

> Thank you very much for sending me the book. [. . .] I found it here when I came back to Chicago at the end of December. We were in Florida for a few months, where I found a quiet place to work on semantics. Since reading Swedish costs me much time and effort, I have not read your book completely. I have gone through the main sections and read closely the section that you pointed out to me. My impression is that the book is very suitable as an introduction to the conceptions of empiricism, and I would be very pleased were it to appear in English. I especially welcome the fact that you pay attention to the historical connections. For many readers this will be very welcome, since in our existing publications the historical connections are mostly ignored.

---

4. Copies of Carnap's letters to Kaila between 1928 and 1940, rescued by G.H. von Wright, are preserved at the Finnish National Library, Helsinki.

How things stand on the question of publication from the business viewpoint of a publishing house, particularly under the current difficult circumstances, I can't say at the moment. Under normal circumstances I would think that the book would be well suited for our *Library of Unified Science*, published in Holland. I will write to Neurath that he should speak with the publisher about this question. You write that in this case you would like to revise the work. Can you quickly estimate whether you should find the time in the near future, in case the publisher will bring out the book, and how long you would need? Perhaps you could write Neurath directly about this question or send him a carbon-copy of your letters to me, so that not too much time is lost.

Nothing came of Carnap's support and suggestions. Holland was soon occupied by German troops and Otto Neurath, the editor and organizing spirit of the unified science movement, escaped on the last boat over the Channel to England. Europe descended into war. Finland went to war against the Soviet Union in the summer of 1941.

Having lost his opportunity to publish his book in English, Kaila turned to what he called his "second contribution to logical empiricism," *Über den physikalischen Realitätsbegriff* (*On the Concept of Reality in Physical Science*). When it appeared in 1942, however, this German monograph was almost completely ignored. After the war, Kaila enjoyed a very successful career in Finland where, from 1948 until his death in 1958, he was one of the first ten members of the Academy of Finland. But he never regained close contact with his old colleagues and friends who had moved from Austria and Germany to the new English-language centers of analytic philosophy. Kaila never visited England, not even when his brightest student, Georg Henrik von Wright, was from 1948 to 1951 Professor at Cambridge University as Ludwig Wittgenstein's successor. In 1948 he travelled to the United States where he met Carl G. Hempel in New York and Kurt Gödel in Princeton, and Kaila's contributions were later acknowledged in historical recollections about logical empiricism. Herbert Feigl, for instance, wrote in 1947 that "the brilliant Finnish psychologist and philosopher, E. Kaila, was present as an active and critical member" of the Vienna Circle.[5] A.J. Ayer discussed Kaila's views, as well.[6] But Kaila had published nothing in English until translations of four of his main philosophical essays appeared in the volume *Reality and Experience*

5. See H. Feigl, "Logical Empiricism," in D. Runes, ed., *Twentieth Century Philosophy* (New York: Philosophical Library, 1947), 406–8.
6. See A.J. Ayer, *The Foundations of Empirical Knowledge* (London: Macmillan, 1940).
7. *Reality and Experience*. For other translations into English, see Haaparanta and Niiniluoto, *Analytic Philosophy in Finland*, and the early essay "William James: The Philosopher of America," *Transactions of the Charles S. Peirce Society* 47:2 (2011), 136–45.

in 1979.[7] Still, Kaila's important position in the history of logical empiricism is acknowledged in Friedrich Stadler's *The Vienna Circle* (2001),[8] and there is a growing body of scholarly work on Kaila.[9]

Now we can add Kaila's 1939 book *Human Knowledge* in this English translation by Dr. Anssi Korhonen. It will of course be of interest to contemporary Kaila scholars, but it can also be expected to serve the function Carnap and Kaila envisioned so many years ago–to stand as a lucid introduction to logical empiricism and some of the main problems in epistemology and philosophy of science.

Eino Kaila was born on August 9, 1890, in Alajärvi in Western Finland, where his grandfather Jonatan Johansson was a vicar. Eino was the oldest son in a family of nine children. His father Erkki, who took the name Kaila in 1906, became associate professor in the Faculty of Theology at the University of Helsinki, and eventually served as the archbishop of Finland from 1935 to 1944. Several of Erkki's uncles were also priests, one of whom, Gustav Johansson, was the archbishop from 1899 to 1930. Coming from a clerical and politically conservative family, the young Eino grew to be an independent thinker, impatient with ready-made systems and world views. After his "philosophical awakening" at the age of 16, he studied for the Master degree at the University of Helsinki in 1908-10.

Academic philosophy in Finland had for a long time been dominated by Hegelian idealism, represented by the "national philosopher" Johan Vilhelm Snellman (1806-1881). His successor, Thiodolf Rein (1838-1919), combined Hegelianism with influences from Lotze and sent some of his students to Wilhelm Wundt's psychological laboratory in Leipzig. Rein had the only chair of philosophy in Finland at the University of Helsinki, but after him the old division between Theoretical and Practical Philosophy was reintroduced. Rein's successor, Arvi Grotenfelt (1863-1941), was inspired by neo-Kantian trends in the philosophy of history, while Anglo-Saxon evolutionary naturalism was introduced to Finland by the moral philosopher and sociologist Edward Westermarck (1862-1939).

8. See Friedrich Stadler, *The Vienna Circle: Studies in the Origins, Development, and Influence of Logical Empiricism* (Vienna and New York: Springer, 2001), 801-5.
9. See Ilkka Niiniluoto, Matti Sintonen, and G.H. von Wright, eds., *Eino Kaila and Logical Empiricism, Acta Philosophica Fennica* 52 (Helsinki: The Philosophical Society of Finland, 1992); Ilkka Niiniluoto and Sami Pihlström, eds., *Reappraisals of Eino Kaila's Philosophy, Acta Philosophica Fennica* 89 (Helsinki: The Philosophical Society of Finland, 2012). Selected works by Kaila, edited with introductions by Ilkka Niiniluoto, have appeared in Finnish in two volumes: *Valitut teokset 1-2* (Helsinki: Otava, 1990-92).

Kaila started his philosophical career by criticizing Haeckel's and Ost-wald's materialist monism, Bergson's speculative metaphysics, and dogma-tism within religion and the church. Restlessly searching for an identity with-in the landscape of science and art, he worked as a cultural editor and reviewer of literature and theatre. But at the same he was preparing his doctoral thesis in experimental psychology, which he defended in 1916.

In his monograph *Sielunelämä biologisena ilmiönä* (*Mental Life as a Biological Phenomenon*, 1920) Kaila argued with broad and extensive refer-ences to research literature that psychic phenomena are physiological and biological. Yet Kaila did not accept reductionism, for he claimed that the laws of psychology cannot be derived from biology and neurophysiology. In the same work, Kaila presented a thoroughgoing critique of vitalism which postu-lates special vital forces (like "elán vital" and "entelechy") to explain organic events, especially regeneration.[10]

In his early period, Kaila struggled intensely with Ernst Mach's positiv-ism. Mach's monism attracted him, but as early as 1913 he defended the reality of atoms against Mach (though he did so not in the coarse "reified" style of the old materialists). Around 1919, Kaila concluded that Mach's program of "phe-nomenological physics" was mistaken–he even criticized Albert Einstein's theory of relativity as too Machian or positivistic. Atoms must be assumed to be real, which means that they belong to "a mind-independent causal nexus." Here Kaila appealed to the psychology of perception: psycho-physiological mechanisms make us to see things in a way that differs from the image on the retina. Even though our picture of the world is biologically conditioned, it also serves as a basis of scientific thinking. Physics operates in the same way as our natural world outlook, when it treats sensations as "signs of real functional connections independently of our consciousness": every physical thing or event transcends "a mere given complex of sensations."

Thus by 1920 Kaila had sided with realism and against phenomenalism in the philosophy of science.[11] He also endorsed cooperation between philosophy and science on the ground that knowledge of reality is not based upon meta-physical speculation, but rather on interpreting the best current theories in science.

In 1922 Kaila was appointed the first Professor of Philosophy of the new Finnish University of Turku. At that time, theoretical philosophy included psychology and Kaila began his career at Turku by establishing a laboratory of experimental psychology and publishing a large volume, *Sielunelämän*

---

10. See Ilkka Niiniluoto, "Kaila's Critique of Vitalism," in Juha Manninen and Friedrich Stadler, eds., *The Vienna Circle in the Nordic Countries: Networks and Transformations of Logical Em-piricism, Vienna Circle Institute Yearbook* (Dordrecht: Springer, 2010), 125–34.
11. On Kaila as a scientific realist, see Ilkka Niiniluoto, "Eino Kaila and Scientific Realism," in Niiniluoto, Sintonen, and von Wright, *Eino Kaila and Logical Empiricism*, 102–16.

rakenne (*The Structure of Mental Life*, 1923), in which he discusses the new Gestalt psychology.

At Turku, Kaila also read extensively in philosophy and science. In 1923, he began to make contact with the new empiricist trends in European philosophy and the new empiricists themselves.[12] In March, he sent a letter to Hans Reichenbach, a young philosopher of science then in Stuttgart (and later Berlin). Kaila had found references to some earlier publications on probability in Reichenbach's book *Relativitätstheorie und Erkenntnis Apriori* (1920), and asked the author for reprints of such further work. This led to an exchange of letters and publications. Two years later Kaila published his first study of this topic, *Der Satz vom Ausgleich des Zufalls und das Kausalprinzip* (1925), followed by *Die Prinzipien der Wahrscheinlichkeitslogik* (1926). In addition to Reichenbach's contributions and his general reading, the critical discussion in the first book was heavily influenced by a Viennese dissertation, Edgar Zilsel's *Das Anwendungsproblem* (1916). In the second book Kaila used *A Treatise on Probability* (1921) by J.M. Keynes. A critical evaluation of both of Kaila's books was given by Herbert Feigl in his dissertation *Zufall und Gesetz* (1927) written under the direction of Moritz Schlick in Vienna. Kaila's next monograph, *Probleme der Deduktion* (1928), shows that he had had closely followed the ongoing debates in the philosophy of mathematics, and was familiar with Russell's and Whitehead's monumental *Principia Mathematica* (1910). *Beiträge zur einer synthetischen Philosophie* (1928), inspired by the Gestalt-theory, was an attempt to formulate an antireductionist philosophy of nature with nonadditive wholes. His Finnish monograph *Nykyinen maailmankäsitys* (Contemporary View of the World, 1929), with central chapters on time and space, matter, life, and mind, discusses philosophical problems by interpreting the best scientific theories. According to Kaila, there is no sharp difference between philosophy and special scientific disciplines, but philosophy is "the highest own life of science," "the alpha and omega of science, its beginning and end."

As early as 1926, Kaila had coined the term "eine logischer Empirismus" for his own position. In an essay contrasting science and metaphysics,[13] he argued that scientific thinking is governed by the "Principle of Verification":

> Every statement about reality must imply something definite about experience which is a ground for the truth or the probability of that statement.

Thus, a scientific statement "must express something about the content of experience itself" (e.g., psychology, history) or it "must logically imply that in

12. See Juha Manninen, "Between the Vienna Circle and Ludwig Wittgenstein: The Philosophical Teachers of G.H. von Wright," in Manninen and Stadler, eds., *The Vienna Circle*, 47–67.
13. See Eino Kaila, "Scientific and Metaphysical Explanations of Reality," in Haaparanta and Niiniluoto, eds., *Analytic Philosophy in Finland*, 49–67.

such and such circumstances this and this will be observed" (e.g., statements about electrons transcending the realm of human observability). Metaphysical systems, on the other hand, abound in statements which violate the principle of verification. According to Kaila, one of the first to formulate it was the metaphysician Leibniz. In his monograph on *Wahrscheinlichkeitslogik*, Kaila spoke about the Principle of Observability (*Prinzip der Erfahrbarkeit*). Two years later, in his study of pseudoproblems, Carnap formulated a Principle of Testability (*Prüfbarkeit*) which requires that for all meaningful statements there have to be conditions under which some experience deductively or inductively supports it.[14] While Kaila's principle was a demarcation criterion for separating science and metaphysics, just like falsifiability in Karl Popper's *Logik der Forschung* (1934), Carnap's principle aimed at distinguishing meaningful and meaningless language.

For Kaila, the crucial example of the application of his principle was the external world hypothesis–in German, *die Aussenwelthypothese*. According to Kaila, the assumption of the existence of the external mind-independent world, and the correspondence of the world picture and the external world, has a very high probability:

> If such a correspondence did not obtain, it would be a 'miraculous accident' that the human world picture in fact can be used to predict observable phenomena.

This correspondence concerns the general relations between things, not the qualities of those things. Even though it does not follow that the external world does not contain those qualities known in our experience (e.g. colors), debates on such qualities are not settled by the Principle of Verification and therefore belong to metaphysics. Kaila called this solution of the problem of reality "critical realism," represented among others by Külpe, Meinong, and Schlick, but he added that these scholars have failed to see the role of probability in this solution.

Kaila also sought contacts with philosophers in Vienna. He sent his monographs on deduction and synthetic philosophy to Carnap in 1928, and received in exchange Carnap's manuscript on the logical construction of the world. On September 28, 1928, Kaila wrote from Turku to Moritz Schlick in Vienna, complaining that "in his remote homeland he lives in an almost complete intellectual isolation." Schlick invited Kaila to visit his circle, and Carnap replied on January 28, 1929, that in Vienna Kaila could find an atmosphere that provides "a good echo for strictly scientific philosophy." Kaila made his first visit to Vienna within months, and when the Vienna Circle (or the Ernst Mach Society) released its manifesto, "The Scientific Conception of the World," later in the year, Kaila was mentioned as one of the thinkers close to the Circle.

14. See Rudolf Carnap, *The Logical Structure of the World* and *Pseudoproblems in Philosophy*, trans. Rolf A. George (Berkeley and Los Angeles: University of California Press), 1967.

Kaila admired the rigor and logical acumen of the philosophers in Vienna and Berlin. His collaboration with them, and his critical view of traditional speculative metaphysics, was well-known in Finland and debated by conservative humanists among the faculty when, in the summer of 1930, Kaila was appointed to succeed Grotenfelt as Professor of Theoretical Philosophy at the University of Helsinki.[15] In his bold statement on the "new method of philosophical research," Kaila made it clear that he saw himself as a representative of scientific philosophy that he contrasted with the literary inspirations of traditional historical approaches.[16]

Still, Kaila's encounter with the Viennese philosophers was in many ways critical. He defended his probabilistic realism in the Circle against Carnap's declaration that the realism controversy is meaningless. A year later he published in Turku a monograph *Der logistische Neupositivismus: Eine kritische Studie* (1930), a detailed analysis of Carnap's phenomenalistic constitution system in *Der logische Aufbau der Welt*.[17] For Kaila, Carnap's conclusions are "catastrophic" and "in fact mean the end of all philosophy," since they deprive empirical research of its "living soul," the "realist" language of science.[18]

Kaila stayed in contact with the new movement. He visited Vienna again in 1932 and 1934, participated in international congresses, and published articles in *Erkenntnis* and *Theoria*. Still, like Reichenbach, he always distinguished his logical empiricism from positivism. He did not accept the principle of verifiability that the once critical-realist Schlick along with Friedrich Waismann had adopted from Wittgenstein. This principle requires that for each meaningful sentence there has to be in principle a method of verifying it by means of observations given in experience. According to Kaila's lecture in the 1933 congress in Prague, this requirement is too narrow, since it excludes "all-sentences," that is, general laws of nature, from meaningful statements.

However, Kaila accepted from Carnap's constitution system the translatability principle that requires that all meaningful concepts have to be reduced to the observational language by explicit definitions. In the monograph *Über das System der Wirklichkeitsbegriffe* (1936), he gave a grandiose summary of his conception of reality on the basis of invariances.[19] Following Leibniz, Kaila regarded "invariance" or general lawful regularity as the criterion of

15. See Ilkka Niiniluoto, "Eino Kaila und der Wiener Kreis," in Georg Gimpl, ed., *Weder-Noch: Tangenten zu den finnisch: österreichischen Kulturbeziehungen* (Helsinki: Deutsche Bibliothek, 1986).

16. See Eino Kaila, "On the Method of Philosophy," in Haaparanta and Niiniluoto, eds., *Analytic Philosophy in Finland*, 69–77.

17. See Juha Manninen, "Eino Kaila in 'Carnap's Circle'," in Niiniluoto and Pihlström, eds. *Reappraisals*. See also A.W. Carus, *Carnap and Twentieth-Century Thought: Explication as Enlightenment* (Cambridge: Cambridge University Press, 2007).

18. See "Logistic Neopositivism: A Critical Study," in Kaila, *Experience and Reality*, 1–58.

reality—even to the extent that a greater degree of invariance indicates greater "degree of reality." He distinguished "phenomenal objects" discussed in the p-language, the "physical objects" in the everyday f-language, and the "scientific objects" in the language of scientific theories. This moves in the direction of epistemological constitution. But, on the other hand, reality can also be divided, by increasing degrees of invariance, into perceptual p-objects, physical f-objects, and scientific objects. This description of reality remains within the domain of logical empiricism, since the thesis of translatability is accepted with the demand that the higher level objects in the hierarchy are reduced to invariances or regularities between lower level entities.

From this perspective, metaphysical pseudoproblems arise when the levels of reality are confused with each other. In metaphysics there is also a confusion between the psychological meaning of a word or statement (experiences and emotions) and its objective or logical meaning. The latter is the same as the real content of a statement in Carnap's sense (the empirical or nonanalytical consequences derivable from the statement).

During his stay in Vienna in the spring of 1934, Kaila worked on experimental psychology with Karl and Charlotte Bühler. That same year he published in Finnish his masterpiece in the psychology of personality, *Persoonallisuus*, which was soon translated into Swedish and Danish. This book turned out to be Kaila's last extensive work in psychology. For afterwards he concentrated, in his lectures and writings, on problems in epistemology and philosophy of science.

As a charismatic teacher in Helsinki, Kaila regularly gave courses in logic and theory of knowledge. The book translated here, *Inhimillinen tieto* (Human Knowledge, 1939), is based on his lectures, documented in shorthand by his student K.V. Laurikainen, later Professor of Theoretical Physics in Helsinki. It consists in three main parts: I, Theory Formation; II, Formal Truth of Theories; and III, Empirical Truth of Theories. Logical empiricism is expressed by four theses: denial of synthetic a priori knowledge, testability, translatability, and logical behaviorism. The concept of invariance is a unifying thread among the main parts of the book. Kaila had introduced it in his 1936 monograph, where he argued for its significance for the problem of reality: the "real" is always something regular. The more law-like something is, the more "real" it is.[20]

In chapter 1, Kaila begins with the observation that the search for invariances is a biological feature of our prescientific experiences. By reference to

19. See "On the System of the Concepts of Reality: A Contribution to Logical Empiricism," in Kaila, *Experience and Reality*, 59-125.
20. See *Experience and Reality*, 102.

the concept of isomorphism, he defends structural realism against Kant. Chapter 2 uses illustrations from Plato, Euclid, and astronomy to argue that the search for invariances created Greek science. Kaila rejects Hume's psychological empiricism and, with reference to Leibniz, defends the equation of reality and invariance.

Chapter 3 discusses Plato's and Aristotle's conceptions of knowledge, while chapter 4 contrasts Aristotle's substantial invariances with Galileo's relational invariances that express law-like regularities or permanent ways of change within the flow of events. With historical evidence from Descartes, Newton, and Leibniz, the Galilean method is shown to combine "rationalized" mathematical theories with their empirical testing.

Kurt Lewin, in the first issue of *Erkenntnis* in 1930, published a paper on the transition from the Aristotelian to the Galilean way of thinking in biology and psychology. Kaila does not refer to Lewin, for it is clear that his contrast between substantial and relational invariances was inspired by Ernst Cassirer's *Substanzbegriff und Funktionsbegriff* (2nd ed., 1923). This theme was so important for Kaila that he proposed it to von Wright as a topic for his doctoral dissertation. Nevertheless von Wright decided to continue his studies in probability and induction.[21]

Chapter 5 deals with induction, Kaila's old theme from the 1920s. With reference to Galileo, he emphasizes the distinction between discovery and proof (or justification). Like Karl Popper in *Logik der Forschung* of 1934, he argues that the discovery of theories is a free an creative process that cannot be formalized in logic. Kaila notes that in concept and theory formation an important role is played by "rationalizations" or "idealizations," e.g., mathematical approximations and limits. Only in special cases can theories be obtained from experience by simple inductive inference. For this reason, he is also sceptical about the possibility of inductive logic: only Reichenbach still believes in numerical inductive probabilities that can be expressed as relative frequencies.

After considering the problems of curve fitting and cryptograms, Kaila comes to an original proposal that he had introduced in an article on Einstein's religion in 1935:[22] the relative simplicity of a theory, T, is defined as the ratio between the number of different facts derivable from T divided by the number of the logically independent basic assumptions of T. In other words, the relative simplicity RS(T, E) of T is the explanatory power of T with respect to observed data, E, divided by the logical complexity of T.[23] Kaila thought that

21. G.H. von Wright's dissertation *The Logical Problem of Induction* appeared in *Acta Philosophica Fennica* in 1941 (Oxford: Blackwell, 1957, 2nd ed.). He discussed the Aristotelian and Galilean traditions in the philosophy of science in chapter 1 of *Explanation and Understanding* (Ithaca, NY: Cornell University Press, 1971).
22. See Eino Kaila, "Albert Einsteins religion," *Theoria* 1 (1935): 58–67.
23. See Ilkka Niiniluoto, *Critical Scientific Realism* (Oxford: Oxford University Press, 1999), 167, 182.

if this number were numerically definable, then the relative simplicity would measure the inductive probability, $P(T/E)$, of the theory given the explained facts. His proposal was independent of Reichenbach's treatment of descriptive and inductive simplicity in *Experience and Prediction* (1938), and it is related to later discussions of theoretical unification in science. Kaila also saw that the requirement of maximal invariance or relative simplicity contains as a special case Mach's principle of economy of thought: as he put it in 1942, science is a "maximum problem," not striving for "parsimonious economy" but a "bold adventure."[24]

But Kaila did not have methods for the quantitative determination of his measure. It was only in 1948 when Hempel defined the systematic power of a theory and showed, against Kaila's guess, that its value is equal to $P(\sim T/E)$.[25] The problem of explicating the syntactical or structural concept of simplicity turned out to be surprisingly complex.[26]

Part II is devoted to basic concepts in formal logic. Kaila himself was not a logician, but he promoted its study in Finland. He clearly knew the relevant literature from Frege and Russell, Hilbert and Bernays, through Carnap, Gödel, Heyting, and Tarski. In 1938-9, Kaila's student Oiva Ketonen–who eventually in 1951 became his successor as professor in Helsinki–went on to Göttingen, Germany, to study proof theory with Gerhard Gentzen.[27]

Kaila discusses logical truth (chapter 6) and mathematical truth (chapter 7). His main conclusion against Kant is the denial of synthetic a priori truths: both logical truths and truths in arithmetic and geometry are analytic and a priori, where analytic truths are consequences of definitions. If the real content of a statement, following Carnap, is defined as the class of empirical sentences derivable from it, then the real content of analytic truths is empty.

The concluding Part III formulates two main theses of logical empiricism:

(L1) The metalogical statements 'Statement L is analytic' and 'Statement L is a priori' are equivalent.

(L2) Every statement concerning reality has to have real content.

Here L2 expresses what Kaila had already in 1926 called the Principle of Observability. Later, with Carnap, he called it the Principle of Testability.

24. See Kaila, *Experience and Reality*, 154.
25. See Carl G. Hempel, *Aspects of Scientific Explanation* (New York: The Free Press, 1965), 278-88. Other probabilistic proposals for explanatory power, degree of confirmation, or degree of corroboration are normalizations of the difference $P(E/T) - P(E)$. See Jaakko Hintikka, "The Varieties of Information and Scientific Explanation," in B. van Rootselaar and J.E. Staal, eds., *Logic, Methodology and Philosophy of Science III* (Amsterdam: North-Holland, 1968), 151-71.
26. See M.H. Foster and M.L. Martin, eds., *Probability, Confirmation, and Simplicity* (New York: Odyssey Press, 1966).
27. See Michael von Boguslawski, *Proofs, Paradoxes, and Probabilities: The Logical Turn of Philosophy in Finland* (Helsinki: The University of Helsinki, 2011).

Kaila begins with reference to Alfred Tarski, whose definition of truth covers both formal and empirical truth. In chapter 8 he returns to the Principle of Testability, which he distinguishes from the narrower Principle of Verification of the "logistic neopositivists." Kaila argues that both general and singular factual statements cannot be required to be decidable–verifiable or falsifiable–by empirical evidence. Still, Kaila wishes to maintain as the third main thesis of logical empiricism the Principle of Translatability:

(L3) Every theory concerning reality has be translatable into the language of experience.

This principle holds for Kaila's 1936 version of the constitution system, since objects on a higher level of reality are invariances between objects in the lower level. Thus talk about scientific objects and everyday physical objects can eventually be reduced to relations between empirical statements.

Kaila points out that assumptions containing idealizations cannot be falsified by empirical evidence in the same way as inductive generalizations. Therefore, testability and translatability do not separately apply to each single term or statement in a rationalized theory, but in a broader sense it concerns the theory as a whole.[28]

In chapter 9 Kaila mentions statements in microphysics as examples of rationalization. He argues that determinism and indeterminism can be formulated as scientific statements in accordance with the broadly interpreted requirement of testability. Further, he argues, it is conceivable that a new form of laws can be found between deterministic causality and statistical average regularities. These remarks anticipate Kaila's growing interest in problems of quantum theory after 1942 and his philosophy of nature in the 1950s, when he tried to make precise the notion of "terminal causality."[29]

Kaila defines metaphysical statements by the condition that "they imply nothing about experience." With inspiration from Carnap, he observes that such statements often violate the logical theory of types and do not satisfy the requirements of "logical syntax." As an example, he mentions thinking about essences, exemplified in German metaphysics by Martin Heidegger's statement, "The essence of time is care." This is a "lyrical outburst," he explains, which admittedly may arouse some deeply felt thoughts.

Besides rationalist philosophers, like Descartes and Kant, Kaila pointed out that many empiricists have used metaphysical statements: in discussions

28. This kind of holism about theories was defended by W. V. O. Quine in his influential paper "Two Dogmas of Empiricism" in 1951. See *From a Logical Point of View* (New York: Harper and Row, 1953). Quine rejects "radical reductionism," i.e., the translatability of all statements into sense-datum language, as a dogma, since "our statements about the external world face the tribunal of sense experience not individually but only as a corporate body."
29. See Max Jammer, *The Philosophy of Quantum Mechanics* (New York: John Wiley, 1974), 165; and Michael Stöltzner, "Terminal Causality, Atomic Dynamics, and the Tradition of Formal Teleology," in Niiniluoto and Pihlström, eds., *Reappraisals*.

about "the mind-independent external world," words like "external," "behind," "transcendent," or "cease to exist" have not been well-defined:

> In so far as every factual sentence can be translated, at least in a broad sense, into the language of experience—and this is what gives the sentence its factual content—no statement about the so-called transcendent reality can have any factual content.[30]

Kaila's internal struggle with this issue of realism is shown by the fact that in his monograph *Über den physikalischen Realitätsbegriff* (1942) he asserted along Carnap's lines that the question of a "consciousness-independent real external world" is a "pseudoproblem," but he added immediately that the realist's talk about the "external world" can be given content: it concerns the third physico-scientific level of the hierarchy of reality, consisting of the highest invariances of experience:

> The controversy between Mach and Planck about phenomenalist and realist physics, if the formulations used by either side are taken *literally*, was a fight about a pseudoproblem; to the extent, however, that the controversy had content, it was rather the realist than the phenomenalist who was right.[31]

Carnap had given up the thesis of translatability earlier in his 1936 article "Testability and Meaning," since he thought that dispositional concepts cannot be explicitly defined by means of the observational terms and that their connections to the observational language have to be given by more liberal reduction sentences. On April 27, 1937, Carnap wrote to his worried friend Kaila to assure him that he was not being unfaithful to empiricism:

> But I think that you have no need to worry that I could be untrue to empiricism. On the contrary, I take my essay only as an attempt to formulate the thesis of empiricism in a more precise and adequate form than we have now, and thus to support empiricism, not to cast doubt on it. I don't think the thesis of reducibility based on definability and translatability—entirely independently of whether it stands or not—has such a profound meaning for empiricism as you seem to. It seems to me that we are dealing here only with the question of the exact logical character of the connection that exists between perception-terms and the terms of abstract scientific language, and thus between perception-statements and scientific theories. That such a connection must exist is the kernel of empiricism. And the more precise analysis has to show in which form this connection can be logically captured.

30. This volume, 192.
31. See *Reality and Experience*, 154.

If we hold that every scientific statement must be capable of either a complete or at least incomplete confirmation, we remain faithful to the main idea of empiricism.

In his 1939 book, Kaila continued this debate by proposing a formula of second-order logic as a definition of dispositional concepts. In a letter of January 15, 1940, Carnap gave a counterexample to Kaila's proposal and suggested that the definition of dispositions may need an intensional language. The status and definability of theoretical terms became one of the hottest topics in the philosophy of science in the 1960s and 1970s, and discussion about "die KAILA-Formel" was continued by Arthur Pap and Wolfgang Stegmüller.[32]

Kaila's own view changed in the 1940s, and he concluded that translatability is a mistaken principle. So he returned to his critical realism of the 1920s, but with new thoughts and conceptual tools. This was clearly stated in his last publication, *Einstein-Minkowskin invarianssiteoria* (The Einstein-Minkowski theory of invariance, 1958).

In the posthumous manuscript *"Arkikokemuksen perseptuaalinen ja konseptuaalinen aines"* (The Perceptual and Conceptual Components of Everyday Experience, 1960), Kaila repeated his hierarchy of objects. But he now argued that everyday physical f-objects cannot be translated into invariances of perceptual p-objects, since such if-then regularities (e.g., a match box rattles if I shake it) always contain references to some activity which is not contained in the original f-object. The same holds for scientific theories and their scientific objects. Kaila concluded that "the thesis of translatability cannot be carried out on any level of objects." For the old debate between phenomenalism and realism, this means that there is "some truth" to realism. In the unfinished manuscript, Kaila attempted to explicate this truth in terms of "limits of perception": a knife cuts better the sharper its blade is ground–even after the point when the tactual appearance of the blade does not change any more.[33]

Kaila's fourth main thesis of logical empiricism, developed in chapter 10, is the Principle of Logical Behaviorism:

(L4) Sentences about a subject's immediate experience are equivalent to certain sentences about the states in the subject's body.

---

32. See Arthur Pap, "Reduction Sentences and Dispositional Concepts," in P.A. Schilpp, ed., *The Philosophy of Rudolf Carnap* (La Salle, IL: Open Court, 1963), and Wolfgang Stegmüller, *Theorie und Ehfahrung* (Berlin: Springer, 1970), 222-26.
33. See "The Perceptual and Conceptual Components of Everyday Experience," in *Reality and Experience*, 259-312.

This is a solution to the problem of the reality of other minds. Kaila mainly refers to Carnap's articles in *Erkenntnis* from 1931 and 1932 that consider scientific psychology on the basis of physical language. Kaila agrees with Carnap that the physical f-language is intersubjective and universal so that psychological statements should be definable by statements about behavioral dispositions or brain states. This does not however assume the view of some primitive mechanistic behaviorists who claim that there is no such thing as consciousness. Rather, it follows from the principles of logical empiricism that the real, intersubjective content of claims about other minds has to lay in physical behavior.

This solution worried Kaila, however, for he realized that the phenomenal language, which is self-centered and qualitative, contains a residue which is not translatable to the f-language. In particular, it is problematic whether the symbol function and gestalts in experience–so important for Kaila's psychology in his *Persoonallisuus* (1934)–can be physicalized. This two-language standpoint was unsatisfactory, for Kaila was seeking a monistic philosophy nature and mind.[34] Together with his growing interest in the problems of microphysics, this tension between mind and matter, quality and quantity, experience and structure, perception and conception, was a driving force in his unfinished quest to articulate a scientific world view, one continued and only partially preserved in the posthumously published parts of the manuscript *Hahmottuva maailma*–"the world as a structuring whole."

---

34. See G.H. von Wright, "Eino Kaila's Monism," in Niiniluoto, Sintonen, and von Wright, *Eino Kaila and Logical Empiricism*, 71-91.

Translator's Note

This translation of Eino Kaila's *Inhimillinen tieto* has been prepared with the modern reader in mind. Kaila's original Finnish often has a solemn and somewhat archaic flavor to it. No special effort has been made to reproduce these qualities. Rather, the original draft translation has been revised and smoothed out, mostly by Dr. George A. Reisch, to enhance its readability for today's readership.

A few very short paragraphs which Kaila has inserted for repetition or emphasis have been omitted from the translation. On a number of details, I have made use of an earlier English translation of Kaila's philosophical works, *Experience and Reality: Four Philosophical Essays* (edited by R.S. Cohen, with an Introduction by G.H. von Wright [Dordrecht: D. Reidel Publishing Company, 1979]). Kaila's philosophical terminology derives mostly from contemporary German sources: Rudolf Carnap and other logical empiricists. Here I have consulted several available English translations; of these, Rolf A. George's translation of Carnap's *Logische Aufbau der Welt* (*The Logical Structure of the World* [University of California Press, 1967]) deserves a special mention.

Kaila's extensive bibliographical references have been edited to make them serve the English reader. References to English translations–and in some cases to an English original–have been added whenever these are available. On some occasions, I have inserted a reference which Kaila has omitted. Sometimes Kaila cites an author apparently from memory or else uses a paraphrase rather than a direct quotation; in such cases, whenever I have managed to identify the source with reasonable certainty, I have added a reference and replaced Kaila's paraphrase with the original, or its translation.

I am grateful to George A. Reisch, who put a lot of effort into improving the translation. I would also like to thank Tuomo Aho and Mika Perälä for valuable discussions, suggestions, and concrete help on a number of details at an early stage of the project. The editors of the present volume, Juha Manninen and Ilkka Niiniluoto, made a number of useful terminological suggestions. The translation was made financially possible by grants from the Finnish Cultural Foundation and Alfred Kordelin Foundation; their support is gratefully acknowledged.

Anssi Korhonen

Preface by Eino Kaila

This book is meant as a guide for anyone who takes pleasure in the pursuit of philosophical problems. It is also intended to be an academic textbook in scientific philosophy as well as a systematic introduction to 'logical empiricism' for professional philosophers. Here I offer a few words to these three circles of potential readers.

A reader in the first group, before beginning a detailed study of this book, may wish to know what requirements the book will impose. To this we reply that it presupposes no special knowledge over and above what is included in standard secondary school education. But it will require sustained work and independent thinking on the part of the reader. Here 'secondary school education' is understood to include an introduction to the elements of philosophy and its history, as well as the basics of logic. The reader who lacks any of these may do well to gather the relevant information before picking up this book. Even a concise textbook in the history of philosophy or an introduction to philosophy will suffice, especially if it addresses developments in the history of scientific ideas.

As a textbook in scientific philosophy, this book is meant to provide a systematic description of what is involved in the concept of knowledge, to clarify, in light of the history of scientific ideas, the developments that this concept has undergone and, finally, to justify important results that contemporary logical analysis has achieved on the questions of what human knowledge is and what it is not.

Finally, with regard to the needs of professional philosophers, the goal has been to fill a gap in the existing philosophical literature. As yet there exists no systematic introduction to logical empiricism, that is, an introduction that, while admitting no compromises in scientific accuracy on any important point, could nevertheless be understood even by a reader with no experience in exact logic or 'logistic'. For this reason, the book includes a summary of the elements of logistic mainly as presented by Hilbert, though concentrating upon points that are significant in epistemological applications.

Some of the basic principles of logical empiricism are to be found in the 'Galilean' concept of knowledge that is part and parcel of modern science. It was first developed by Galileo and Newton, who not only founded their research on this conception but also endeavored to explicitly formulate this conception. In the late nineteenth century and at the turn of the century, a number of distinguished mathematicians, among them Ernst Mach and Henri Poincaré, developed it further in important respects. Nevertheless, the type of philosophical research that is best known as 'logical empiricism' has received its contemporary form only after philosophers have begun to appreciate–and this development has taken place mainly after the Great War–how important exact logic is to their work. Exact logic, that reform in logical thought that can ultimately be traced back to ideas of Leibniz, has been quietly taking place in the course of the last century

This book attempts to synthesize the most important results of logical empiricism into a systematic whole, the core of which is to be found in four fundamental theses of logical empiricism. These will be worked out and given a justification in the course of the following investigations. Apart from a few details, my own contribution is confined to this systematization and a number of insights and observations relating to it; these have to do, mainly, with a number of questions belonging to the psychology and history of knowledge and constituting the background for logical empiricism. In light of these insights, the logical empiricist conception of knowledge is the culmination of two and a half millennia of development in human ideas.

In the references found at the end of the book* I have mentioned the most important advocates of logical empiricism together with their most significant works. The list is by no means exhaustive; it mentions those sources from which the present author has benefited the most, on the one hand, and those, on the other, that the reader is likely to find useful for more deeply understanding the issues introduced here.

This work was prompted by my experiences as an academic teacher. In this capacity I have on a few occasions addressed issues examined on the following pages and they have led me to numerous exchanges of thoughts with my students. I have not always been only on the giving end of these exchanges.

* Not included in the present volume.–Eds.

Now that this book, which means a great deal to me, is to be brought before the public, part of the gratitude that I feel belongs therefore to some of my pupils. As a teacher I have occasionally felt as if the light from the logical height that I have seen moving upon the face of the deep was visible to my audience, too. If this book gives the reader a similar glimpse of clarity, its purpose will have have been served.

Christmas, 1938
The Author

Human Knowledge

Part 1. Theory Formation

Chapter I

Search for Invariances

Were one to ask, What are the aims of the human pursuit of knowledge? the answer could be given in one word: *invariances*. What do we mean by this word to which we attach so much importance? A short answer would be: by 'invariance' we mean regularity, or lawfulness. The meaning that we naturally associate with these words, however, does not quite capture the quite general meaning of 'invariance'. And, it may be asked, shouldn't the concepts 'regularity' and 'lawfulness' themselves be explained? Let us begin then by giving some examples of what we mean by invariances.

Of all invariances, the most important are the so-called laws of nature, that is, constant regularities between events. Another important class of invariances is constituted by so-called physical objects, or material objects. After all, every object contains a regularity, for objects are constituted by distinct properties that hold together in a regular manner. Space is a system of invariances; it is part of our conception of space that it possesses a structure described by a certain geometry, a structure that remains the same everywhere, does not vary, and is therefore invariant. Every science, be it physics, psychology, or something else, is concerned with this sameness, these constancies and stabilities–these *invariances*. As the invariances that we discover are more general, the more we succeed in satisfying our pursuit of knowledge.

This conception of human knowledge may seem strange, perhaps even one-sided. Yet as we pursue the matter further, this impression will soon change. For we will see that not only science but also prescientific thought,

3

including the kind of immediate understanding that is present in sense perception itself, is fundamentally concerned with invariances. Perception is constantly on the lookout for these invariances; one could almost say that this is all it ever does.[1] We shall now consider a few examples.

Most of the time, we are interested in perceptual phenomena only insofar as they are signs or signals of some other phenomena that we expect to occur under certain conditions. A given appearance of white signals chalk; it is a sign of something that under certain conditions yields, for example, a white streak on a blackboard. We say that we see objects like pieces of chalk. In fact, however, we must *learn* to 'see' in exactly the same way that we learn to read, that is, to comprehend certain groups of letters as expressions of thoughts. In reading we grasp the meanings of what we read and take notice of the expressive signs themselves only to the extent that is necessary for us to comprehend the meanings. Similarly, in perception we become aware of physical objects and events and do not usually attend to the underlying perceptual phenomena. What interests us in our perceptions, in other words, are the regularities that govern the course of phenomena and, in the simplest cases, are comprehended without any conscious effort.

Consider another kind of example. Even in cases where we do not comprehend perceptual phenomena primarily as signals of something physical, their comprehension still leads to the establishment of invariances. Consider

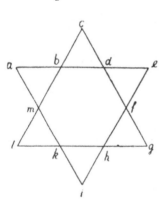

figure 1. It is a so-called ambiguous figure. It can be understood in several different ways, for example, as a whole that is made up of two equilateral triangles, placed on one another. Or it can be understood as a ring consisting of six small, congruent triangles, or still other ways. Yet no matter how we see the figure, each of those articulations that can really be seen is to a great extent invariant, simple, regular, and symmetric. In each case, we see the upper part of the figure constructed in the same manner as its lower part, and so on. Geometrically, there are countless other articulations that are equally

Figure I

possible and, so to speak, equally justified, but which are highly nonsymmetric. Articulations that fail to satisfy the invariance requirement in these ways cannot be *seen*; they cannot be brought about visually. They can be produced only conceptually, such as the articulation one part of which consists in the figure *cfhl*, the other in *aefghi*. It is easy to show by means of such examples—and these can be found in almost every instance

1. Cf. here the very apt words of Kant: "Understanding . . . is always occupied in investigating appearances, in order to detect some rule in them" (*Critique of Pure Reason*, A126).

of visual perception–that the immediate, unconscious, and unintentional articulations that perception searches for and finds are invariances.

Let us next consider Meumann's figure. Of course, we immediately see it as articulated or organized. However, if, after looking at the figure for a while, we try to reproduce it from memory, it may well happen that our attempt fails completely. We then take a fresh look at the figure, this time not resting content with nonconscious articulation that is independent of our will, but trying to grasp the figure consciously and deliberately. In this case we analyze the figure and if possible try to identify elements that repeat themselves according to some rule. When we grasp something in this way, through a conscious effort and analysis, we are searching for invariances. Soon we realize that in the figure in question a curve of the following kind ⌒⌒ repeats itself according to a law that is easily recognized. Once we have identified the law, we can retain the figure in our memory; we come to possess knowledge of it as soon as we have found the invariance contained in the figure, and our knowledge is no more than knowledge of its underlying law. Suppose the figure is a map of a peculiar network of roads. Once we have grasped it in this way, we can keep the network in our thoughts; it has become clear to us.

Figure 2

If we continue to study such figures, it will soon become clear that this search for invariances lies very deep in our nature. Our biological need to find means for survival forces it upon us. At the same time, however, it is an innate law of our nature, as it were; it manifests itself wherever the human spirit is active. It would be of interest to consider how invariances are searched for and implemented in the different walks of *aesthetic* life. What, for instance, is artistic style? It is a uniform pattern that repeats itself in a multiplicity. What is appropriate in style in the artistic sense is that which consistently follows some invariance. Clarity, unity in multiplicity, balance, harmony, and *beauty*; in all of these there is some invariance that manifests itself in a concrete form.

Finally, a few examples help to show that these considerations apply even to advanced scientific research which can itself be seen as a search for invariances.

Experience presents itself to us as a boundless field, a colorful multiplicity of phenomena. In our search for knowledge, we try to comprehend this multiplicity in a way that is as simple and unified as possible, that is to say, invariant.

Aristotle presents a comprehensive theory of motion. He classifies all forms of motion into definite kinds: straight and circular motions, natural and forced motions. The motion of a simple body is simple, that of a composite body is compound. These different forms of motion are not comparable, says he; they do not constitute any uniform field. Sublunary motions, or motions taking place on the Earth, are completely different in nature from the super-lunary motions of the celestial bodies. According to Aristotle, there are no general laws of motion, laws that would hold of any motion, whatsoever.

Next consider Galileo, the founder of the modern theory of motion. How does he proceed? How does he think? Let us consider again Meumann's fig-ure. Trying to grasp it, we looked for some element, as simple as possible and repeating itself according to some law. Galileo, a man of genius, moves at an immeasurably higher intellectual level, but does *exactly the same* as we do when we try to grasp the content of the figure. He asks himself: What are those recurring conceptual elements that can be combined in accordance with some simple law so as to yield the actual phenomena pertaining to motion? This is his famous analytic method, or as he himself calls it, the method of resolution.

Eventually, Galileo determines that three facts constitute the conceptual basis for all motion: continuity, the parallelogram of forces, and uniform ac-celeration. (It was not, however, until Newton that these concepts were made absolutely clear.) As regards acceleration in particular, Galileo assumes that the increase in velocity that we observe in free fall takes place in the simplest imaginable way, to wit, in such a way that speed increases by a constant amount per unit of time. Then he *'sees' in his thought*, for example, the fall of a stone thrown in the air as dividing into a certain uniform, rectilinear motion and a certain uniformly accelerating motion which "unite, but do not disturb one another," and then it is easy to ascertain that the trajectory is parabolic. In-spired by considerations like these, Galileo himself says: "Facts which at first seem improbable will, even on scant explanation, drop the cloak which has hidden them and stand forth in naked and simple beauty."[2]

There is thus a continuous striving towards more and more general laws; for the more general a law is, the greater the invariance of the field to which the law applies, and the more we perceive the multiplicity contained the field to be *of the same kind*.

Toward the end of the seventeenth century, Newton built his celestial me-chanics on the foundation laid by Galileo. What is added, in fact, is just one new conceptual element–the supposition that bodies give acceleration to one another in accordance with the well-known inverse square law. This law is as-sumed to be valid for celestial bodies, or superlunary motions, as well as for those taking place on the earth. (Acceleration is thus no longer a constant, as it was for Galileo.) Thus, again, Newton *'sees' in his thought*, for example, the orbital motion of the moon as its fall towards the earth, and he calculates that if the distance which the moon descends from the tangent of its orbit towards

2. *Dialogues Concerning Two New Sciences by Galileo Galilei*, trans. H. Crew and A. de Salvio, with an Introduction by A. Favaro (New York: Macmillan, 1914), 4.

the center of the earth is multiplied according to the inverse square law, the moon, falling on the earth, ought in the space of one second describe 15 Paris feet, 1 inch, and 1 4/9 lines. In fact, a body falling on earth describes in the first second 15 Paris feet, 1 inch, and 1 7/9 lines.[3] Since these values are almost exactly the same, there is no doubt in Newton's mind that these are both cases of gravity; that is, that what takes place in the heavens when the celestial bodies revolve around one another is *the same* as what happens on our earth when an apple falls from a tree. Newton's contemporaries, staggered by the result, came to believe that they witnessed the discovery of a law governing the entire universe.

'Economy of Thought'

The fact that our search for knowledge can be understood as an attempt to ascertain invariances was not discovered yesterday. People grasped it clearly as soon as they began to apply the biological standpoint to the human search for knowledge. Of those thinkers who have expressed opinions of this kind, first and foremost was Ernst Mach (d. 1916), the Austrian historian of physics and philosopher. At every turn in his works there are references to the *economy of thought* ('*Ökonomie des Denkens*') that he considers to be the core of all scientific understanding and theory formation.[4] Thus he is fond of emphasizing the *parsimonious* character of thought; every law of nature attempts to give an economical, condensed description of *how things are*–and nothing else. Here one might point out that Mach perhaps puts a little too much emphasis on the purely biological, life-supporting function of the search for invariances and the economy that is involved in it. As we have mentioned, the search for invariances lies so deep in our nature that it is present wherever the human spirit is active, for example in artistic creation which does not serve any purely biological needs. What we have here is something more than just a tool in the struggle for survival; we have something of intrinsic value, even if it was originally no more than just a means serving some end. This is a fundamental feature of the life of the human spirit, which even in its highest spheres has a biological foundation and can be understood on the basis of the laws of biology.

Even if these remarks are to some extent critical of Mach, the point is merely to emphasize that what he means by talk of economy of thought is in fact something even deeper than what he has in mind. Mach's own considera-

---

3. Newton, *Mathematical Principles of Natural Philosophy*, Book 3, Prop. 4.
4. Ernst Mach deals with the economy of thought in almost all his works. In this connection, the most important of these are *The Science of Mechanics: A Critical and Historical Account of its Development* (see ch. 4 in particular); *Popular Scientific Lectures* (see ch. 13 in particular); *Knowledge and Error–Sketches on the Psychology of Enquiry*; *The Principles of Physical Optics*.

tions suffice to make this clear. One of Mach's favorite examples was Ptolemy, the ancient astronomer.[5] Even in the second century A.D., Ptolemy knew that a light ray on entering a denser medium from a less dense one approaches the normal and recedes from it when the direction is the opposite, from the denser to the less dense medium. He made experimental observations and drew up refraction tables from 10 to 80 degrees. He was already searching for the law of refraction and assumed the ratio $\alpha : \beta$ to be constant for each pair of media, an assumption contradicted by his own observations. Later, at last, Snellius, a contemporary of Galileo, discovers the law $\sin \alpha : \sin \beta = k$ for each pair of media. What a splendid gain in economy! Refraction tables become quite superfluous! After the discovery, it suffices to know the constants k; these are all that one has to keep in mind. Each angle of refraction can be computed, once the incidence angle and the relevant constant are known; that is to say, the angle can be *inferred*. If the law possesses general validity, our knowledge, which Ptolemy and his many refraction tables represented as an indefinite multiplicity, has been transformed from a compilation of distinct facts into a deductive unity. From the law we *infer* particular instances. Thus we see that the discovery of general invariances transforms knowledge into something deductive. A law of this kind, Mach remarks, is no more than an economic, parsimonious description of how things are in a certain respect; actually, what it describes is never more than a particular *aspect* of the relevant phenomenon, an aspect which happens to interest us in the context of our study; Snell's law is just a description of a geometrical aspect of the behavior of light.

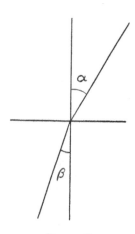

Figure 3

Rationalization

We shall now take a closer look at two important cases of the search for invariances. As we have seen, we attempt to arrange what we have seen in as simple and uniform a manner as possible. In one important respect, however, there is more to the search for invariances than this. Imagine we are looking at a growing tree. We say that its trunk is a cylinder or that its leaves are shaped like a heart. We say this even though we can see perfectly well that what we have are only rough approximations of these simple geometrical shapes. We say that

---

5. Mach, *The Principles of Physical Optics*, ch. 3.

the earth is round, although its surface is full of hollows and bulges. In our thought, that is, we add to the invariances established in experience.

This figure, representing inscriptions of the letter I, has been copied from the exercise book of a child in elementary school who is learning to write. In producing the drawings, the child has copied his own inscriptions rather than the model letter. The series thus shows how he has understood the letter I. Here there is an interesting detail, namely, the strong internal specialization of the figure that is revealed in the drawings: step by step it becomes articulated into a certain straight line and a certain curve between which there is a strong contrast. This is a consequence of the fact that understanding involves an increase in the invariance of the figure; for when each of its main constituents condenses in itself the diversity of the parts of the original figure and articulates in itself as simple a figure as possible, they must gradually become

Figure 4

quite different from one another. This kind of specialization, or differentiation, which readily gives rise to contrasts, is typical of our intellectual activity even on its highest levels. In due course we shall see remarkable illustrations of this phenomenon, taken from the development of scientific ideas.

Let us return for a moment to Galileo's kinematics and consider his conception of uniform acceleration. What does experience teach us? Experience shows, for example, that for a body in free fall, its increase in velocity in equal, perceptible units of time is approximately the same. Galileo's many experiments with inclined planes show, as he puts it, "no appreciable discrepancy" between the increments in velocity and this law of free fall.[6] In fact, however, minor discrepancies can always be observed. In an experiment conducted with utmost care, the following increases in velocity were observed in consecutive units of time:

9.6, 9.6, 9.5, 9.7, 9.5, 9.6, 9.6, 9.5, 9.7 units.

We say that these minor deviations are attributable to different sources–air resistance, deficiencies in the measuring instrument, etc. And we think that under ideal circumstances, free of such disturbances, the increase in velocity would be constant and the acceleration strictly uniform. In fact, however, the situation here is ultimately like the example of the geometric tree. Although

6. Galileo, *Dialogues Concerning Two New Sciences*, 179.

Aristotle goes a little too far when he says that nothing in nature is exactly a straight line or a circle, what he says is quite correct in most cases; we *round off* everything in our thought. No matter how precise we make them, our measurements, when repeated, will always exhibit minor deviations. In our thought, we add to the invariance of our experience so that even those perceived regularities that are often subject to gross deviation receive an ideal simplicity. We *rationalize* our concepts–for instance the concept of acceleration–to give them that exactness, precision, and simplicity that is not possessed by the corresponding phenomena of experience.

We should be clear from the outset what is really accomplished in rationalization. If we fail to observe the gulf between the imperfect invariances of experience and the perfect invariances of idealized or rationalized systems, we shall run into difficulties that have proved fatal in the history of science and philosophy, as we shall see.

As we have already indicated, rationalization and its results, namely rational concepts and hypotheses, play a decisive role already in prescientific, everyday thought. Good examples are found in the geometrical concepts that are involved in our natural conceptions of time and space. According to these conceptions, spatial and temporal quantities are *continuous*. Here it suffices to consider the vague, as it were intuitive, conception of continuity that we seem to possess. We think that *certain relations that hold for experience within certain limits and with certain, possibly quite glaring, exceptions are valid without restrictions or exceptions*. It is this operation of thought that we call *rationalization*, and the concepts it yields are what we call rational concepts. We may see already how this process of rationalization takes us to the concept of 'infinity'. According to the natural conception, between any two points there is always another; which implies that there are infinitely many points between any two points. But we nowhere perceive or experience infinity. Every concept in which infinity is presupposed is rational; we have formed it by rationalizing the content of our experience. When we observe a dot, or a particle so minuscule that our eyes cannot divide it into parts–say, a right side and a left side–we readily call it a point; but we can easily see that it is not a geometrical point. When we draw two such specks close to each other, we can see that only a finite number of such dots can be drawn between them. Berkeley is quite right in saying that there is no such thing as ten-thousandth part of an inch–that is, not in perception.[7] 'Point' is a rational concept, for a point is something that exists to satisfy the dictates of geometry: in this case, between any two such points, there is always another.

Let us consider another example of how crucial a role rationalization plays in so-called 'exact thought' and how we could not manage without it, not even in our pre-scientific thought. We toss a coin for 'heads or tails'. The result is

7. Berkeley, *A Treatise Concerning the Principles of Human Knowledge*, Sec. 127.

a sequence of throws in which, for example, the first 10 throws yield 6 heads and 4 tails, the first 20 throws yield 11 heads and 9 tails, the first 30 throws yield 13 heads and 17 tails, the first 40 throws yield 21 heads and 19 tails. The number of heads in the entire sequence of tosses, or their *relative frequency*, that is, 6/10 for the first ten tosses, 11/20 for the first twenty, and so on, fluctuates around the value 1/2, but the mean deviation from this value decreases as the number of tosses increases. Now, we rationalize this fluctuating relative frequency by supposing that if the number of trials increases without bound, the perceived ratio, if it continued to behave in the same way, would converge to the limit 1/2. We call this the rational concept of mathematical probability, and we define it as the limit of a relative frequency converging to a definite value. In calculating probabilities we operate with a given constant number–in our example 1/2–whereas the relative frequency that we meet in experience deviates more or less from this idealized value. All uses of mathematical statistics, as for instance in insurance activities, are based on this kind of rational concept formation.

We cannot investigate all of the many difficulties involved in the formation of rational theories and concepts. Some of these are among the deepest problems in epistemology. For our purposes, we need only see that rationalization is an evident manifestation of the search for invariances; in rationalization, we simplify and unify some field in a way that often goes far beyond what is found in our experience. It regularly happens–as we have already pointed out–that this introduces the mysterious concept of the infinite to our intellectual world. We may also notice that this process of rationalization is in a sense something paradoxical; for it seems we must say that rationalization does violence to experience, and nevertheless no science that is based on experience can do without it.

Isomorphism

We gain a new perspective on the nature of human knowledge when we consider the following special case of a high-level invariance. Think of a geographic map. Points on the map correspond to places in the depicted area and relations between the points correspond to relations between the places. Within the limits determined by the map's scale, moreover, this correspondence is *one-to-one*. This means that corresponding to each position on the map, there is one and only one point in the area; conversely, for each place in the area there is one and only one position on the map. This applies to relations, too; corresponding to each relation between two points, there is a fixed relation holding between positions on the map and conversely. For instance, if the distance between two positions on the map, m_1 and m_2, is 1 millimeter, and this corresponds to a distance of 1 kilometer between two points, a_1 and a_2, of the depicted area, then, if the distance between two other positions on the map, m_3 and m_4, is likewise 1 millimeter, the distance between the corresponding points, a_3 and a_4, must be 1 kilometer. (We assume, that is, that our map does not 'stretch distances'). This map is correct or gives *knowledge* of the depicted area only to the extent that the correspondence holds. We call this kind of correspondence a 'correspondence in logical structure' or *structural similarity* or *isomorphism*. We say that wholes corresponding to one another in this way share a common structure. That is, an isomorphism holds between two wholes, classes, or systems, S_1 and S_2, when there is a one-to-one correspondence between their parts (members, elements) and also between the relations of S_1 and S_2.

With the help of the map example, we can make a remarkable observation: the existence of an isomorphism does not presuppose that the relevant relations should be qualitatively similar. A map usually represents altitudes, for example, without there being in its surface any bulges and hollows that rise or sink like mountains or valleys in the depicted area. Instead these altitude relations are usually represented by the map's colorations and a one-to-one correspondence between differences in color intensity and differences of altitude in the depicted area. The one-to-one correspondence between the relations means in this case that if, for instance, the difference in darkness between two positions, m_1 and m_2, on the map is 10 units and this corresponds to an altitude difference of 1 kilometer between the corresponding places, a_1 and a_2, in the depicted area, then, if the difference in darkness between two other positions on the map, m_3 and m_4, is, say, 5 units, the altitude difference between the corresponding places, a_3 and a_4, must be 500 meters, and conversely. *Thus, isomorphism by no means presupposes that the wholes between which there is an isomorphism should be qualitatively similar.* For instance, there is an exact isomorphism between the spiral groove of a gramophone record in which the needle runs and the musical piece thus reproduced. Small protrusions in the groove correspond one-to-one with notes, and their interrelations correspond with relations between the notes. In the same way that a musician can 'read notes', he could, with the help of a microscope, 'read' the music from the gramophone record. Yet these two isomorphic wholes are qualitatively about as different as possible. One, the groove, is a permanent physical object in space, the other a temporal series of musical tones.

Applied to our concept of knowledge, these observations are important. A whole, S_1, like a map, represents another whole, S_2, to which it stands in the relation of isomorphism. Someone with knowledge of S_1 thereby possesses knowledge of S_2, insofar as mere logical structure is concerned. He possesses this knowledge in spite of the fact that, again, S_1 and S_2 may be qualitatively very different. *To possess knowledge of some domain, it is not necessary to know its perceptible properties, its absolute qualities.*

What then is this logical structure of which we can have knowledge, even if we know nothing about the quality of the material in which the structure is realized? Structure is a purely logico-mathematical likeness, a likeness that can be expressed using only logical and arithmetical concepts. In exactly the same way that 'red' is the likeness in color that obtains, for instance, between blood and a poppy, an isomorphic structure, although it occurs at an immeasurably higher level of abstractness and generality, is the likeness that obtains, for instance, between a musical score and a musical piece. *Isomorphism is invariance of logical structure.* Whenever our search for knowledge succeeds in establishing this kind of invariance, it has attained one of its highest goals.

When this happens, prescientific, everyday thought has long since been left behind. We can come to possess knowledge about an important domain of experience, for example, even if the qualities belonging to the domain and the relations in it are unknown to us. In such cases the domain is *alien to our thought* in the sense that we lack all images representing it, and yet we can give an exact *description* of its logical structure. Our knowledge may be constituted solely by representations that correspond to their objects only in this logico-mathematical sense.

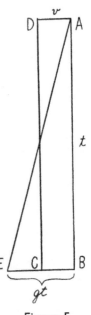

Figure 5

What role has this search for high-level invariances played in the development of human knowledge? Looking at the development of exact science, we can easily see that its role has been crucial. When Galileo created his kinematics, one of his fundamental insights seems to have been as follows.[8] An expression of the form xy represents geometrically the area of a rectangle if x and y are the lengths of two adjacent sides. In kinematics, xy denotes the distance, d, travelled at constant velocity, if x is velocity, v, and y is time t (for $d = vt$). In this way, a geometric quantity, the area of a rectangle, and a kinematic quantity, the distance travelled at constant velocity, are isomorphic. Thus, in figure 5, the rectangle ABCD represents one such distance, when AD denotes velocity and AB denotes time. Let us next consider the phenomenon of uniformly accelerating motion, as for example in free fall. In this case the velocity AD is not constant, but increases from 0 at every point at a constant rate, until at point B a certain final velocity BE is reached. Because acceleration is uniform, AE is a straight line and ABE a triangle, the area of which is $1/2 \cdot AB \cdot BE$. On the other hand, it is easy to see (in differential geometry) that the area of this kind of triangle is isomorphic to a

8. Galileo, *Dialogues Concerning two New Sciences*, 173.

distance travelled at constant velocity. But $AB = t$ and $BE = gt$, where g denotes the velocity change per each unit of time; hence the distance $d = 1/2 \; AB \cdot BE = t \cdot gt = gt^2/2$. Hence the distance that an object falls is directly proportional to the square of the time it has been falling. In this way the observation that there is an isomorphism between certain geometrical quantities and certain kinematic quantities leads to one of those great discoveries in which all exact science is based.

The discovery of such invariances is a thread running through the entire development of modern science. Invariances open up novel and often unifying perspectives on domains that have hitherto remained distinct. Our present task does not permit a consideration of further examples; many—and the best—of these would require more thorough knowledge of science than may be presupposed here.[9] It suffices merely to mention the insight of Descartes when he developed analytical geometry, the discovery of an isomorphism between geometry and algebra establishing a correspondence between geometrical points in the Cartesian coordinate system and pairs of real numbers, between straight lines and equations of first degree, and so forth.

What then is the general philosophical significance of the concept of isomorphism? While our previous examples show that it has played a crucial role in the development of exact sciences, its philosophical significance is to be found, first and foremost, in the fact that it introduces into the very concept of science a new and abstract feature. It raises the question, Could all knowledge, once it is subjected to a detailed investigation, turn out to be a matter of isomorphic representation? Perhaps all qualitative similarity between our thought and its objects is no more than a psychological feature which may be useful, perhaps even indispensable, in practice, but which may be irrelevant to the representative function of knowledge itself and, therefore, irrelevant to its truth. At this point we are not in a position to go deeply into such far-reaching questions, so the following remark must suffice. As is well known, Kant argued that knowledge pertains to appearances only and not to 'things-in-themselves'. And yet he clearly thought that there is an isomorphic relation between appearances and things-in-themselves. That is to say, appearances are representations of things-in-themselves; they share a structure, although, according to Kant, that structure is realized in material that is completely different in the two cases.

We can see therefore that it is wrong to say that we know *nothing* of things-in-themselves; after all, we do know their structure. And if the extreme view turned out to be correct that our knowledge is in the last analysis just a matter of mere isomorphic representation, we would have to say that we know just as much about things-in-themselves as we do about appearances.[10]

9. The importance of isomorphism is appropriately emphasized by Rolf Nevanlinna in his lecture "Ueber das Wesen der Exakten Forschung," *Sitzungsberichte der Gesellschaft zur Beförderung der gesamten Naturwissenschaften zu Marburg*, 67. Band, 4 (Heft, 1932).
10. Russell, *Introduction to Mathematical Philosophy* (London: George Allen and Unwin. 1919), 61.

In any case, Kant's conception of human knowledge is in certain remarkable respects reminiscent of our everyday conception, according to which knowledge is a kind of acquaintance with the qualitative character of what is known; it is not just conceptual representation, in which the decisive factor is logical correspondence and not qualitative similarity.

We illustrate this point with the help of the following example, which has often been used in epistemology. Let us imagine a father teaching color words to his little son; because of some physiological anomaly, however, the son's perception of color qualities is the reverse of his father's in accordance with this schema:

Father:	white	red	yellow	green	blue	black
Son:	black	green	blue	red	yellow	white

Having learned the color words from his father, the son, when his father shows him a white windflower, sees it as black but calls it 'white'; when his father shows him a red strawberry, he sees it as green, but calls it 'red', and so on. The two would agree in all their statements about the colors of objects. In fact, *there is a complete isomorphism between the respective color worlds of the father and the son.* For instance, the father points to a yellow streak in the spectrum and says to his son: "Notice that yellow is the lightest of these colors." The son replies: "That's right, and that other color, blue, is the darkest of the spectrum." He would reply in this way because, although he sees yellow as the darkest and blue as the lightest color, what he calls 'light' is dark, and vice versa; he calls yellow blue and blue yellow. Now, if the Kantian conception of knowledge were correct, the father would have no knowledge of his son's color world, although they would agree about every detail, whenever the subject of color came up in their conversations.

Furthermore, we can make a rather striking observation: when it comes to the sense-qualities experienced by our neighbors, everyone of us is exactly in the same position as the father of our example is to his son's color world. Even the ancient Cyrenaics pointed out that, at most, we can have a guarantee of structural similarity, that is isomorphism, between our own experiences and those of other people–but not of any qualitative similarity. One may well argue, then, that insofar as we have knowledge of the experiences of our neighbors, it is not about the intrinsic qualities of these experiences, and not even about the qualities of their relations. Our knowledge is rather about their structure in the sense we have been explaining above, as this structure manifests in verbal reactions and other types of behavior. And we may perhaps add that if our knowledge is to be 'intersubjective', that is, if it is to possess a content that is the same for all individuals, then this content can only consist in the structure of experience, or of reality, and not in its absolute qualities.

As a matter of fact, any modern psychologist who examines the foundations of his own science must admit that when he sets out to study the color worlds of his test subjects, for instance, he does not and cannot study their intrinsic qualities but only the structure as this manifests itself in behavior.

In considering such questions, we begin to appreciate the import of the question, "What is human knowledge and what it is not?" In particular, we find ourselves forced to reject many different kinds of conceptions of knowledge familiar from history; these conceptions–Kant's, for instance–may bear striking similarity to everyday thought; but they are alien to exact thought. We shall here consider a few examples.

Kant's follower Schopenhauer, whose understanding of man and of life is in certain respects extraordinarily deep and who depicts them so eloquently, shows no sensitivity to exact thought. "Where mathematics begins, there understanding ends," he once wrote. Schopenhauer is an example of how severely limited even the greatest minds can be. He offers an argument to express his negative attitude towards all scientific explanation of reality, that is, towards an economic description of reality that is mostly concerned with its relations or structure.[11] Let us suppose, Schopenhauer asks, that this kind of scientific description has been completed. In that case, he says, the feeling of a philosophical explorer would be that of a person who, upon finding himself in the company of complete strangers who introduce other members of the group as their friends or cousins or some other relatives, duly expresses the pleasure of meeting these people; but who at the same time cannot help asking himself, Who are these people? As Aristotle once said, "relations do not seem to indicate the substance of anything," so Schopenhauer holds relations, the structure of some whole, in such a low esteem that if structure is all that is known, this knowledge is all but indistinguishable from total ignorance. The remarkable thing, though, is that it is precisely relations or structures that become more and more important when our knowledge becomes more and more general; that is, when our grasp of some domain becomes more and more unified. We could use Schopenhauer's own example, pointing out, for example, that in our time a scientist who studies biological or psychological heredity, trying to gather knowledge of some group of people, might well say that for him the most important things about the group are precisely the kinship relations within it.

In our day, the Schopenhauerian attitude towards exact thought is found in the famous French philosopher Bergson. He wants to draw a sharp distinction between positive science–above all the relational and structural knowledge established in exact science–and the absolute knowledge of essences that is supposedly delivered by metaphysical philosophy. The former, he says,[12] examines its object from the outside; it is based on analysis, and no concept utilized

11. Schopenhauer, *The World as Will and Representation*, Second Volume, §17.
12. Bergson, "Introduction à la métaphysique," *Revue de Métaphysique et de Morale* 11 (1903).

in it has any content other than what the relevant object–for instance, some human personality–has in common with other similar objects. What is unique to this object and different from everything else falls outside the sphere of this knowledge. Metaphysical knowledge, on the other hand, is said to be intuitive and able to penetrate the unique essence of its object, grasping it as such.

Against this view, it must be pointed out that it fails to draw a distinction between *acquaintance* and *knowledge*.[13] If they were the same, we would have complete knowledge of that with which we are fully acquainted–as we perhaps are with our own self. Why, then, is psychology such an arduous science? Why has it made so little progress and achieved so few results? In his chief work, *Dialogue Concerning the Two Chief World Systems*, Simplicio, the representative of the Aristotelian standpoint, has this to say about the causes of falling motion: "The cause of this effect is well known; everybody is aware that it is gravity." Salviati, Galileo's spokesman, replies:

> You are wrong, Simplicio; what you ought to say is that everyone knows that it is called 'gravity.' What I am asking you for is not the name of the thing, but its essence. [. . .] I except the name which has been attached to it and which has been made a familiar household word by the continual experience that we have of it daily. But we do not really understand what principle or what force it is that moves stones downward than we understand what moves them upward after they leave the thrower's hand, or what moves the moon around. We have merely, as I said, assigned to the first the more specific and definite name 'gravity'.[14]

These considerations show how far-reaching issues are involved in the concept of knowledge. In fact, the question, "What is knowledge?" is the same as philosophy in its stricter, scientific sense; this can be seen in ancient philosophy and, with increasing clarity, in modern philosophy. Modifying a well-known statement, we could say: "Tell me your conception of knowledge, and I'll tell you what your philosophy is!" In what follows we shall try to show, by considering briefly the development of some scientific ideas, that the human search for knowledge can indeed be regarded as a search for invariances; and that human knowledge itself, being the result of this search, can be understood as the discovery and representation of such invariances. If, furthermore, we succeed in showing that other conceptions of human knowledge in fact presuppose this self-same search for invariances, but err because of some prejudices and misconceptions, we will have accomplished something.

13. Schlick, "Experience, cognition and metaphysics," in: Schlick, *Philosophical Papers*, Vol. II (1925-1936), ed. H. Mulder and B.F.B. van de Velde-Schlick, trans. P. Heath (Dordrecht: D. Reidel, 1979), 99-111. (German original in *Kant-Studien*, Band 31, 1926.)
14. Galileo, *Dialogue Concerning the Two Chief World Systems*, ed. S. Drake (Berkeley,CA: University of California Press), 234.

Chapter 2

How the Search for Invariances
Created Greek Science

The French historian of religion Ernst Renan once wrote that the Greeks are the only miracle in history. With them the European spirit first rises to self-consciousness; to them we owe the best of what we possess, namely, the elements of our culture. Has the might of human reason, one may well ask, ever been given a more eloquent expression than in the well-known words of Archimedes: "Give me a place to stand and I shall move the earth"? Has anyone ever exhibited a more striking awareness of the value of the life of the human mind than Euclid, who replied to the King of Egypt–who had complained to him how difficult geometry was–"There is no royal road to geometry"? Before the Greeks, had anyone truly understood the original, Greek sense of the word 'theory' as disinterested intellectual enquiry or contemplation, in which the human spirit, like some 'world eye,' inspired by nothing but the striving for knowledge, surveys the endless diversity given in experience? The dialogues of Plato, the best of which remain fresh as morning dew, reveal to us the entire depth of the struggling human spirit. Everything to which the ancient Greeks put their minds grew to become exemplary. Thus they created European art and European science.

Euclidean Geometry

The Greeks did not create their science from nothing. They assimilated everything useful, but in their hands it was given a new shape. On the intellectual
side, they were the first to build scientific theories, that is, systems of assumptions that give a simple and unified formulation of the invariances constituting a given domain. Egyptian surveyors knew that a rope with knots 3, 4, and
5 units apart constitutes a right-angled triangle with sides of these lengths.
First in the Pythagorean school and then in Plato's Academy, these seeds grew
into scientific geometry, in which all known geometric facts are derived from
a few simple basic assumptions and which is crowned by the beautiful theory
of the five regular so-called Platonic solids. Euclid of Alexandria systematized
these results around 300 B.C. in the thirteen books about the "Elements" of
mathematics, a work said to be the most read after the Bible. In this way the
Greeks provide us with the subject we shall examine on the following pages,
namely the concept of *theory*. We shall now consider the nature of scientific
theories in a preliminary way, using Euclid's system as an example.

When we set about finding invariances within some domain, our ultimate
aim is to establish a theory of that domain; for a theory in its ideal form is a system of assumptions, as simple and as few as possible, from which the relevant
facts can be derived. In derivation or inference, in turn, one demonstrates that
the derived facts are already contained, as a matter of logical fact, in the basic
assumptions; for when we infer something, we try to make completely clear
to ourselves what is involved in asserting the basic assumptions. As soon as
these assumptions have some nontrivial content, this clarification can only be
accomplished step by step, showing that any seemingly new cases are in fact already contained in the basic assumptions, even if they should occur in new connections. Consider, for example, the proof given by Plato's pupil Theaetetus
that there are five, and no more than five, regular polyhedra or solids bounded
by equilateral, congruent polygons.[1] The gist of the proof, which comes last in
Euclid's system, is the discovery that if the sum of given angles whose vertices
meet is four right angles, they constitute a plane, and hence that only angles
whose sum is less than four right angles can form a solid angle. In this way the
theory of five Platonic solids, a theory which made a huge impact on Plato,[2] is
reduced step by step to a number of basic assumptions in which it is already
implicitly contained. A proof is nothing but an *explicit* statement of what is
implicitly involved in the basic assumptions. Psychologically, as a procession
of thoughts, the chain of proof may be series of surprises. But logically, it is a

---

1. Cf. Eva Sachs, Die fünf platonischen Körper, *Philologische Untersuchungen* 24, 1917.
2. This is shown by the fact that in *The Republic* we find complaints about there being no geometry of space, while *Timaeus* is replete with speculations relating to the geometry of solids.

series of 'tautologies' or 'repetitions' showing that each apparently new case is the *same* as those already asserted in the basic assumptions.

Thus, the search for invariances is satisfied in an ideal way by a theory, that is, by a hypothetico-deductive system in which the transition from basic assumptions to derived assertions or theorems is made using nothing but logical inferences. Here the domain under scrutiny has been comprehended in as simple and unified a way as possible so that it can be perceived, as much as possible, as everywhere *the same*. Simple conceptual basic elements—here, the point, straight line, and plane—and the simple basic relations that hold between these elements—coincidence, congruence and the relation of lying between—repeat themselves everywhere in accordance with the basic laws expressed in the axioms. Yet they do so in ways that are psychologically surprising. Our knowledge of some domain, once we have succeeded in formulating an ideal theory of it, is so formally perfect that this "knowledge equals the Divine," as Galileo once put it.[3] Man seems to have achieved something that is almost superhuman.

We cannot but admire the infallible intellectual 'instinct' possessed by the first Greek mathematicians—men like Eudoxus, Theaetetus, Theodorus and Euclid, most of whom were either Plato's congenial spirits or his followers. They had their goal perfectly clear before their minds.[4] The question here is this: If we make such and such assumptions, what follows from them? Axioms are *laid down* and are not subject to discussion. It is precisely this conscious limitation in which we can recognize the master. These mathematicians were perfectly clear about the nature of the *logical* before anyone had ever used the concept 'logical'. As always, logic comes first in practice; only much later did Aristotle, clearly inspired by mathematics, create a theory of logic.[5] This theory, however, is no more than a defective and *partial picture* of the logic that was in fact being used by mathematicians.

Euclid's system is nevertheless not perfect. It contains presuppositions that are unnecessary and never used; on the other hand, a number of presuppositions that are in fact used in proofs are missing. The ancients themselves pointed this out.[6] Euclid defines the concepts 'point', 'straight line', and so on, but makes no subsequent use of his definitions: 'a point is that which has no part', 'a straight line is a line which lies evenly with the points on itself'. It seems that with these definitions Euclid wants to show that his system is about our natural conception of space. Thus we may well interpret his obscure state-

3. Galileo, *Dialogue Concerning the Two Chief World Systems*, 103.
4. Cf. here H. G. Zeuthen, *Forelæsninger over matematikens historie*, two volumes, 1893-1903; in particular, vol. 1, 102. (German translations as H.G. Zeuthen, *Geschichte der Mathematik im Altertum und Mittelalter*. Verlag von Andr. Fred. Höst et Sön, Köpenhagen 1896; *Geschichte der Mathematik im XVI. und XVII. Jahrhundert*, Leipzig: B.G. Teubner, 1903).
5. H. Scholz, *Die Axiomatik der Alter, Blätter für Deutsche Philosophie I*, 4. Band, Heft 3/4.
6. See, for instance, T.L. Heath, *The Thirteen Books of Euclid's Elements*, vol. 1, second edition. (Cambridge: Cambridge University Press, 1926).

ment about straight lines as an attempt to capture that conception which we all seem to share, and the Euclidean system ought to be seen as a rationalized theory of our natural conception of space. Euclid's definitions, however, are quite unnecessary in the logical development of the system; the only assumptions referred to in the course of a proof are what the basic assumptions–in Euclid these are divided into postulates and general axioms–state about these points, straight lines, etc., that is, about the relations in which they stand to one another, according to the axioms. If, then, we imagine that these definitions have been omitted, we may give the basic concepts 'point', 'straight line', 'congruence', etc. whatever content we wish, as long as the axioms are satisfied. No matter what entities we wish to scrutinize, and no matter what relations they bear to one another, if these entities stand to one another in relations expressed in the axioms, then such and such a theorem follows. Once we have dispensed with the definitions, we can see more clearly what is really asserted in a theory formulated in this way. The point is to show that *if* the axioms are true, such and such further states of affairs are valid. In this case we say that *the basic concepts have been implicitly defined by the axioms*; for the content of these concepts is determinate only to the extent that it satisfies the axioms.

Axiomatic System

Keeping in mind what was said above about isomorphisms, we can easily see what this means. If we dispense with definitions–if, that is, we do not 'fix' the meaning of our basic concepts–then our theory is not only about the natural conception of space, say, but about any system that is isomorphic with it, such as, say, a certain Cartesian number space. This is an enormous step forward in the search for invariances; yet this step was not definitively taken, nor was its meaning fully understood, until our own time. Our theory has now been transformed into an *axiomatic system to which different 'interpretations' can be assigned*, to use the modern phrase, a system that is realized in different isomorphic '*models*'. What is most remarkable is that this step forward towards generality is eminently natural; it requires only that we eliminate from a theory everything that is irrelevant to its logical development, that is, to inference. Our system is then no longer a theory with content; it has been transformed into a system that can be expressed in logico-arithmetical terms and that describes a certain invariant logical structure. We shall pick up this point again later, when study the logic of scientific theories and consider the question of what is really involved in logical inference and logical truth.

As for those assumptions necessary to Euclid's system that are not made explicit, it is said in the first postulate that a point can be drawn from any point to any point. This means that there is a straight line between every two points.

But to this it should be added that there is exactly *one* such line between every two points, for otherwise it does not follow that two distinct straight lines can have at most one point in common, and it cannot be proved that two straight lines cannot form a closed figure. This, however, is how Euclid's first postulate is supposed to be understood, as is shown by its use. This inaccuracy is in itself minor, but in one respect it has had grave consequences. One of the examples that Kant used to support his remarkable view that mathematical inference is something different from logical inference was precisely that we cannot prove "from the concept of straight line"–that is, from the Euclidian axioms–that two straight lines cannot form a closed figure. Strictly speaking, this is quite correct, but this is only because Euclid's axiom system is not fully adequate on this point.

We must point out against Kant that Euclid's system, when it is considered as a whole and measured by reasonable criteria, possesses a remarkable logical perspicuity. In the fifth book, which contains the theory of proportions created by Eudoxus, the concept of limit was in fact used, although only *in casu*. This was done in a way that meets such stringent standards of logical rigor that only in the last century has mathematical thought again reached a similar perspicuity.[7] In the eighteenth century, after the invention of the Calculus, mathematicians had no qualms about using infinitesimal quantities whenever they wished to 'smooth' a curve or 'square' a round; Euclid makes no mention of such entities, but speaks always about finite quantities which in given cases can be made smaller than any previously introduced quantity. He uses this rigorous notion of limit–although it is not recognized as such–when he proves, for example, that the areas of circles are to one another as the squares are on their radii. It has been argued that one reason why Newton hesitated so long with the publication of the differential calculus–the calculus of fluxions, he himself called it–was that he could not attain the "rigor of the Ancients."

Greek Astronomy

To see how deeply ingrained the search for invariances was in Greek science, we shall look at the emergence of another science that the Greeks created, namely astronomy.[8] This science, too, received a definitive form in Plato's Academy. It seems, moreover, that the incentive for it may have come from Plato himself who required that invariances be established for celestial phenomena, that is, for the movements of celestial bodies.

---

7. See, for instance, H.G. Zeuthen, *Forelæsninger*, vol. 1, 146, 151; M.H. Hasse and H. Scholz, "Die Grundlagenkrisis in der griechischen Mathematik," *Kant-Studien* 33 (1928), 4–34.
8. The following presentation owes a great deal to Duhem's excellent discussion in his *Le Systéme de Monde*, first two volumes (Paris, 1916).

Let us be clear about how these celestial phenomena appear to us. First, the firmament of stars, the celestial sphere, seems to revolve around the earth in twenty-four hours with a constant angular speed, its axis of rotation perpendicular to the so-called celestial equator. Second, like the celestial sphere, the sun completes one cycle in twenty-four hours, but falls behind it regularly in the course of the year, thus moving slowly in the opposite direction, from east to west. If we could see stars in daytime, we could observe the sun occupying different locations on the celestial sphere at different times of the year. These locations constitute the arc of a great circle called the zodiac, or the ecliptic. The angle between the celestial equator and the ecliptic is approximately twenty degrees. These observations were well established long before the Greeks. It was only in Plato's time that the seasons were observed to be of unequal lengths; that, for example, the length of time from the vernal equinox to the summer solstice is not exactly one quarter of a year. Hence the apparent orbital velocity of the sun is not constant. (This is readily understood from our point of view, since the orbit of the earth is an ellipse.) Third, the revolution of the moon exhibits further irregularities. Not only does it occupy different locations on the celestial sphere in the course of a month; it does not stay on the ecliptic. Its orbit plane is therefore different from that of the sun. Furthermore, its apparent size varies slightly, namely by 1/11 of its diameter. Finally, the celestial bodies to which the Greeks gave the name 'wanderers' exhibit irregularities similar to those exhibited by the moon. Sometimes they are ahead with respect to the sun, sometimes they fall behind; sometimes they stand still and sometimes they deviate from the zodiac. Mercury and Venus always remain near the sun. Their brightness varies considerably; at its brightest Venus—or the 'evening star'—casts a shadow like the moon.

Now, in this embroidery of the heavens—as Plato calls it in his *Republic*—should we remain content with these irregularities? No, the irregularities must be explained away, if possible. There can be no wandering in the heavens, for celestial objects provide as accurate a reflection as possible of what is perfect among the perishable! We cannot bring ourselves to believe that perfect celestial motions would be subject to changes in direction and speed, so Plato, according to a story that goes back to his own time, gave astronomers the following task: *What are those completely regular circular motions that, if assumed, would save planetary phenomena?* This remarkable phrase—"to save the phenomena"; in Greek, "sozein ta phainomena"—occurs repeatedly thereafter. In its Latinized form "apparentia salvare" it is even used by Copernicus in his great work *On the Revolution of the Celestial Spheres.*[9] The phrase means: *Which invariances would define the motions of stars in such a way as to render their wanderings only apparent?* This was the beginning of scientific astronomy.

9. P. Duhem, *To Save the Phenomena* (Chicago: University of Chicago Press, 1969). (The French original published in: *Annales de philosophie chrétienne* 79 [1908].)

The development of Greek astronomy introduces a philosophically significant perspective that helps advance our discussion. In his dialogue *Timaeus*, Plato himself offered an astronomical sketch intended to "save the phemomena," one that was further developed by Eudoxus and Aristotle. This was the theory of so-called homocentric spheres. Imagine a number of concentric spheres, each possessing a constant rotation axis and rotation speed, but in such a way that the rotation axis and direction of rotation of a sphere may be assumed to differ, if need be, from those of the nearest outermost sphere. Thus, for example, according to Eudoxus, for each planet there is a sphere, the motion of which is identical with that of the fixed stars. Inside the first sphere there is another, the axis of which is inclined to that of the first and which rotates slowly in the opposite direction. There may be one or two additional spheres, if needed, with the planet itself located on the innermost sphere. In this way we have "saved" the direction of its rotation axis as well as its speed of rotation. It seems that the majority of Greek astronomers regarded celestial spheres as no more than mathematical fictions, with the help of which one could describe the apparent motions of celestial bodies and satisfy Plato's invariance condition. Aristotle, however, clearly thought that these spheres were material surfaces.[10]

Aristotle's contemporaries, however, were quite aware that many celestial phenomena could not be saved by the theory of homocentric spheres. It could not account, for example, for variation in the apparent size and brightness of celestial bodies. Here entirely new ideas were introduced. First there was Heraclides of Pontus, a disciple of Plato, whose views were so strange that they earned him the nickname 'paradoxologos' or 'writer of absurdities'. Heraclides formulated a picture of the heavens that was very similar to what Tycho Brahe would present some two thousand years later.[11] Suppose that the earth rotates around its axis; and also that of the planets at least Mercury and Venus revolve around the sun and not around the earth. These assumptions give us a very natural way to 'save a number of wanderings'. Finally, there is Aristarchus of Samos, who substituted a heliocentric picture of the heavens for the geocentric picture accepted by everyone mentioned above. From the historical point of view, it perhaps not surprising that not even the name of Aristarchus's chief work has survived. According to Archimedes, Aristarchus's main argument for heliocentrism held that since the fixed stars do not have a parallax, their distance from the earth must be enormous. The earth, moreover, is such a minuscule object in the cosmos that it would be very unnatural to suppose that the entire heavens revolves around it.

In the fifteenth and sixteenth centuries, the ideas of Heraclides and Aristarchus were known mainly through some references to them by Plutarch,

---

10. Aristotle, *De Caelo*, 287a.
11. There was a difference between the two, though, in that Heraclides thought that the earth rotated around its axis in the course of a day, whereas Tycho held the earth to be immobile.

a Greek author from the first century A.D. It is very unlikely that Copernicus would have dared to reintroduce the heliocentric picture of the heavens had he not known that some among the ancients had already suggested it. One amusing detail is that among his predecessors Copernicus mentions not only Heraclides and Aristarchus but other Greek names as well–names that modern scholars now regard as pure fictions invented by Heraclides for dialogues he wrote following Plato's style.

When we ask why the heliocentric hypothesis was so completely ignored in later Greek astronomy, we notice something remarkable. As is well known, the geocentric view remained prevalent until the time of Copernicus. The next great astronomer after Aristarchus, Hipparchus (second century B.C.)–a man whose observations were so accurate that it was not until the invention of the telescope in the early seventeenth century that his standards could be improved upon–advocated the geocentric picture of the heavens. The reason is clear. Even Aristarchus's question was, What are those *circular* motions with which "the celestial phenomena can be saved?"–a question ensuring that phenomena caused by orbital eccentricity, or, as we would now say, by elliptical orbits, cannot easily be explained. The remarkable fact is that Greek astronomers, without exception, assumed that orbits must be circular; only Kepler, after great inner and outer struggles, succeeded in establishing that they were elliptical.[12] Yet even many of Kepler's contemporaries found the idea incomprehensible; it cannot be, they said, that the orbital radius could be constantly changing.

Here we see a limitation that was characteristic of the Greeks as well as all subsequent scientific thought that relied on the Greek model. The limitation is extremely interesting, and we shall shortly consider it more closely, for it bears an evident connection with the special status within Greek thought of the search for invariances. When it became clear that one could not avoid orbital eccentricity–the assumption, that is, that the earth is not always the center of orbital motions–and yet one had to preserve the assumption that orbits are circular, the result was the complicated theory of epicycles. The theory was established by Ptolemy in the second century A.D. in a treatise on astronomy known by its Arabic name, *Almagest*. The idea was to add a sufficient number of additional cycles–epicycles–to each heavenly body in such a way that they all execute uniform circular motions (thus complying with the requirements imposed by Plato) and that the center of an epicycle was on another sphere and went around it, as is shown in figure 6.

From the kinematic point of view, this kind of description is fully equivalent with the elliptic hypothesis. According to Archimedes, it was Apollonius, the creator of the theory of conic sections, who proved that each epicyclic hypothesis was equivalent to the corresponding eccentricity hypothesis without

12. See, for example, E. Apelt, *Die Reformation der Sternkunde* (Jena: Druck und Verlag von Friedrich Mauke, 1852).

epicycles. Thus, the theory of epicycles saved celestial phenomena quite well, but the price that one had to pay for the explanation was unnaturally high: the theory was exceedingly complicated.

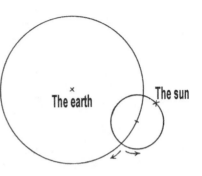

The earth The sun

The minds of these great theorists were hemmed in by certain curious prejudices. What makes these prejudices philosophically interesting is that they have a clear connection to the conception of human knowledge that is found everywhere in Greek thought. This is *the concept of knowledge that was definitively established by Aristotle* and which dominated all European scientific thought

Figure 6

until the fifteenth and sixteenth centuries. This concept and its thoroughly Aristotelian spirit is clearly expressed by Ptolemy in the introduction to his *Almagest*. There Ptolemy writes that physics cannot develop into a genuine science "because of the unstable and unclear nature of matter."[13] The only general science that can give "certain and trustworthy knowledge" is astronomy; for it is "concerned with the study of things which are always what they are," and is therefore "able itself to be always what it is." It is remarkable that the Greeks did not see the circular motion of heavenly bodies as a kind of *change*. They instead conceived of circular motion as a qualitatively constant *state* of a spherical heavenly body, a state manifesting its eternal essence. We can only have knowledge of what is in this way *thing-like and not subject to change* or degeneration, they assumed. Of anything else, knowledge is not possible.

The Demands of Reason or the Postulates of Rationality

In this way the Greek concept of knowledge presents a deep philosophical problem. A thorough examination of this problem sheds surprising light on the earlier development of European science. We have noted, to begin with, an extremely strong urge for understanding, a most intense search for invariances. To the examples mentioned above others could be added, all of them showing how the search for invariances created Greek science. These examples help us to see that the conception of human knowledge and its origin that is found in *psychological empiricism* is very probably wrong. This 'copy theory' holds that all our concepts have emerged gradually by abstraction from the contents of our experience, and that we have arrived at all our assumptions

---

13. Ptolemy's *Almagest*, *Preface to Book I*, translated and annotated by G.J. Toomer (London: Duckworth, 1984), 36.

concerning reality by gradual generalization from the facts of experience; in other words, that all our knowledge is a kind of generalizing copy of reality. Yet in considering the emergence of the great scientific theories in the early days of science as well as in its later phases, it seems that the crucial factor underlying their invention was instead an urge to understand by intellectually detecting patterns. If we wish to assign some tolerably clear sense to the word 'reason' or 'ratio', we should define it as this urge to understand, together with the *postulates of rationality*, or 'demands of reason', that are consequent upon this urge. In this case it seems evident that this urge is prompted precisely by the manifold of experience we encounter.

One of the most consistent advocates of psychological empiricism was David Hume, who thought in particular that our conviction that all events are governed by laws is a general habit of mind, produced by the repeated perception of regularities in particular cases. It is easy to show, however, that this conception cannot possibly suffice as an explanation; in Greek science, from its very inception, when men did not yet possess much knowledge of particular regularities in nature, it was precisely this conviction that received most eloquent expressions. Almost all Greek thinkers possessed some *principle of causality*, that is, a principle to the effect that events in nature are governed by a law. "Nothing happens by chance, but everything has some definite cause," said Democritus. "Similar causes always produce similar effects," Plato wrote in his *Theaetetus*. In Lucretius we find again and again the phrase "foedera naturai"–archaic Latin for 'the decrees of nature', that is, the laws of nature. Order appears to reign in nature, so that not just anything can happen. Horses, for instance, do not give birth to mice or elephants to ants. This is admitted even by the most ardent skeptic.

In the same way, most Greek schools of thought were convinced that in every change there is something that is preserved and that in all multiplicity there occurs something that retains its identity. Indeed, the whole of Greek science was begun when the Ionian 'physiologists'–this is Aristotle's term for the first philosophers–set out to look for the primordial matter which, while it recurs everywhere, retains its identity. "How much does smoke weigh?" they asked and gave the following answer: "Subtract the weight of ashes from the weight of the body, and you get the weight of the smoke." Even thought there is a slight chemical inaccuracy in this reply, it shows that these men firmly believed in the conservation of matter–more than two thousand years before Lavoisier showed through a series of experiments that this view was at least approximately correct.

There is, however, even more convincing proof that in the search for invariances we have found the true incentive behind all scientific thought and theory formation. The early thinkers we have been considering here did not hesitate to assume that *reality complies with the 'demands of reason' or the postulates of rationality*. The same conception is later found in early modern rationalists, particularly in Descartes, and in a very strong form. "The senses are poor witnesses" and similar statements are found everywhere in Greek thinkers, including Plato. What does not satisfy the demands of invariance–the indefinite multiplicity and variation of experience–is said to belong to the appearance, to be delusion or unreal. The real is *defined* in such a way that it satisfies the demands of reason. As we shall see in due course, the procedure which we follow in creating a concept of reality is, in a sense and within certain limits, exactly the same; the only difference is that we acknowledge that what is at issue here is a definition of nothing more than a concept of reality. Leibniz may have been the first to see this clearly, when he said that the real differs from the dream, delusion, or the unreal only in being–in accordance with its concept–a *regular* 'dream', that because of this we can predict the future on the basis of what is present, and hence that 'real' is an invariance of experience. By contrast, early Greek thinkers, including Plato, were in the habit of putting the reality that satisfies the demands of invariance *'behind'* the realm of appearances, which in this case is at best a mirror of reality. In this way the 'true reality', the object of scientific knowledge sought by these thinkers, became that which cannot be reached through the senses, but only through *reason*. Thus this optimistic belief that the desire to understand can be fully satisfied brought to European thought *metaphysics*, that is, the assumption that 'behind' experience there is another, intellectually more perfect, more invariant, world. Only very gradually there began to emerge an awareness of how imprecise this talk about a world 'behind' our experience really is.

The Origins of the Mechanistic Conception of Nature

In considering the origins of Greek astronomy, we saw that their conception of scientific knowledge itself imposed insurmountable internal obstacles to the yearning for knowledge that the Greeks felt so intensely; we saw how Greek science cut off its own wings, as it were, wings which had brought it far into the recesses of the heavens. Traces of this conception of knowledge are found throughout the development of European science and can in fact still be found in our day. We can throw important new light on this conception by considering the origins of Greek atomism, i.e., of the mechanistic conception of nature. This is the view that all changes in nature are changes of position, that is, motions in which physically indivisible particles or atoms unite and separate. In its most extreme form, the mechanistic conception of nature assumes nothing beyond mutual proximal action by these particles, such as repulsion and attraction. Its more moderate form–one that gained popularity particularly after Newton in modern era–includes actions at a distance in accordance with some law, depending on the distance of the particles and taking place in the direction of their connecting straight line. Even in modern age this view has, from time to time, almost completely dominated scientific thought. How did this view originate and wherein lies the secret of its power?

Ancient atomism is best known through the didactic poem, *De rerum natura*—"On the Nature of Things"—by Lucretius Carus, a name we have already encountered. According to contemporary scholarship, this work follows Epicurus's main work in detail,[14] whereas Epicurus himself mostly follows his predecessors, Leucippus and Democritus. Again, the decisive impetus to Greek science was given by the multiplicity and change that is encountered in experience. Eleatic thinkers denied the very possibility of all 'variance'. They held that one could conceive no such thing without being caught in contradiction. Zeno presented his famous and logically sharp paradoxes to this end. According to a currently common interpretation, they are mainly concerned with the inconsistencies found in the unclear concept of 'infinitely small'.[15] When the Pythagoreans found out about the incommensurability of the diagonal of a square with its side, the story goes, someone invented the intrinsically confused idea that if the relevant measure is imagined infinitely small, this would give the sought-after common measure. According to Simplicius, Zeno's reaction was to say, Look at the contradictions we find ourselves in if we assume there exists a multiplicity! If there is a multiplicity, it must be both infinitely large and infinitely small; and it even has to be infinitely large and infinitely small simultaneously.

Zeno's argument may be interpreted like this: if it is legitimate to assume that a line segment is constituted by an infinity of infinitely small unit line segments, then there are two possibilities. Either these units have a finite extent $\neq 0$, in which case a line segment composed of such units must be infinite. Or else their length equals zero, in which case, evidently, their sum equals zero as well. This is how far the Eleatic thinkers went to deny, in the name of reason, all multiplicity and change, that is, all 'variance', and to conclude instead that all our experience is delusion.

"This is impossible," replied the atomists, who said, according to Aristotle, "There is some measure of truth in phenomena, and they are infinitely varied." In this way the demand for invariance demands that it be reconciled with the varieties of experience. The entire development of European science can be considered a similar compromise between the demands of reason and experience, whereby these two lines of thought, whose origins are to be found in quite opposite directions, increasingly converge and finally coincide—as we shall seek to demonstrate—within the movement known as logical empiricism.

The atomists themselves tried to do justice to the diversity of experience, going as far as they could without renouncing the demand for invariance, as they understood it. They thought that the Eleatic absolutely invariant 'Being'

14. C. Bailey, *The Greek Atomists and Epicurus* (Oxford: Clarendon Press, 1928).
15. M.H. Hasse and H. Scholz, "Die GrundlagenKrisis."

or 'plenum' was divided into infinitely many parts differing from one another only in their figure, size, and order but not possessing any sensible qualities like color, sound, or warmth. Hence, "all nature consists of bodies and of void; anything else is mere supposition." Lucretius shows in detail why atoms must be absolutely indivisible and why they cannot, therefore, possess any qualities. We see, he says, that the 'foedera naturai'–the laws of nature–everywhere determine the being of things and the amount of force. How can it be that "the same always brings about the same?" This can be understood only on the assumption that there are absolutely immutable 'primordial rerum' or germs of things whose immutability *guarantees* the uniformity of nature. These are the fixed 'seeds' of all things, without which anything could come out of anything. No more than anything can come from nothing–for everything needs its own 'seeds'–can anything disappear into nothing–for if something were perishable down to its ultimate parts, it would have already disappeared through an infinity of time. This, however, goes against our experience, in which likes are always produced by likes. Therefore, there must be something that admits no change "lest all things return to nothing utterly."[16] This is why atoms can only possess unchanging properties; they have no color, warmth or coldness, no sound, no taste or odor, for "anything with these properties would be brought utterly to naught."

Here we meet a clear expression of that very same Greek peculiarity that we encountered when discussing the development of astronomy, namely, the Greek habit of reification or framing thought in terms of things. All lawfulness, they were inclined to think, is a matter of *substantial causality*. Like the celestial bodies, which perform their circular motion that manifests their eternal, spherical essence, so order prevails in nature, more broadly, according to the atomists, only because there are *unchanging basic objects revealing their unchanging properties in the course of events. It is only through these objects that lawfulness is guaranteed.*

No Greek thinker ever gave a clear formulation of the idea that lawfulness might be first and foremost a matter of invariant dependence relations holding between changes in nature. This idea of *dynamic causality* belongs to a modern, 'Galilean' conception of knowledge. From its point of view, it may well be that there is nothing beyond the continuous flux of phenomena; but this does not mean that there cannot be unchanging laws governing the flux. But this is not the Greek way of thinking–at most Heraclides the 'Obscure' may have been inclined towards such a view.

To see the enormous influence that Greek thought has exercised in this respect on the development of European science, consider the following passage at the end of Newton's *Opticks*. Here the author–in spite of being one of the

16. Lucretius, *On the Nature of Things*, Book II, 842 seqq.

creators of the modern, 'Galilean' conception of knowledge–repeats almost verbatim some Lucretian ideas:

> These primitive Particles being Solids, are incomparably harder than any porous Bodies compounded of them; even so very hard, as never to wear or break in pieces [. . .]. While the Particles continue entirely, they may compose Bodies of one and the same Nature and Texture in all Ages: But should they wear away, or break in pieces, the Nature of Things depending on them, would be changed. Water and Earth, composed of old worn Particles and Fragments of Particles, would not be of the same Nature and Texture now, with Water and Earth composed of entire Particles in the Beginning. And therefore, *that Nature may be lasting*, the Changes of corporeal Things are to be placed only in the various Separations and new Associations and Motions of these permanent Particles.[17]

The mechanistic conception of nature must evidently have been supported by an exceedingly strong habit of thought, one quite independent of any supporting evidence from experience for the reality of atoms (which in any case was not obtained until relatively late in the modern period, as for example in the kinetic theory of heat and gases, or the law of relative atomic weights in chemistry). The mechanistic conception of nature was not decisively undermined until it became evident in contemporary physics that electromagnetic phenomena could not possibly be given plausible explanations using the principles of Leucippus and Democritus.

These considerations may help explain why this conception has been so powerful; for we see that it concerns nothing less than the search for knowledge itself and the underlying 'demands of reason', captured in their characteristically Greek form. It is therefore worthwhile to pursue the matter a little further, enriching our discussion of the mechanistic conception with a few remarks.

Greek atomists believed that atoms did not, in the strict sense, possess any qualities. That this really was their view is shown by the following objection, well known, according to Plutarch, by the ancients. It shows, at the same time, how the seeds for almost all modern discussions in philosophy had already been sown in ancient thought.

The atomists generalized the mechanistic conception of nature, applying it even to mental life, a step that turned their doctrine into what is known as 'materialism'. This gave rise to the following often-repeated objection. We experience qualities like warmth. According to the atomists, this quality is

---

17. I. Newton, *Opticks*, Based on the fourth edition London, 1730 (Dover Publications, Inc. New York, 1952), 400.

produced in our sense organs when their atoms are combined in a suitable way. But, says Plutarch,[18] either these atoms possessed this quality beforehand, or else it was the combination that lent them this quality, which means that they underwent a change. Both possibilities, however, contradict the atomists' own presuppositions.

Even if we refuse to generalize the mechanistic conception of nature in the direction of materialism, we nevertheless find ourselves in insuperable difficulties. Early modern philosophy introduced the terminology of *primary* and *secondary qualities*; the former are figure, shape, order, motion and rest, while the latter include color, sound, and so on. This distinction, however, entirely overlooks the fact that shape, size, motion, etc., can mean two quite different things: on the one hand, it may mean *immediately perceived shape, size*, etc., which are qualitative matters, like color. On the other hand, it may mean *measured* size, etc., which involves *relations* between the measured things and units of measurement, together with a relational determination thereby ascribed to the measured thing. This distinction is in fact drawn in prescientific, everyday thought; there, however, it is all but forgotten, for our everyday conception is not familiar with relational thought. Let us consider the well-known Hering's figure (see Figure 7). When it is said that the main lines of the figure are straight and that the distance between them is 'really' the same everywhere, this means that their *measured* shape is straight, their *measured* distance is everywhere the same, and the curving of the main lines and the increasing of the distance between them around the star-like figure is an 'illusion'. *Here we can already see that the 'real', as opposed to what is 'apparent', is that which possesses greater invariance.* When we place the star-like figure between the main lines, a change occurs in the perceived shape and size, while the measured shape and size remain the same. We can then see how the entire dispute about primary and secondary *qualities* is based on a confusion, a failure to distinguish between a qualitative, immediately experienced shape, size, motion, and so on and their relational, measured counterparts.

Against the atomists, ancient skeptics presented several proofs that shape, size and other so-called primary qualities vary exactly like color or warmth and that there is therefore no reason to prefer them. These objections have been repeated by modern radical empiricism, which is in the main nothing more than a further development of ancient skepticism. The skeptics noted that, seen from one end, a colonnade seems to narrow and the lines of pillars curve towards the other end; seen from the middle, it seems to narrow and curve towards both ends. What, then, is its 'real' shape? What is remarkable is that neither the skeptics nor their followers hesitate to call this kind of variation 'apparent', saying, for instance, that the colonnade has, of course, a real, measurable shape and size independent of these shifting appearances. Yet when they start to philosophize, they seem to forget about this relational con-

18. Plutarkhos, *Adv. Colot.* 8.

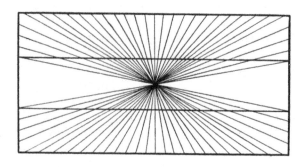

Figure 7

cept of the 'real' that they use routinely in everyday life. The relational manner of comprehension is indeed alien to everyday thought and early philosophy.

Measured, 'real' shape, size, motion, etc., are thus in fact nothing more than *relations*. But relations of what? As soon as we begin to talk about relations, we presuppose some objects whose relations we are talking about. It is precisely at this point that consistent atomism falls into insuperable difficulties.

Consider first the atomist conception of the void, understood to be the same as Eleatic nonbeing. Aristotle argues forcefully that this concept contains a contradiction.[19] If, for instance, the interval between two bodies is, in the atomist sense, strictly and absolutely empty, so that one can only speak of the distance or volume of this interval, this kind of determination cannot be assigned to something that is intrinsically nothing; for that which is nothing cannot possess any properties, such as distance. "That which really is empty is 'empty'," says Aristotle. Descartes repeats the same idea.[20] Imagine a vessel whose inner surface surrounds what is strictly a vacuum; in that case, the sides of the vessel must come into contact, for that which is not cannot possess even a distance.

We say, *The emptiness that belongs to the 'void' we perceive* is always only relatively and never absolutely empty. We see a tree at a distance. This *perceived* empty interval is empty only in the sense that it contains no color, warmth, hardness or any other perceived qualities. That it nevertheless is a certain *sense datum* is shown, for example, by the fact that a void seen in front of us is perceptually different than one that we imagine behind us. If they were the same, there could be no experienced difference between the two.

Even as early as the atomists—the first to develop a physicalist picture of the world—we see a tendency to *eliminate all qualities* from the conceived or physical world. Such an elimination, however, cannot be carried out consistently without facing the contradiction that Aristotle emphasized, the contra-

19. Aristotle, *Physics*, 214a.
20. Descartes, *Principia Philosophiae*, II, 16.

diction of arguing that something is real when, on the other hand, it must be recognized as unreal and nothing. If, for instance, we eliminate from what is physically void the qualitative content that belongs to the experienced, relative void of perceptual space, there will be nothing left.

This very same contradiction appears in the other main ingredient of the atomists' physical picture of the world: the notion of an atom. If atoms have no qualities, how can they be different from the void? How can they have a size and a shape, if not through the fact that there is a quality existing in a part of space that has a certain shape and size? What is this quality? Some, like Newton, said atoms are hard. To this Aristotle had already replied: On what grounds do we assign one or more tactile qualities to atoms while eliminating others?

By modern standards, this physical, atomistic conception of reality may well strike us as exceedingly primitive. Be that as it may, it engages us deeply in those epistemological problems that are typical of all physical theories of reality. We see that, even at this primitive level, the atomist conception developed out of a search for invariances that sought to replace, in a sense, variable qualities with relations. If, however, the resulting invariant world is conceived as the 'real world' existing 'behind' the world of appearances, contradictions ensue—and this happens quite independently of the fact, itself a decisive argument against atomism, that the word 'behind' has been left undefined and has in fact no real content.

As a first and very rough approximation, this physicalist conception of reality is a way of speaking about immediate experience. Like any other theory that is concerned with reality, it is 'reducible to experience' in a sense that will be explained later on: it must be capable of being 'translated into the language of experience', for it is nothing but a certain high-level 'logical construction' from elements found in experience. It is only at a much later stage, however, that this claim—which is one of the main 'theses' of logical empiricism—can be shown to be correct.

One feature of the atomist conception of the void is significant from the standpoint of the history of scientific ideas and their development. According to the atomists, the void is *absolutely* void, while atoms are *absolutely* solid. Atoms are 'atoms', that is, indivisible, precisely because there is no void in them. Compared to the Eleatic philosophers, who gave the impetus to this idea, experience and its content have brought about a deep differentiation in concept and theory formation. What is real is now divided into two, the solid and the void. Between the two there is a sharp opposition, but considered on their own, both are homogeneous: the solid is always the same solid, the void always the same void. Here we have a concrete example of how a law characterizing intellectual development—one to which we have already referred—is no less applicable when we consider the development of higher and more refined scientific ideas. The first impetus for the development lay in the requirement of invariance. Yet the content of experience forces one into a constant refinement in the formation of concepts and theories. Whenever this sort of differentiating step is taken–when what was formerly considered homogenous becomes divided, like the Eleatic 'Being' divided into the atomists' void and plenum– the search for invariances makes its breakthrough: in the pair of concepts the differentiation has produced, the sphere of each, at least when it is considered on its own, is understood to be maximally homogeneous and simple. Usually, the opposition between the members of the pair becomes maximal, as well. In *perception* the void and the solid pass into one another, with innumerable transitions like the shadings on the neck of a dove; in *thought*, by contrast, following the requirement of invariance, the rationalizing formation of concepts and theories seeks to reduce this continuous transition to one absolute opposition. Examples of this are found throughout the history of science.

Chapter 3

The Aristotelian Conception of Knowledge

We have glimpsed the gigantic figure of Plato in earlier chapters. The Academy he had founded was for decades the center for all Greek science.[1] Has European science ever flourished as Greek science did in Plato's Academy in the latter half of the fourth century BC?

In Plato we encounter the first large-scale attempt to discover what is fundamental to the life of the human spirit, not only intellectually but in all respects. To appreciate Plato's importance to science it suffices to point out that the great struggle of ideas that took place in the sixteenth century and inaugurated modern science was, in one respect, a struggle between Aristotelianism and a resuscitated Platonism. Kepler, for instance, the inventor of the laws of planetary motion, was in his youth a committed Platonist, so much so that his first work, *Mysterium cosmographicum*, takes up where Plato had left off in his dialogue *Timaeus*. One can also discern Platonist tendencies in Galileo's intellectual background, not to mention Descartes or Leibniz, both of whom were in many respects committed Platonists who combined their Platonism with the new, Galilean conception of knowledge.

And it is really only with Plato that *philosophy* in the strict, scientific sense of the word is born; that is, with Plato the eye of the intellect is now turned inward so that the *concept of knowledge itself becomes an object of scientific*

1. According to recent Plato scholarship, Platonic science was more independent of its predecessors, in particular, the Pythagoreans, than has been assumed; see, in particular, E. Frank, *Platon und die sogenannten Pythagoreer* (Halle: Niemeyer, 1923). Cf. also J. Stenzel, *Zahl und Gestalt bei Platon und Aristoteles* (Leipzig: B G. Teubner, 2nd ed., 1933).

consideration. In this way, the theory of theories, the theory of knowledge, is born.

Plato's pioneering attempt to sketch a theory of scientific knowledge was thoroughly Greek. The peculiar limitations inherent in the Greek conception of knowledge that we have already glimpsed become explicit in his endeavor to articulate the elements involved in human knowledge. Some nineteenth-century philosophers, namely certain neo-Kantians, have tried to make Plato into a kind of predecessor to Kant, arguing that he in fact supported the modern conception of knowledge;[2] such constructions are entirely arbitrary, however.

All Greek thinkers were inclined to consider existence as if 'being', in fact, was synonymous with 'being unchanging'. There is a fragment from Melissus that says, "If earth, water, air and fire were what they appear to be, appearances could not change, but would have to remain as they appear." Why would that be? Because Melissus assumes that 'being' this or that means 'being this or that unchanging'. What does Heraclitus the Riddler mean when he says: "Everything is and is not"? Or, "We are sick and healthy"? Or, "What is real is contradictory"? He can only mean this: Since we may well be healthy today and sick tomorrow, we are, in a contradictory way, both and neither. If we really *were* healthy, that is, we would *always* be healthy.

This identification of being with being unchanging is repeated time and again in Plato. In *Phaedo* it is said that each of the real beings "remain unchanging and constant, never admitting any sort of alteration whatsoever."[3] "Philosophers," we learn in *Republic*, "are able to grasp the eternal and unchangeable, and those who wander in the region of the many and variable are not philosophers."[4] This is why philosophers must be the rulers of the State, and why they must prepare themselves for this duty by pursuing scientific knowledge of unchangeable things. He who possesses knowledge of the unchangeable possesses something lasting and can therefore accomplish something that will be lasting. "For mind and science," it is said in *Philebus*, "when employed about changing things, do not attain the highest truth."[5] 'Knowledge of the changeable' would be a contradictory notion, for knowledge is something unchanging, yet knowledge of the changeable would mean that knowledge is itself changing. In *Theaetetos* we are taught that when we are concerned with the world of constantly changing appearances, we should only use the term 'becoming' and not 'being'; for this reason even material things cannot be spoken of as having any absolute existence or by any name that would bring them to a standstill, for "he who attempts to fix them is easily refuted."[6]

2. P. Natorp, *Platos Ideenlehre: eine Einführung in den Idealismus* (Leipzig: Verlag der Dürr'schen Buchhandlung, 1903). (English translation as P. Natorp: Plato's *Theory of Ideas: An Introduction to Idealism*, ed. with an introduction by V. Politis [Berlin: Academia Verlag, 2004])
3. *Phaedo*, 78d.
4. *Republic*, 484b.
5. *Philebus*, 59.
6. *Theaetetus*, 157.

All of this is a consequence of what Plato regarded as the true nature of knowledge. "Words," Plato once said, "must be akin to the matter which they describe; when they relate to the lasting and permanent and intelligible, they ought to be lasting and unalterable, and, as far as their nature allows, irrefutable and invincible."[7] The description of phenomena, by contrast, is akin to these phenomena; it is nothing but opinion or doxa, subject to variation and change, whereas scientific knowledge or episteme aims to capture what is invariant, the real as it is, and is therefore unalterable.

Do we then possess genuine scientific knowledge, Plato asks, and not mere opinions about 'shadows in a cave' or 'reflections' found in the world of experience?[8] Yes, Plato insists. Here we encounter the Kantian turn that is given so much emphasis by the neo-Kantians. Perceptions, if considered on their own, remain separate from one another but they are brought together by reason–so teaches Plato–to form a 'unity of an idea'. "Perceptions come from the body, their similarity and difference from the thought." Not all concepts are generalizing copies acquired through experience, but at least some of them are originally within us, as memories from a world that is intellectually more perfect and more invariant, that is, the world of 'ideas' or forms (eidos). Several passages in Plato address what we earlier called the rationalization of concepts. General concepts–those belonging to mathematics in particular–provide the standard that we ourselves set for phenomena, such as when we form a judgment about the equality of things by starting from a notion of complete equality that, according to Plato, we simply do not find in experience. We could not, according to Plato, possess such rationalized concepts–mathematical concepts in particular–if there was no corresponding invariant world, the world of being as it is in itself; for knowledge is an unchanging description of something that is unchanging.

The only things that remain stable, relatively speaking, in the flux of phenomena are the *kinds* of things (eidos). These are an imperfect reflection of the invariant world of ideas, reified forms of kinds; in Plato's case, this world does not remain purely intellectual or *'ideatic'*. It has an ethico-religious tone that transforms it into an *ideal* world, as well. This explains why Plato holds mathematics in such high esteem–and why it acquires even more prestige as he continues to refine his thinking. Indeed, "Let no one enter the Academy who does not know his mathematics!" "God always calculates."[9] When the Creator as the craftsman of the world (the demiurge of *Timaeus*) constructs the cosmos, he realizes the 'idea of the good'–that is, first and foremost, the *invariant*–as much as is possible within the realm of the perishable. For this reason a mathematical astronomy and a mathematical physics can be created; although these do not constitute proper scientific knowledge, they can never-

---

7. *Timaeus*, 29b.
8. *Republic*, 510e.
9. *Timaeus*, 30 seqq.

theless constitute a 'probable story'. In this kind of mathematical physics, it is assumed that matter possesses a crystalline structure constituted by Platonic solids, and the regular solids in turn are constructed out of equilateral triangles; these are regarded as atoms of a kind.

As Plato grew older, he came closer and closer to the atomist picture of the world. What distinguished him completely from the atomists, however, was the vision of life that gave an idealist tone to his philosophy. It is for this reason that he so abhorred the 'uninitiated', those who "think that nothing is save what they can grasp in their hands"[10]–which is a false accusation, for the second main element in the atomists' reality, the void, is something that cannot be touched. Both Plato and the atomists thought that geometrical quantities are the basic elements of the world of experience. Aristotle goes so far as to call atoms 'numbers'; sometimes, on the other hand, they are referred to as 'eidos' like the Platonic ideas, and the latter, in turn, are very much like numbers.

In this way Plato gave a powerful impetus to the development of mathematical natural science. Its ultimate purpose is ethico-religious. It teaches us to know the 'idea of the good'. In terms of the intellectual aspects that interest us, this means that we must know invariances. We may learn better to appreciate this task now assigned to the natural sciences once we realize that similar ideas were endorsed by the men who created modern science. It belongs to Natural Philosophy, Newton said in an important passage of his main work, to reason about the nature of God "from the appearances of things."[11] With Leibniz, Plato's words become, "When God calculates and exercises his thought, the world is made"[12]–although the calculation that Leibniz's God practices is no longer the elementary mathematics of the Greeks, but rather the mathematics of the differential calculus and continuously changing quantities. When the same Leibniz considers this world to be the most perfect of all possible worlds, this should, again, be understood after the manner of Plato. Here, perfection is primarily a matter of reality possessing rational perfection in a way that satisfies the requirements of invariance. Such a world, Leibniz argues, "is at the same time the simplest in its hypotheses and the richest in phenomena, as might be a geometric line whose construction would be easy but whose properties and effects would be very remarkable and of a wide reach."[13]

How did it come about that this powerful impetus to exact research eventually came to a halt, dying out in its infancy in general physics and even in areas such as astronomy where it had achieved considerable results? The subject that Aristotle treats so extensively under the title of 'physics' is in our view not

10. *Theaetetus*, 155e.
11. *The Principia: Mathematical Principles of Natural Philosophy*, Book III, General Scholium.
12. G.W. Leibniz, *Dialogue*, in G. W. Leibniz: *Philosophical Papers and Letters: A Selection*, trans. and ed., with an Introduction by L.E. Loemker (Dordrecht: D. Reidel Publishing Company, 1969), 183 n. 4. (*Die Philosophische Schriften von Gottfried Wilhelm Leibniz*, Hrsg. von C.I. Gerhard. Band VII. [Berlin, 1890] 191.)
13. G.W. Leibniz, *Discourse on Metaphysics*, §6; *Philosophical Papers and Letters*, 306.

physics at all; and Archimedes's statics, though undeniably a great achievement, remained an isolated initiative that was not taken up until much later by Galileo and his contemporaries.

There is a connection between this stagnation and the Greek conception of knowledge as an unchanging picture of a reified, unchanging reality. According to this conception, there can only be knowledge of unchanging things and of nothing else. In Plato we find a number of radical requirements of invariance, even of exact mathematical invariance. But he insists, first, that these invariances should be in a sense the simplest ones; a theory of the heavens should consist in the geometry of the circle, and the physics of the sublunar world must be the geometry of the equilateral triangle. Second, he insists that these invariances are to be understood as *structural laws*, that is as laws for *structures* and not for events. And when experience seems to only partly satisfy the sought-for invariances, sometimes even deviating from them entirely, this does nothing to undermine the requirements; given the 'unstable and obscure nature of matter', it is only to be expected, Plato says, that perishable things should be no more than a partial reflection of the rational perfection belonging to 'true Reality'. For this reason Plato regards all mathematical natural science as no more than a 'probable story'[14] which is not even supposed to be valid as a full, exact account. *The requirement of verification by experience is weak*. It is at this point that Plato's heir, Aristotle, enters the stage, taking the main role in the development of scientific ideas.

Aristotle

With the instinctive certainty that is characteristic of a great master of empirical research, Aristotle sets "the unimpeachable evidence of the senses" as the criterion for all knowledge relating to reality.[15] He does not really provide any reasons for this *postulate of verification*, the basic element of all empiricism; indeed, conclusive reasons for it have been given only within modern logical empiricism. To Aristotle it is self-evident, as he himself puts it, that "principles must be judged from their results."[16] That is, explanatory principles must be judged by whether what is found in experience complies with the experiential consequences of a theory. For a theory can have no other purpose besides explaining the facts of experience.

Aristotle's reasons for the requirement of verification—in so far as talk of such reasons is at all appropriate—were psychological. Aristotle was the first *psychological empiricist*, and a very radical one at that. For in him we find two

14. *Timaeus* 59.
15. *De Caelo*, 306a.
16. *De Caelo*, 306a.

problems linked and confused in a way that was not noticed clearly until logical empiricism, namely the *logical* question about the validity of knowledge, and the *psychological* question about its origin. According to Aristotle, general concepts emerge as generalized copies of repeated, particular perceptions. This copy-theory extends to mathematical concepts as well, including number concepts.[17] In this way, "there is nothing in understanding that was not first in sense," as the Scholastic philosophers would put it centuries later.

Starting from these premises, Aristotle subjects Plato's theory of ideas to a devastating criticism; the curious thing about it is that the reasons brought against the theory can already be found in Plato's own dialogue *Parmenides*–a remarkable fact that Aristotle fails even to mention. One of Aristotle's criticisms is of particular interest to us. If it is assumed, he says,[18] that corresponding to each species of perceptible things there is a reified concept, its idea, which has itself been made into a substance, then a search for the causes of things yields as many extra causes. The theory, that is, does not simplify, but rather doubles, what it is supposed to explain. Here we encounter a basic principle of epistemology, Ockham's razor. When applied to epistemology, it is commonly formulated as follows: explanatory principles must not be multiplied beyond necessity. It involves the idea that every theory must possess a certain *relative simplicity*. This important concept together with the reasons for the principle we have just stated will be explored later on.

In Plato's search for knowledge the focus is on an extraordinarily radical postulate of invariance, whereas in Aristotle the emphasis is on the requirement of experiential verification. In Plato the postulate of invariance is given a remarkably narrow formulation: he insisted upon thing-like invariances of the simplest possible kind. *Rather than freeing the search for invariances from its peculiarly Greek limitations, Aristotle rejected, in the name of experience, the requirements imposed on it by Plato.* This fact underlies one of the remarkable features of the Aristotelian conception of knowledge: *it rejects the very idea of rationalizing concept and theory formation.* This means, above all, that attempts to create a mathematical natural science are given up. "The method of mathematics," Aristotle says, "is not that of natural science."[19] The forms of sense perception are not those that are found in geometry. No perceptible thing is exactly straight or circular, and in perception no circle touches a straight line only at one point.[20] The very requirement of mathematical exactness is discarded as being somehow contrary to nature; Aristotle even says that this mathematical accuracy–what he calls "pettifoggery"[21]–is something 'mean', that is, something that belongs literally to handicraft. This is a fatal step, for a good hypothesis or a theory is such that, *if* it is false, it can clearly

17. *Posterior Analytics*, 100a.
18. *Metaphysics*, 992a.
19. *Metaph.*, 995a.
20. *Metaph.*, 998a.
21. *Metaph.*, 995a.

be shown to be so. Because of this step, however, typical Aristotelian assumptions become formally bad hypotheses because they are inexact. They could not be easily verified or falsified, because they had no *exact* empirical consequences to be clearly confirmed or refuted.

It is helpful even at this early point to consider the brilliant reply that Galileo would give, almost two thousand years later, to this rejection of the mathematical conception of nature. In *Dialogue Concerning the Two Chief World Systems* we find Simplicio, the Aristotelian, repeating the very claims about the nonmathematical character of nature that we have just been considering. Galileo's spokesman first points out how imprecise it is to say that a sphere in a nature never touches a plane only at one point.[22] If this were the case, he argues, it would not be a sphere and a plane. That is to say, the mistake that is committed when simple geometrical concepts are applied to matter, in which they can only be approximated, is neither a mistake of geometry nor of physics, that is, of nature; it is simply a mistake made by the *calculator*. Bodies have always some shape, and therefore a geometrical shape, no matter how complicated that shape may be. We start with concepts that are as simple as possible and take into account the 'perturbations caused by matter', to use a Platonic phrase; in this way, by approximation, we come closer and closer to the actual geometrical forms that are found in nature. This means that we refuse to compromise the ideal, namely, the search for invariances; but neither do we compromise the requirement of testability by experience. We bring the two ideals closer together through gradual approximation.

Aristotelianism, on the other hand, compromises the very ideal of knowledge and turns Aristotelian natural science into a somewhat trivial enterprise. To a considerable extent Aristotle returns to the viewpoints of pre-scientific everyday life and then develops them in a systematic manner. This, though, he accomplishes with the awe-inspiring thoroughness and consistency of a great logician, so much so that, in a sense, his picture of the world has no gaps in it; he has an answer to all questions. This Aristotelian conception of knowledge, even if it began with a false step, is so exemplary that even today theories that are grounded in everyday thought without the fruitful impact of science are often reminiscent of Aristotelianism.

Aristotle's conception of knowledge was most characteristic of Greek epistemology and has played an immense role in the development of scientific ideas. He formulated his conception in his so-called first philosophy–what later generations began to refer to as 'metaphysics'–and in his psychology.[23] It holds, first, that there can be knowledge only of the universal; second, that knowledge is always of the unchanging; and third, that knowledge is of that which is always, or is most of the time, and not of what is a matter of chance. We shall investigate each of these features in turn.

22. Galileo, *Dialogue Concerning the Two Chief World Systems*, 206–7.
23. *Metaph.*, see Books B and Z in particular.

Consider, then, the first feature: "Knowledge is knowledge of the universal." The reason for this view, above all, is that words must possess some general meaning if their meanings are to be grasped. That is to say, words must be able to be used not only in a given particular situation, but in other situations as well. Hence, "every conceptual determination relates to something general." Here we meet one of those logical insights that we encounter time and again when we study Aristotle. It is an essential feature of human knowledge, and we shall consider it in more detail on a later occasion.

Second, there can be knowledge only of what is not corruptible, and this means: there can be knowledge only of what is thing-like and not subject to change. Aristotle speaks entirely in the spirit of Plato when he says that of perishing things there can be no scientific knowledge (episteme), but only opinion (doxa). "Not even a land surveyor can have knowledge of things that he experiences, for his knowledge would disappear as soon as the things have disappeared." "Perishing things are obscure to those who have the relevant knowledge, when they have passed from our perception."[24]

Third, all knowledge of nature is generic and concerns what is generally and mostly the case, but not what is subject to chance. We shall defer this point until later and consider here the second feature in more detail.

In and of themselves, our sense perceptions are always particular, but what we remember of them are 'universal forms'. The relationship that sense perception bears to the particular is analogous to that of the intellect to what is general. For this reason "one must indeed applaud those who say that the soul is the place of form."[25] What is general is in the mind, as it were, in itself, as a thing-like 'idea'. To possess knowledge is to be in a possession of such general forms, and it cannot be true unless it remains in the intellect as a thing-like entity, corresponding to the thing "like a wax imprint repeats the form of the seal." If there occurs a change on the surface of the earth, the corresponding map is no longer correct. Just as a geographic map can only be of a surface that does not change, representation and knowledge in general can only concern that which is thing-like and unchangeable.

From the modern point of view we recognize that even in what changes, if it is subject to laws, there is something unchangeable, namely regular relations of dependence, like the relation between distance and time in falling motion. To the ancient Greeks we could put the question, Are these *relational invariances* not the most important ones? None among the Greek scientists or philosophers had a clear vision of this possibility. "Like perceives like," they all said, including Plato and Aristotle.[26] Knowledge is something unchangeable and not one thing today, something else tomorrow. How could it be like that if it did not remain in the mind, retaining its thing-like, unchangeable

24. *Metaph.*, 1040a.
25. *De anima*, III.4.
26. *Timaeus*, 45; *De anima*, III.8

character? In such a case–this seems self-evident–its object must be thing-like and unchangeable as well. Knowledge of the changeable would not be knowledge at all but, at most, mere opinion that is liable to change. In fact this is the gist of the Greek conception of knowledge. It is even found in full measure in those Greek thinkers who deny the very existence of anything invariant, such as the skeptics who maintained that there is no knowledge, only opinion.

Let us next consider some of the fatal consequences that this conception of knowledge had throughout Aristotle's thought. To begin, it cuts off his wings when he sets out to create a theory of theory, that is, *logic*. We cannot but be surprised at how far Aristotle could develop his logic, given the Procrustean nature of his conception of knowledge. Even Kant said that since the time of Aristotle logic had not taken a single step forward. This was an exaggeration, but the fact remains that it is really only in our time, namely during the past hundred years, that logic has broken these fetters, a development that derives its inspiration ultimately from Leibniz.

We saw that in Euclid's system–created approximately at the time of Aristotle–we have a logical theory that comes reasonably close to perfection; that is, in Euclid we have logic *in practice*. Aristotle's theoretical logic–or, as Kant was to call it, "formal logic"–is a scientific description of logic that is really being used: it is a theory of theory.

A number of logical insights receive surprisingly precise and clear formulations in Aristotle's theory. These include the following: An assertion or a judgment is a "speech" affirming or denying something. Universal affirmations and particular denials as well as universal denials and particular affirmations stand to one another in the relation of affirmation and negation; "everything is perishable" and "something is not perishable" would be an example of such pairs. One of these must be true, and the other must be false; there is no third possibility ("tertium non datur"). A judgment that both affirms and denies something is not true–this is known as the law of noncontradiction. But we also find limitations: In every judgment some property is ascribed to a thing or else is denied of it[27]–a claim that is blatantly wrong, but which continues to be repeated in modern textbooks, thanks to Aristotle's authority. From the standpoint of modern logic, this would mean that all judgments or logical sentences possess either the form '$A(a)$' or 'not-$A(a)$', that is, in them a property is either ascribed to or denied of a *single* thing. Hence, Aristotle recognizes nothing but thing-property judgments like "a is perishable." Relational judgments, on the other hand, like the judgment "a is more perishable than b," in which some common determination is affirmed of two or more things, are entirely neglected. It is impossible to make such judgments by means of thing-property statements, and yet they are the most important of

---

27. Aristotle's most important logical doctrines, which will be discussed in the text, are found in his works, *On Categories, De Interpretatione,* and *Prior Analytics.*

all. What is more, this renders Aristotle's logic trivial, for it is scarcely possible to find a single interesting system that is specified only by means of 'unary predicates', to use modern parlance, that is, statements like '$A(a)$', in which something is said of some one thing. For instance, it is impossible to state the logical structure of the series of natural numbers, 1, 2, 3, . . . without 'binary predicates' of the form $A(a,b)$, in which some determination is ascribed to two things (such determinations can be extended to more than two); without, that is, determinations like 'successor of' or 'greater than'. From the formal point of view, thing-predicate sentences are a relatively trivial special case among all possible logical sentences.

This shows how Aristotle's reifying manner of thought, dominated by the pair of concepts 'thing' and 'property', mutilates his logic. Aristotle's logic in fact becomes mere *classification* and nothing more; it is a theory of classes and their corresponding properties, and this characterization applies to his science as well. Thing-property sentences fail to capture any system beyond classifications; not even the general concept of *order* can be given a definition. And a concept cannot be defined except by stating its position in some classification of concepts, that is, by stating the 'distinguishing mark' that separates it from other members of the class and the 'nearest kind', or genus proximum, that is, the class itself. If it is assumed, for instance, that the concepts of sum and unit are known, we can define number 2 through the equation $1 + 1 = 2$, but this is not a definition in the Aristotelian sense. Hence from the Aristotelian point of view, the majority of actual definitions are in fact impossible. What is more, this point of view involves the further restriction that exactly one definition is possible in each case, for "as there is one essence, there is one definition."

There is one respect, however, in which Aristotle has given a correct–and even exemplary–account of the elementary theory of classification. One of his most important steps consisted in what is today known as *formalization of logic*. For simple cases he introduced a logical language that is precise in the following sense. In natural language it often happens that one and the same thing can be expressed in different ways. For instance, "everything temporal is perishable" means the same as "if something is temporal, it is perishable." In logic it is for technical reasons necessary to proceed as Aristotle did: it is necessary to pick one of these logically equivalent expressions and use it systematically, condensing it, furthermore, into a formula that is as simple as possible. In modern terminology, Aristotle's formulae consist, first, of 'logical constants'. These are words or symbols expressing logical concepts, for instance 'every', 'some', 'is', and 'not'. On the other hand, they also contain 'logical variables', symbols like M, P, and S that are used to indicate indefinite classes or properties corresponding to them. Logical constants are thus the so-called forms of thought, and their interrelations are the subject matter of logic. These constants cannot be replaced by others in a given formula without changing its so-called *'logical form'*, that is, without changing the relevant rule of inference or turning the formula into nonsense. Logical variables in turn indicate the changing *'content'* of thought that is indifferent to the logician. In a given formula, these variables can be replaced by others according to certain rules without changing the logical form. In this respect Aristotle and modern logic agree as to the proper task of logic: logic is the theory of theory. A theory is a system in which, from certain basic statements certain other, derived statements are inferred. Thus, logic is first and foremost a theory of inference; it has completed its primary task as soon as it has supplied the necessary rules of inference and furnished proofs that they are consistent and sufficient. Aristotle gave a number of elementary rules for cases that have to do with classes or properties corresponding to them, and part of his presentation here is both complete and free of error. The fundamental formula here is the so-called modus Barbara, which is the name the scholastics gave to it:

> Every M is P
> Every S is M
> Therefore, every S is P

Here we see the gist of the logical apparatus that Aristotle used to explain nature. The narrow structure of his logic is visible everywhere, a feature that comes from his conception of knowledge. In compromising the radical requirement of invariance for the benefit of experience, which is otherwise typical of the Greeks, he reveals his conception of knowledge and reality to be primarily a reflection of the peculiar limitations of Greek thought. "What is lacking here," it has been said, "are tools with which change can be conceptualized."[28] What is lacking here is the concept of a law-like dependence, that is, the concept of function. The very form of thought is here determined by the type of invariance that dominates prescientific everyday thought: a thing, an object together with its properties. Early modern philosophers would call this the 'school philosophy' or scholasticism that lost its hegemony only after a vehement battle of ideas. It nevertheless still dominates philosophies that remain alien to modern scientific thought.

To elucidate this point, consider Aristotelian 'first philosophy', aiming to study 'unchanging being' and Aristotelain physics that studies 'changing being'. The former introduces into philosophical thinking the concept–or rather word–'essence' (*ousia* in Greek), i.e., *'what something is'* as opposed to 'what it is like or how it is'. To answer this question, one looks for that 'underlying support'–*hupokeimenon* in Greek; *substratum* in Latin–of which properties

---

28. This is Kurd Lasswitz's phrase from his work, *Geschichte der Atomistik vom Mittelater bis Newton* (Hamburg und Leipzig: Verlag von Leopold Voss, 1890). –Cf. here the important work by Ernst Cassirer, *Substanzbegriff und Funktionsbegriff*, 2nd ed. (Berlin, 1923). (English translation in E. Cassirer, *Substance and Function and Einstein's Theory of Relativity*, trans. W.C. and M.J. Swabey [Chicago and London: Open Court Publishing Company, 1923].)

and relations are predicated. These latter exist only insofar as they are unchangeable; only the essence, the substance, is or has being. The deepest of all questions concern the determination of this being. It is not until relatively late in the early modern period, under the influence of Leibniz and the empiricists, that it becomes clear that this question is empty.

The important point here is that the question underlying and guiding all scientific theory and concept formation is '*What?*' rather than '*How?*' Let us be clear about what is involved in this. Suppose, for instance, that we are studying some particular kind of change (which brings us to Aristotle's physics). The question one then asks is not how that kind of change occurs; one asks *what* it is. For example, one does not set out to study the laws of motion but tries to classify the different kinds of motions. Once the requirement of invariance is compromised, there is little reason to engage in analysis, for analysis is nothing but search for hidden invariances. In this way, one comes to accept everyday experience in all its coarseness. Experience seems to teach that every rectilinear motion comes to a rest. *If we do not ask the question, how this coming to a rest happens*, we fail to see what is really crucial here, namely that how quickly a moving object stops will depend upon the strength of resistant forces, and hence that cessation is dependent upon certain factors that we may imagine to be missing altogether so that, in a limiting case, rectilinear motion could continue forever. Aristotle in fact considered the idea of infinite rectilinear motion and found it to be absurd.[29] For he believed that every motion (rather than only a *change* in motion) implies a cause of that motion; if the cause ceases, the motion stops. It follows that all motion in the world, including the rotational motions in the Heavens, must have an ultimate cause, the so-called 'unmoved mover'.

This applies to every other kind of change, as well. The basic idea is this: Every change presupposes that the relevant object is capable of that change. "In each kind of motion it is that which is capable of that motion that is in motion [. . .] and so there must be something capable of being burned before there can be a process of being burned."[30] In every change some latent 'potentiality' (Greek *dynamis*; in Latin *potentia*) becomes real or actual (Greek *energeia*; in Latin *actualitas*). Change takes place when something that is in itself a mere possibility, like the stuff out of which something is made (*hyle*), obtains some 'form' (*eidos*; *morfe*). *A thing, thus, has two kinds of properties: manifest and latent*; the latter are the potentialities. When a thing changes, something latent becomes manifest.[31] (We could say that from a deeper perspective every change is only apparent.) This applies to motion as well. In motion the moving body takes on the 'form' of a new place.

29. *Physics*, 214b.
30. *Physics*, 251a.
31. *Physics*, 257b.

In this way changes, too, are considered exclusively within the framework of things and their properties. In all change there is present–to use a scholastic term–a 'qualitas occulta' making itself manifest. Action follows being, 'operari sequitur esse'. When the potentiality that is present in a change has been named, everything to say about that change has been said.

The latent capabilities of things, their 'potencies', are teleological factors, as well. When a particular change reaches its final state, this state is at the same time the purpose of the change.[32] For the Greek word *telos* means not only 'end' but also 'purpose'. Often, Aristotle's thought even follows linguistic hints. Thus the word 'teleion' means that which has been brought to an end and, hence, what is in a sense complete. Therefore, he concludes, the finite must be more complete than the infinite.[33] For the former has its limit; it is something that has been brought to an end, 'teleion'. This is one of the roots of the often-mentioned finitism that was characteristic of Greek thought.

We have now outlined the peculiar, vaguely indefinite 'teleological' or 'organic' explanation of the world that is found in Aristotelianism. When something happens in nature, this is because "everything craves for its form, like a woman craves for a man," that is, seeks to realize its own potentiality. When things are in motion, they strive to move to their natural places, heavy things downwards and light things upwards. If somebody had told Aristotle that this is not always so, he would have replied that it is valid in *most* cases and one should not demand mathematical exactitude from nature, for that is "pettifoggery," the sort of precision that is suitable for craftsmen only. Our knowledge is indeterminate in the way that nature itself is indeterminate. For example, the earth is "by nature a sphere," although not exactly a geometrical sphere. Our knowledge is only about what "nature strives for," although what nature strives for is not always what it achieves.

This is the origin of the way of thinking that dominated all European thought until it was finally superseded by the birth of modern science. It is the origin of such doctrines as, for example, "nature abhors the void," a doctrine that would explain why the level of water rises in a vacuum tube. The point behind such a conception was not only to describe how nature in fact behaves; it was to say something more; for why else would people have stopped talking about this "horror vacui," when Torricelli, a student of Galileo, showed that under normal atmospheric pressure this 'abhorrence of the void' is active only up to the height of seventy-six centimeters? Aristotelianism had deep roots because, in some respects, it accords so well with everyday thought, permeated as it is by the relatively primitive type of invariance that is characteristic of everything 'thing-like'.

A few examples show how persistent this Aristotelianism was, and still is. When the modern, Galilean conception of knowledge emerged, its protago-

32. *Physics*, 194a.
33. *Physics*, 207a.

nists—Galileo himself and even more strongly Newton—emphasized that they wanted to find out, first and foremost, *how changes take place* and that they therefore ignored the question of their so-called causes. The question 'How?' gives rise to *relational* rather than property concepts. The concept 'forces of nature', for example, refers to a law underlying certain courses of events occurring in nature and not to some hidden property of things. At the end of his *Opticks*, Newton emphasizes that 'Forces', as he uses the term, arise not from 'occult qualities' but from Laws of Nature.[34] How difficult it is to adopt such a view becomes evident when we consider that even the philosophical empiricists of the seventeenth and eighteenth centuries were inclined to regard these 'Forces' as hidden properties. Locke, a great admirer of Newton's natural science, nevertheless thought that the study of nature could not be developed into a genuine science; that we can discover *how* changes take place, but not the 'real essence' underlying these changes.[35] Another illustration, out of many possible, is the case of Schopenhauer. Natural forces like weight, elasticity and electricity, he says, are nothing but unknown properties of things.[36] Hence natural science does nothing but classify phenomena. The 'inner essences' of these forces will remain forever closed to it.

In this way Aristotelianism—the illicit assumption that we come to understand nature by somehow deriving changes from the underlying 'essences' of things—has led, and continues to lead, people to metaphysics. This reifying thinking, which operates with 'substances', remains committed to the notion of cause that was so thoroughly criticized by Hume—the belief that between cause and effect there is some necessary, intrinsic connection, that is, that causes, in the end, are hidden properties of things whose effects are built into those things as potentialities. Still further, this manner of thinking leads to the belief that there could be a higher road to knowledge that what is provided by ordinary scientific experience; that there could be an 'intellectual vision' capable of penetrating the 'essence' things or their hidden properties in same the way that ordinary perception reveals to us visible properties.

34. *Opticks*, 401.
35. J. Locke, *Essay Concerning Human Understanding*, book IV, ch. XI.
36. Schopenhauer, *The World as Will and Representation*, I, § 15.

Chapter 4

The Galilean Conception of Knowledge

The concept of knowledge is based on two main elements: the search for invariances and the requirement of verification. Both were handed down to us by Greek science and philosophy. When we emphasize the former, we follow the rationalist line of thought; when we emphasize the latter, we agree with empiricism. The Greeks themselves, however, could not find a balance between these two elements. They assumed from the start that the invariances they were seeking had to be thing-like. It is for this reason that Greek science and philosophy eventually reached a deadlock that was not broken until the early modern period. After a prolonged battle of ideas, the concept of knowledge itself was given a new meaning and liberalized as the Aristotelian conception was replaced by the Galilean concept of knowledge, the concept that is characteristic of modern science.

The gist of the change is found in the following idea. Insofar as the object of knowledge is constituted by experiential invariances, one can continue to agree with the Greeks that there can be knowledge only of the unchangeable. However, the most important kind of unchangeable thing is no longer to be found in things themselves, but rather in the relations between changes; it is to be found, that is, in *relational invariances* or functions, not in substances. We may readily admit that things do change all the time; they come into being and are destroyed. It does not follow from this, however, that there is nothing unchangeable in *how* they come into being and are destroyed, as long as this unchangeable would not be substantial but functional.

This we begin to find when we study *how things are*. Commenting on one of the key points in the modern conception of knowledge, Leibniz points out that one is free to claim that experience is nothing but 'somnium sive phantasma', a dream or illusion; it is, nevertheless, an ordered, law-like 'dream or illusion', in which the future can be predicted on the basis of the past and knowledge of the laws that regulate this stream of changes. This makes it possible that the *world of ideas we are looking for, the 'true Reality', is in fact materialized in those 'reflections' that we find in the stream of experience*; in the relations of dependence obtaining between the 'shadows of a cave'. Everything perishes but laws remain. There were a few occasions when Greek thinkers nearly recognized this possibility. Heraclitus the Riddler may have come closest, but Plato should be mentioned, as well. For example, when the Sophists argued vigorously that there could not be scientific knowledge of phenomena (because these are not only changeable but thoroughly dependent upon the observer) Plato replied that everyone is the best judge of the taste he is picking up at the moment, but the cook will be a better judge than the guest of the pleasure to be derived from the dinner being prepared.[1] *This so-called relativity of phenomena, that is, by no means excludes the possibility that we may obtain generally valid knowledge of them.* The Greek conception of knowledge, however, stands in the way of any further development of this idea. It is only with the emergence of the Galilean conception that the 'gigantomachy', the primordial battle of giants that Plato mentions in *The Sophist*,[2] takes a new turn: the 'real' is the law for the 'apparent'.

This is why the Galilean conception of knowledge constitutes one of the most remarkable moments ever in the development of scientific ideas. The Aristotelian conception of knowledge, operating with the concepts of thing and property, was grounded in the habits of everyday thought. Now, though, human thought took a decisive step as consciously developed relational concepts, often quite detached from everyday experience, came to occupy an ever greater role in the comprehension of reality.

In the course of the following centuries, this new direction in the development of scientific ideas gradually gained strength and stability. How and why this happened is a question to which historians of ideas have probably not yet given a satisfactory answer.[3] It is fascinating to follow the gradual change occurring in intellectual climate in the course of the transition from the Middle Ages to the modern era: the most conspicuous sign of this change–though by no means its cause–was a turn from books to nature, from Aristotelian scholasticism to experience. Our task leaves us no time to explore in any depth the earliest phase in the gradually emerging new type of thinking, with such

1. *Theaetetus*, 178.
2. *The Sophist*, 246a,
3. The most ambitious attempt in this direction is probably Ernst Cassirer's *Das Erkenntnisproblem in der Philosophie und Wissenschaft der neueren Zeit*, 2 vols. (1906, 1907).

forerunners of modern thought as William of Ockham and Nicholas of Cusa. At the turn of the fifteenth and sixteenth centuries, the new movement of thought succeeded in establishing its first tangible results, with Copernicus entering the stage and Leonardo writing in his notebooks striking aphorisms, thoughts with an extraordinarily wide range. "Even when truth dwells on humble and lowly matters," he says, "it is still infinitely above uncertainty and lies, disguised in high and lofty discourses." With developments like these, the craving for mathematical precision that Aristotle so despised is becoming transformed into the *mark of nobility* for scientific thought. "And I deem useless all knowledge which is not produced by experience, the mother of all certainty, and which does not return to experience." A scientific theory, that is, must be a bridge, constructed with mathematical precision and leading from experiences to other experiences. Independently of one another, in different places and in different ways, the program for a new kind of scientific thought is propagated by such men as Francis Bacon, Joannes Vives, a Spaniard who excelled particularly in psychology, and Giordano Bruno, the martyr of the new conception of the world, among many others. Beginning his career as a pure Platonist, Kepler develops into a modern mathematical physicist who is convinced that an error of eight angular minutes suffices to show that one of his earlier conjectures about the orbit of the Planet Mars cannot be correct. All of this brings us to Galileo.

Why should one call the modern conception of knowledge 'Galilean', as we have here? It is because in his two main works, *Dialogue Concerning the Two Chief World Systems* and *Dialogue Concerning Two New Sciences*, both written in the form of a Platonic dialogue, Galileo tried to clarify to himself the *new conception of science* in more detail than anyone had before. The two treatises and especially first one belong as much to philosophy, specifically to epistemology, as they do to physical science. The *Dialogue Concerning the Two Chief World Systems* contains what must be the most detailed criticism of Aristotelianism ever. Together with some of his other treatises, these works will be the primary sources for us, for they reveal the modern conception of science not only in theory and in a schematic and vague form as in Bacon but, above all, in practice.

Several features of the Galilean conception of knowledge made Galileo one of the forerunners of logical empiricism, the view whose correctness we are defending here. We may begin with Galileo's remark that the "way of demonstration is distinct from the way of discovery." Discoveries are made by the analytic method or the 'method of resolution', as Galileo calls it. It consists in a conceptual and experimental analysis of simple paradigmatic cases in which one tries to identify their invariant, very general elements. These are then rationalized in order to formulate a mathematical theory. Throughout, the process of inquiry is guided by the question, *how* something is; the question about the so-called causes of events is ignored for the time being. Tempting though it may be to enter speculation about what causes the acceleration of a falling body, one must first try to establish *how* this acceleration takes place.[4] Questions about essences are ignored altogether.

Suppose, for example, that one looks through Galileo's telescope to examine the sunspots it revealed. Here Galileo says,

> In our speculating we either seek to penetrate the true and internal essence of natural substances, or content ourselves with a knowledge of some of their properties. The former I hold to be as impossible an undertaking with regard to the closest elemental substances as with more remote celestial things. The substances composing the earth and the moon seem to me to be equally unknown, as do those of our elemental clouds and of sunspots. I do not see that in comprehending substances near at hand we have any advantage except copious detail; all the things among which men wander remain equally unknown, and we pass by things both near and far with very little or no real acquisition of knowledge. When I ask what the substance of clouds may be and am told that it is a moist vapor, I shall wish to know in turn what vapor is. Peradventure I shall be told that it is water, which when attenuated by heat is resolved into vapor. Equally curious about what water is, I shall then seek to find that out, ultimately learning that it is this fluid body which runs in our rivers and which we constantly handle. But this final information about water is no more intimate than what I knew about clouds in the first place; it is merely closer at hand and dependent more upon the senses. In the same way I know no more about the true essence of earth or fire than about those of the moon or the sun [. . .] But if what we wish to fix in our minds is the apprehension of some properties of things, then it seems to me that we need not despair of our ability to acquire this respecting distant bodies just as well as those close at hand—and perhaps in some cases even more precisely in the former than in the latter. [. . .] Hence I should infer that although it may be vain to seek to determine the true substance of the sunspots, still it does not follow that we cannot know some properties of them, such as their location, motion, shape, size, opacity, mutability, generation and dissolution. These in turn may become the means by which we shall be able to philosophize better about other and more controversial qualities of natural substances.[5]

In Newton we shall meet precisely this same basic attitude towards the study of nature. As Newton put it,

4. Galileo, *Dialogues Concerning two New Sciences*, 166-67.
5. Galileo, *Letters on Sunspots*, in *Discoveries and Opinions of Galileo*, trans. with an Introduction and Note by Stillman Drake (New York: Anchor Books, 1957), 123-24.

To tell us that every Species of Things is endow'd with an occult specifick Quality by which it acts and produces manifest Effects is to tell us nothing: But to derive two or three general Principles of Motion from Phaenomena, and afterwards to tell us how the Properties and Actions of all corporeal Things follow from those manifest Principles, would be a very great step in Philosophy, though the Causes of those Principles were not yet discover'd.[6]

Concepts deriving from this problem setting, one which concentrates upon relations, are of course *relational concepts*. For example, the concept of motion is transformed from an absolute property of a moving thing–the form it took in Aristotle's philosophy–into a relational concept. In his first main work, Galileo seeks to establish the Copernican doctrine. The major obstacle standing in its way is the Aristotelian concept of absolute motion. If the earth moves, then a stone thrown straight up in the air should fall behind the earth. Rectifying this elementary mistake, Galileo develops in detail the principle that is today known as the 'Galilean principle of relativity'. It may strike us as self-evidently correct, but it was a tough nut to crack to his contemporaries. Let us imagine, Galileo says, that on a ship moving uniformly and rectilinearly a stone is thrown straight up in the air by someone standing on the deck. If there is no air resistance, the stone will land exactly at the same place where it was thrown. What is its 'real trajectory'? Seen from aboard the ship, it is perpendicular to the deck; seen from ashore, it is a parabola, because the place where the stone falls is different from the place where it was thrown in the air. "Motion," says Galileo, "insofar as it is and acts as motion, to that extent exists relative to things that lack it."[7] This means, first of all, that the impression of motion that is present in immediate perception and is a perceptible quality is something different from 'real' or physical, that is, *measured* motion–a change in distance relative to something. Thus, second, every motion presupposes a coordinate system–to use modern parlance–in which it is measured. Trajectory varies depending on which coordinate system is chosen. There can be no absolute or 'real trajectory', for motion is a relation. Furthermore–and this is the gist of the Galilean principle of relativity–in a coordinate system that is in uniform and rectilinear motion relative to the earth, as, for example, the ship that moves in this way, everything happens as if there was no motion at all.

Let us suppose that we have discovered the fundamental invariances pertaining to the subject-matter at hand, notions such as continuity, acceleration, and the parallelogram of forces in kinematics. What comes next is Galileo's 'way of demonstration'. This consists in finding out what consequences given assumptions have. Galileo is explicit that the general principles of his kinematics are assumptions–he uses the word "hypothesis"[8]–that are shown to be

6. Newton, *Opticks*, 401-2.
7. Galileo, *Dialogue Concerning the Two Chief World Systems*, 116.
8. Galileo, *Dialogues Concerning Two New Sciences*, 172.

correct by establishing that their consequences agree exactly with experience. On the other hand, it may have escaped Galileo that when he infers from certain *consequences*, that is, from facts of experience derived from a theory, to certain *grounds*, namely to the assumptions he has made, this inference cannot be a matter of logical proof. For proofs proceed not from consequences to grounds, but only the other way round. He appears to think that when experience delivers exactly what follows from an assumption with respect to experience, we may take the assumption to be "demonstrated."[9]

It did not take long before the leading proponents of modern science clarified this last point. They came to see that their science was no more than a 'likely opinion', to use Plato's phrase, though this opinion was now given a mathematical formulation; and they realized that there could be no other kind of knowledge of reality. Huygens, the inventor of the wave theory of light, has this to say in the Preface to his *Treatise on Light*:

> There will be seen in it demonstrations of those kinds which do not produce as great a certitude as those of geometry, and which even differ much therefrom, since, whereas the geometers prove their propositions by fixed and incontestable principles, here the principles are verified by the conclusions to be drawn from them; the nature of these things not allowing of this being done otherwise. It is always possible to attain thereby to a degree of probability which very often is scarcely less than complete proof. To wit, when things which have been demonstrated by the principles that have been assumed correspond perfectly to the phenomena which experiment has brought under observation; especially when there are a great number of them, and further, when one can imagine and foresee new phenomena which ought to follow from the hypotheses which one employs, and when one finds that therein the fact corresponds to our prevision.[10]

Newton is equally clear that his science contains assumptions and not demonstrated truths. He says:

> Although the arguing from Experiments and Observations by Induction be no Demonstration of general Conclusions; yet it is the best way of arguing which the Nature of Things admits of [. . .]. And if no Exception occur from Phaenomena, the Conclusion may be pronounced generally. But if at any time afterwards any Exception shall occur from Experiments, it may then begin to be pronounced with such Exceptions as occur.[11]

9. Ibid.
10. C. Huygens, *Treatise on Light*. In *Great Books of the Western World*, vol. 34 (Chicago, London, Toronto: Encyclopaedia Britannica, Inc., 1952), 551.
11. Newton, *Opticks*, 404.

To return now to Galileo, he was one of the first to realize that logical, that is, *formal truth* is something different from empirical or *material truth*. The latter obtains when the general sentences of a theory, as he says, "agree with all particular phenomena derived from them"; which in turn means that in empirical sciences truth is always 'probability'. Formal or logico-mathematical truth, on the other hand, is something absolute because from a logical point of view it is always 'tautological'. He shows clearly how conclusions drawn from the presuppositions of a system are, as he puts it, 'virtually included' in the presuppositions from which they are developed step by step. "For what more is there," he asks, "to the square on the hypotenuse being equal to the squares on the other two sides, than equality of two parallelograms on equal bases and between parallel lines?" "And is this not ultimately the same as the equality of two surfaces which when superimposed are not increased, but are enclosed within the same boundaries?"[12] It is only because our understanding is limited that we must work out this chain of identities step by step, a task that amounts to giving a logical proof. An infinite intellect would grasp all conclusions the moment it grasped the assumptions. Thus we may argue against Plato, "the Creator needs neither mathematics nor logic." Leibniz's conception of the nature of logical and mathematical demonstration is approximately the same. "What was concealed in the proposition," he says, "or was contained in it only potentially, is rendered evident or explicit by the demonstration.[13] Here we begin to glimpse one of the basic insights of logical empiricism, namely that logical truths are '*analytic*' (in a sense that we will define later on) while empirical sentences, sentences with factual content, are always '*synthetic*'. In these insights Galileo and Leibniz were ahead of their times. Compared to them, most empiricists–but also even Kant, for instance–held views that must be regarded as reactionary. More about this later.

There is a deep logical insight in Galileo's observation that logic, considered as a theory, is something completely different from logic in practice. The situation, he points out, is similar to someone who understands the art of poetry, and yet is inept at composing a poem himself.[14]

One of the remarkable features of the Galilean conception of knowledge is that it perfectly balances the two main ingredients of our quest for knowledge, to wit, the search for invariances, on the one hand, and the requirement of empirical verifiability, on the other. The search for invariances leads to a strongly rationalized mathematical theory in which the multiplicity of experience is idealized and simplified. Then this simplicity of a rationalized theory descends to the multiplicity of experience through approximation. When we test the laws of motion, for example, we do this fully aware that in setting their consequences against experience, we must take into account a number of in-

12. Galileo, *Dialogue Concerning the Two Chief World Systems*, 104.
13. G.W. Leibniz, "On Freedom," in Leibniz, *Philosophical Papers and Letters*, 264-65.
14. Galileo, *Dialogue Concerning the Two Chief World System*, 35.

terfering factors. For example, the trajectory of an object thrown in the air is never an exact mathematical parabola. In addition to the resistance of the air and other such factors, the derivation of the law itself assumes something that does not in fact hold in the actual world, namely that the center of the earth is an infinite distance away. This assumption generates errors, but these are so small that they can be ignored as long as we are dealing with distances that are extremely small in comparison to the distance from the center of the earth.[15] Epistemologically, however, the point remains that the error is there, and even more importantly, that one acknowledges it.

On the other hand, a number of Platonist and Aristotelian elements can be found in Galileo's writings. Notice in particular how, according to him, *a rationalized theory of natural phenomena is more than just an appropriately simplified description of the contents of experience.* Corresponding to such a theory, Galileo seems to believe, there is a world of quantities hidden behind the world of qualities.[16] "The book of nature," he says, "is written in the language of mathematics." "I think that if ears, tongues, and noses where removed, shapes and numbers and motions would remain, but not odors or tastes or sounds. The latter, I believe, are nothing more than names when separated from living things."[17] "Nature is comprised of triangles and squares, circles and spheres, cones and pyramids." These geometrical and mechanical determinations are what he calls "real or primary properties" of things, a phrase that is thus found already in Galileo.[18] They are what can be grasped. "Qualitative changes," Galileo says, "cannot be grasped."

A similar Platonist and atomist intellectual framework can in fact be detected in most of the pioneers of modern science. The nature that science investigates, Kepler says, is 'nudae quantitates', comprised of 'bare numbers'. Natural objects, Descartes believed, have only purely geometrical and mechanical properties, and Newton seems to have shared this opinion, as we have already pointed out. It is surprising to see this in Galileo, given that he demonstrates with striking clarity that motion, for example, is physically a relational concept, one that can only with difficulty be understood as a primary *property.* Similarly, Galileo occasionally mentions the 'deception of senses' that is revealed through reason. This reminds us that we are still far away from

16. See in particular his work *The Assayer* (Excerpts translated into English in *Discoveries and Opinions of Galileo*, 229–80).
17. Galileo, *Il Saggiatore. Le Opere di Galileo Galilei.* Edizione nazionale. vol. VI (Firenze, 1896), 350. (A Selection from *Il Saggiatore* is translated into English as "Excerpts from *The Assayer*", in *Discoveries and Opinions by Galileo*, trans. with an Introduction and Notes by S. Drake [New York: Anchor Books, 1957], 229–80; the quotation is from 276–77.)
18. Kaila does not give reference here, but what he has in mind is probably a passage in *Il Saggiatore* where Galileo calls the shapes, numbers and motions of things their "primary or real accidents"; see Galileo, *Il Saggiatore*, Opere, vol. VI, 348. Galileo also uses the phrase "true accident, affection and quality" (347). An English translation of the relevant passage can be found in E.A. Burtt, *The Metaphysical Foundations of Modern Physical Science* (London: Kegan Paul, Trench, Trubner & Co., Ltd., 1925), 75. -Trans. note.

Leibniz and logical empiricism and their insight that reason reveals not the Real Being 'behind' illusions, but rather invariances that exist in the relations between them.

With Descartes—arguably the one among the pioneers of modern science who comes closest to Galileo—we find a complete victory of Platonist rationalism over empiricism. This distinguished mathematician, despite being given the honorific title 'father of modern philosophy', was far behind Galileo in his conception of knowledge. In Galileo we find a fruitful balance between the search for invariances and the requirement of empirical verifiability. But with Descartes this balance tilts toward Plato and a postulate of invariance. Empirical verifiability, it is suggested, is not necessary in principle, for we are supposed to know the laws of nature in advance. For they are the laws of geometry and mechanics—the latter, incidentally, receive only a very incomplete formulation in Descartes's hands. And not only this. We also know *why* the laws of nature comprise just these laws and no others; other laws would not be in agreement with the Creator and his permanence[19]—all of which means that these laws are derived from the requirement of maximal invariance. The archaic assumption is made once again that natural objects can only have determinations that are common to all things. It follows from this, for example, that weight is not an original property, because fire, which is matter, nevertheless lacks it. What remains with Descartes are only geometrical and mechanical characteristics: shape, size, and motion. Parts of bodies are not indivisible—that is, atoms—because they are not *geometrically* indivisible. On Descartes's view, matter is nothing but extension, filled up with an infinitely divisible, homogeneous medium, in which there occurs nothing but contiguous action: attraction and repulsion. Physics becomes indistinguishable from geometry. While Galileo, thinking that principles can be correct only insofar phenomena can be derived from them, had derived 'causes' from 'effects', Descartes proceeds in the opposite direction, "deriving effects from causes."[20] The only thing that matters for him are those 'clear and distinct notions'—'notiones clarae et distinctae'—which exist implanted in us as the 'germs of truth', as Plato had taught, and whose validity is evident *a priori*—that is, independently of experience—and can be shown to be correct by the 'light of reason'. Galileo's question, 'How?' now gives way to Descartes's question, '*Why?*' Against Galileo, Descartes insists that he has not established the 'ultimate causes' of natural phenomena[21] and for that reason has failed to answer such questions as, for example, *why* do bodies fall? The concept of substance is also reintroduced and is given pride of place. "All we have are substances and their states," Descartes says. "When we perceive any attribute, we conclude that some exist-

19. Descartes, *Principles of Philosophy*, II, 36, 37; *Discourse on the Method*, Part V.
20. Descartes, *Principles of Philosophy*, III, 4.
21. In Descartes's letter to Mersenne, quoted in L. Olschki, *Galileo und seine Zeit*, 1927, 124. [Descartes to Mersenne, October 11, 1638–Trans.]

ing thing or substance to which it may be attributed, is necessarily present."[22] This axiom of Greek philosophy explains Descartes's dictum, "Cogito, ergo sum"–"I think, therefore I am" (that is, I exist as a thinking thing or substance). Consciousness, cogitatio, belongs necessarily to some thing, as the property of a spiritual substance ('res cogitans').

With Descartes, the content of experience, of which pure consciousness (thought) and perceptible extension constitute the two extremes (with, however, indefinitely many experienced items occurring between them) is now divided into two substances: thinking and extension. This is an important step in the process of differentiating fundamental concepts. Throughout Greek thought, 'soul' was one aspect of organic life. For Aristotle, the soul was the 'entelechy' of the body, that is, its perceptible 'form'. Soul was an indefinite vital force. With Descartes, the soul instead becomes *consciousness* and essentially distinct from organic life. In this conceptual differentiation we meet, again, a phenomenon we see in other, analogous cases: new concepts–in this case 'cogitation' and 'extension'–are homogeneous within their own spheres but sharply contrast to one another; in this they are just like the empty void and the full plenum in Greek atomism. And again it strikes us that in *experience* we find all manner of intermediaries between these two extremes, and yet, as we form rational concepts, these are crystallized into two absolute opposites: a mechanism that is purely geometrical, on the one hand, and intentionally acting consciousnesses, on the other hand, with nothing between the two. This Cartesian dualism has had an extraordinary influence by requiring that everything be explained either as a mechanism or else teleologically, as a spiritual substance. As a conceptual structure, from a formal point of view, this dualism is exactly the same as the absolute void and the absolute fullness in the atomist picture of the world.

Starting from such mechanical principles, Descartes sets out to provide a complete explanation of nature. It is true, he does not neglect experience entirely, for, he says, it is often difficult to know, without resorting to experience, which of the many possible ways a given phenomenon has been brought about.[23] But we know independently of experience, *a priori*, that the effect always can be deduced, one way or another, from the 'clear and distinct notions' that are revealed through the 'natural light of reason'. It is only a matter of secondary importance, when it is pointed out[24] that the 'key to the code of nature' that is found in these notions must be correct, because otherwise it would remain incomprehensible how natural phenomena can agree so well with mechanical principles.

22 Descartes, *Principles of Philosophy*, I, 52; II, 54.
23. Descartes, *Discourse on the Method*, VI; *Principles of Philosophy*, IV, 204.
24. Descartes, *Principles of Philosophy*, IV, 203-4.

During the latter half of the seventeenth century, many scientists believed that the 'key to the code of nature' had really been found. The key was mechanics, and so the time had come to ask the question, 'How?' with respect to all natural phenomena; the time had come, that is, to ask what the mechanical causes of these phenomena were.

Newton

Here the gigantic figure of Newton enters the stage, and once again we admire the certainty of that scientific 'instinct' that directs him in theory formation. Newton redirects the course of modern science, rescuing it at a moment when Cartesianism was leading it away from the right path. Newton thus saved the Galilean conception of knowledge. This is how we can understand the battle against "hypotheses" that Newton fought throughout his life. For by "hypotheses," Newton means Aristotelian and Cartesian *a priori* assumptions, ill-founded speculations about the essences of phenomena and their *causes*. This battle is all the more significant because Newton is in fact fighting against his own spirit; he, too, accepts the mechanistic conception of nature. So the notion of action at a distance, a notion that experience itself forces upon him, strikes him as almost impossible to swallow because it is incompatible with a strict mechanistic approach.

Newton's pupil, Roger Cotes, who published the second edition of *Principia*, writes in its preface, giving voice to his master:

Those who have treated of natural philosophy may be reduced to about three classes. Of these some have attributed to the several species of things, specific and occult qualities, according to which the phenomena of particular bodies are supposed to proceed in some unknown manner. The sum of the doctrine of the Schools derived from *Aristotle* and the *Peripatetics* is founded on this principle. They affirm that the several effects of bodies arise from the particular natures of those bodies. But whence it is that bodies derive those natures they don't tell us: and therefore they tell us nothing. And being entirely employed in giving names to things, and not in searching into things themselves, they have invented, we may say, a philosophical way of speaking, but they have not made known to us true philosophy.

Others [i.e. the Cartesians] have endeavored to apply their labors to greater advantage by rejecting that useless medley of words. They assume that all matter is homogeneous, and that the variety of forms which is seen in bodies arises from some very plain and simple relations of the component particles. And by going on from simple things to those which are more compounded they certainly proceed right, if they attribute to those primary relations no other relations than those which Nature has given. But when they take a liberty of imagining at pleasure unknown figures and magnitudes, and uncertain situations and motions of the parts, and moreover of supposing occult fluids, freely pervading the pores of bodies, endued with an all-performed subtilty, and agitated with occult motion, they run out into dreams and chimeras, and neglect the true constitution of things, which certainly is not to be derived from fallacious conjectures, when we can scarce reach it by the most certain observations. Those who assume hypotheses as first principles of their speculations, although they afterwards proceed with the greatest accuracy from those principles, may indeed form an ingenuous romance, but a romance it will still be.[25]

This was Newton's scientific attitude from the very beginning of his career. As far as this method goes, his first published work, *New Theory of Light and Colours* of 1671, is as perfect as his last.[26] Science has no other task than to start from experience and state the exact laws of phenomena that will help other phenomena to be predicted. That famous slogan, "Hypotheses non fingo," I frame no hypotheses, is already presupposed in this first work. When his distinguished contemporaries–Huygens among them–enchanted with mechanistic metaphysics spoke about this "new hypothesis concerning colours," Newton replied indignantly that he had made no "hypothesis as to the cause or nature of colour." That is to say, he had not asked what light rays are, nor why they behave as they do. His interest had been simply *how* they behave. Against his contemporaries, for whom the main issue was whether the corpuscularian hypothesis (the emission hypothesis) or the wave hypothesis was correct, Newton emphasized,

It is true that from my theory I argue the corporeity of light; but I do it without any absolute positiveness . . . . But I knew that the properties which I declare of light, were in some measure capable of being explicated, not only by that, but by many other mechanical hypotheses. And therefore I chose to decline them all, and to speak of light in general terms . . . . You see therefore, how much *it is beside the business* in hand to dispute about hypotheses."[27]

The reason Newton eschewed hypotheses is hardly some failure to reflect on the supposed mechanical causes of natural phenomena; very few engaged

25. *Newton's Principia*, trans. into English by Andrew Motte in 1729, Cotes's Preface to the Second Edition, xx.
26. Cf. here L.T. More, *Isaac Newton, a Biography* (New York, London: Charles Scribner's Sons, 1934), 86.
27. More, *Isaac Newton*, 105 [*Philosophical Transactions*, No. 88, 5084–Trans.]

in such reflections as intensively as Newton. Rather, it is to be found in that deeply ingrained 'instinct' which guides him whenever he works, so to speak, in full responsibility, and dictates to him that his proper task is to answer the question, *how things are.* Guided by this instinct and with superhuman effort, he creates his main work, *Naturalis philosophiae principia mathematica,* which for two centuries has served as a kind of Bible in scientific research.

In the beginning of Book Three, Newton provides a few "rules of reasoning in philosophy"–regulae philosophandi–that very clearly express that experimental research is a generalization from experience and is therefore no more than "probable." Verification by experience is needed continually. "In experimental philosophy," he says, "we are to look upon propositions inferred by general induction from phenomena as accurately or very nearly true, notwithstanding any contrary hypothesis that may be imagined, till such time as other phenomena occur, by which they may be either made more accurate, or liable to exceptions."[28] Thus, when Newton fights the battle against 'hypotheses', he has in mind not assumptions *per se,* for he is well aware that his own science rests on just such a system of assumptions. The method of natural philosophy, he writes at the end of *Opticks,*

> consists in making Experiments and Observations, and in drawing general conclusions from them by Induction, and admitting of no Objections against the Conclusions, but such as are taken from Experiments, or other certain Truths. For Hypotheses are not to be regarded in experimental philosophy. And although the arguing from Experiments and Observations by Induction be no Demonstration of general Conclusions; yet it is the best way of arguing which the Nature of Things admits of.[29]

And similarly in *Principia,* at the end of Book Three:

> But hitherto I have not been able to discover the cause of those properties of gravity from phenomena, and I frame no hypotheses; for whatever is not deduced from the phenomena is to be called an hypothesis; and hypotheses, whether metaphysical or physical, whether of occult or mechanical, have no place in experimental philosophy. In this philosophy particular hypotheses are inferred from the phenomena, and afterwards rendered general by induction.[30]

Newton's "hypotheses," therefore, are plainly Aristotelian and Cartesian assumptions framed so as to provide answers to *what-* or *why*-questions without providing an adequate grounding in experience. Newton's real concern,

28. *Newton's Principia,* Book III, Rule IV, 400.
29. Newton, *Opticks,* 404
30. *Newton's Principia,* 547.

rather, is to answer the question, *how?* And yet the prevalent mechanistic metaphysics of his contemporaries was a kind of siren song that even Newton found hard to resist, as much as it offended his scientific conscience. Thus it remained inconceivable to him, for example, how "inanimate brute matter" should affect other matter without mutual contact.[31] Furthermore–and this we have already pointed out–it strikes him as just as inconceivable that regularity in natural phenomena could have any other basis than immutable particles, particles that the Creator, the Master Clockmaker, has arranged so as to build the entire mechanism that is the Universe. Finally, Newton assumes that absolute time and absolute space exist in the sense that one can speak of temporal and spatial determinations independently of any material coordinate system.[32]

Leibniz

On this last point, Newton is staunchly resisted by Leibniz, the other inventor of the Differential Calculus. He is the fourth and last of the scientific sages of the seventeenth century whom we shall discuss. Among his contemporaries and throughout most of the following two centuries, this man was known for the 'best of all possible worlds' and the fantastic doctrine of windowless monads. According to Leibniz's theory, there exist indivisible basic objects, "monads," which are soul-like and produce all of their experiences from within themselves, in accordance with their internal law and a pre-established harmony prevailing among them. Once we have fought our way through the spider's web that Leibniz has spun from these elements he inherited from Scholastic metaphysics, we find a number of modern scientific ideas with far-reaching consequences. Only in our time have we recognized these ideas for what they really are, and this new perspective has forced a reappraisal of Leibniz's metaphysics, as well.

Here we shall consider only how the *modern conception of knowledge* is reflected in Leibniz's peculiar philosophy.[33] The impression one sometimes receives from reading textbooks in the history of philosophy is that it was not until the British psychologizing empiricism–of Berkeley and Hume–that the old concept of substance was finally shown to be essentially empty; that only when these empiricists reinvigorated Ancient Skepticism was the distinction between primary and secondary qualities given up; and that Kant was the first

31. Letter to Bentley, in More, 379.
32. *Newton's Principia*, 6-7.
33. For the interpretation of Leibniz's philosophy, see B. Russell, *A Critical Exposition of the Philosophy of Leibniz*, 2nd ed. (London: Allen & Unwin, 1937); L. Couturat, *La logique de Leibniz: d'après des documents inédits* (Paris, 1901); Cassirer, *Leibniz' System in seinen wissenschaftlichen Grundlagen* (Marburg: Elwert, 1902).

to achieve the insight that space and time are 'phenomena'. All these ideas, however, can already be found in Leibniz.

In almost all seventeenth-century scientists we find a mechanistic conception of nature in the form of a metaphysical doctrine positing a purely quantitative world lying 'behind' and 'supporting' a phenomenal world of qualities. By far the best indication of how modern Leibniz was in his conception of knowledge is that although he did in a sense advocate the mechanistic conception of nature, for him this theory had nothing to do with metaphysics; it was simply *a way to describe the phenomenal world.* He is inclined to think that "all other material phenomena can be explained through local motion,"[34] including those that occur in living bodies and which concern human behavior, even speech. Thus, Leibniz says, "everything takes place in the body as if man himself were only a body or an automaton," that is, "as if the evil doctrine of Epicurus and Hobbes [i.e., materialism] were true."[35] But this does not imply that matter with its mechanical and geometrical properties would be a substance concealed 'behind' the world of phenomena, for the only reality are the soul-like monads with their qualitative contents that follow one after another in a law-like succession. The radical geometrico-mechanical conception of the world is a scientific description of these contents. "Not merely light, heat, color and similar qualities are apparent but also motion, figure and extension."[36] All these phenomena are on a par. They are, as it were, "an exact and persistent dream" and are, therefore, "a well-founded phenomenon."[37] To look for something more, something that is hidden 'behind' the perceived qualities of things and their laws, would be just as inappropriate as it would be to ask what substance lies behind the rainbow. "To look for something *behind* phenomena is, in my view, to act like someone who, even after the cause of mirror images has been indicated to him, is not content with that, but wishes to have the hidden *essence* of a mirror-image explained to him."[38] Leibniz emphasized again and again how the so-called reality of phenomena has a sufficient and necessary ground in the possibility of predicting the future from the present, in the law-like character of phenomena. "Even if," he says, "this whole life were said to be only a dream, and the visible world only a phantasm, I should call this dream or this phantasm real enough if we were never deceived by it when we make good use of reason."[39] That is to say, the 'real' is nothing but a

34. Leibniz, *Specimen dynamicum*; Leibniz, *Philosophical Papers and Letters*, 437.
35. Leibniz, *Reply to the Thoughts on the System of Pre-established Harmony*, in Leibniz, *Philosophical Papers and Letters*, 577.
36. Leibniz, *On the Method of Distinguishing Real from Imaginary Phenomena*, in Leibniz, *Philosophical Papers and Letters*, 365.
37. From Leibniz's draft letter to Remond, Leibniz, *Die Philosophische Schriften von Gottfried Wilhelm Leibniz* Band VII, 623.
38. From Leibniz's draft letter to de Volder, *Philosophische Schriften*, Band II, 282.
39. Leibniz, *On the Method of Distinguishing Real from Imaginary Phenomena*, in Leibniz, *Philosophical Papers and Letters*, 364.
40. Leibniz's letter to de Volder, January 21, 1704. In Leibniz, *Philosophical Papers and Letters*, 534.

relational invariance that is present in the 'apparent'. The only reality is to be found in the monads, together with their perception-like successions of qualitative contents. This is all there is to their 'substantiality';[40] it is nothing but a law in accordance with which substances act.

Every monad experiences the world from its own perspective. And reality is a law-like system constituted by these different world perspectives. Every such perspective is a miniature picture of the entire infinite universe and is therefore inexact in the way that a map drawn in a very small scale is inexact. Hence, to use a modern phrase, the geometrico-mechanical conception of the world is an isomorphic description of the system of world perspectives that has been drawn up using a specific set of principles. And it is not the only such description, for monads are soul-like and they can be considered in that capacity as well. If we imagine, Leibniz says,[41] the brain enlarged a thousand times so that we could move inside it as if we were in a mill with its cogs and wheels, we could give a purely mechanistic description of the brain and its functioning. Yet this functioning would constitute, at the same time, an isomorphic description of certain mental episodes. With this famous thought experiment Leibniz expressed the real meaning of the principle of psycho-physical parallelism more clearly than anything written by Spinoza and probably more deeply than any other author. We see, then, that Leibniz's scientific program already accommodates consistently the idea of 'behavioristic' psychology holding that mental life can be described through isomorphic physical episodes, namely, certain events in the physical life of an organism. The mechanistic limitations of this program, it must be admitted, constitute a weakness, but this is really only a secondary issue.

It is no surprise that Leibniz, in formulating these doctrines, occasionally says that there is much that he should add to them but that "this century is not yet mature enough to receive it."

The imaginary opposition between thinking and extension, or between matter and spirit, has been overcome in Leibniz's philosophy. There is a smooth transition leading from spirituality of the most elevated kind to matter of the most mundane, and this applies as much between different monads as it does within a single world perspective. One could say that there is a contrapuntal play of a single, all-comprising melody by the monads, and that this universal symphony is what constitutes reality.

Once we disentangle these deep thoughts from the spider web of scholastic metaphysics, we come relatively close to the conception of reality that is characteristic of logical empiricism, as we conceive it here.

41. From Leibniz's draft letters to Bayle, December 1704, in Leibniz, *Philosophical Texts*, ed. and trans. R.S. Woolhouse and R. Francks (Oxford: Oxford University Press, 1998) 255–56; *Monadology*, §7 (*Philosophische Schriften*, Band III), 66.
42. Leibniz, *Monadology*, §1.

It is easy to see the shackles of tradition that bind Leibniz and hamper the movements of his thought. Starting from the illicit assumption that everything 'composite', that is, everything that involves some multiplicity, must be a combination of some absolutely simple parts, he arrives at the doctrine of indivisible and indestructible soul-like monads.[42] In logic, hard as he tries, he fails to free himself from the Aristotelian assumption that every judgment is to be understood as taking the subject-predicate form, a view that bears an important relation to his doctrine of pre-established harmony. For anything that a monad experiences during the different phases of its life-dream, Leibniz thinks, are consequences of its 'complete individual concept' as this exists in the mind of God, and is included in it in the same way that a predicate is included in a subject.[43] In principle he is a radical rationalist, for he believes–like Plato and Descartes–that the laws of nature can be derived from the requirement of maximal invariance. This world is the 'best of all possible worlds' precisely because it is characterized by a kind of rational perfection.

Yet even when Leibniz strays from the right path in his thinking, as he does here, his genius never deserts him. Starting from the requirement of invariance, he formulates some of the most important principles of modern science. These include the principle of conservation of energy–here he finds himself in opposition to a person no less than Newton–and the principle of least action, which he derives from the requirement that events must be definite.[44] For example, a light ray coming from a point A is reflected from a point B on a mirror to another point, C, in such a way that the angles of incidence and refraction are equal; this law can be derived using the requirement that the distance ABC must be the shortest of all possible paths for the light to follow. Otherwise the path could not be fixed under the given circumstances, since there are longer paths with distances that are equal to one other. According to Leibniz, we can be *a priori* certain of all such principles like this whose validity derives from the requirement of invariance.

Even so, Leibniz's commitment to rationalism is not unconditional. It is limited by the presupposition that human experience is an isomorphic description of reality, although it is drawn up in a scale that renders it less than adequate. Therefore, he says, "everything should be deduced from phenomena"[45] so that, for example, "there is no criterion for the real over and above what is found in phenomena and the laws with which they are in conformity." And thus it happens that Leibniz, a man who in principle was a radical rationalist, is the first to give a relatively clear formulation of the basic principle of logical empiricism, the postulate of empirical verifiability. In his famous con-

43. Leibniz, *Discourse on Metaphysics*, §8.
44. Leibniz, *Discourse on Metaphysics*, §22; *Philosophische Schriften*, Band VII, 272.
45. Leibniz's letter to de Volder, 1705, *Philosophische Schriften*, Band II, 276.
46. Leibniz's Fifth Letter to Clarke, §52. In Leibniz, *Philosophical Papers and Letters*, 705-6.

troversy with Newton it appears as *"principe de l'observabilité,"* the principle
of observability,[46] which says that every statement about reality must have determinate consequences with respect to experience; if a statement has no experiential consequences, it is empty, without factual content. Leibniz uses this
principle primarily to refute Newton's doctrine of absolute space and time.
Imagine, for example, that the material world in this imagined absolute space
turned 180 degrees around itself, so that east would become west, and west
would become east; this would make no difference to our experience. Hence
the idea is empty; although it seems to, it actually says nothing about reality.
In this respect, too, we may follow Leibniz and take up where he left off.

Leibniz's greatest bequest to logical empiricism, though, is his logic; and
this independently of the Aristotelian limitations we mentioned above. For he
is well aware, to begin with, that school logic is no more than "a kind of alphabet"[47] in comparison to the logic that is in fact used in science. He thinks,
furthermore, that the whole of mathematics is a special, enormous development of logic.[48] Mathematics is much more than just a science of quantity. On
the contrary, every theory that is exact in the true sense is mathematical, and
hence we can even speak of the 'mathematics of qualities', insofar as these can
be given an exact treatment. *'Mathesis universalis'*, a term that Leibniz often
uses, signifies a general theory of structures in which logic and mathematics
merge together. He is also the first to apply the modern term 'logistic' to general, theoretical logic.[49] Beyond that—and it is this point more than anything
else that makes him a predecessor of modern logic—he extends the requirement of formalization much further than anyone before him. With Leibniz,
one must introduce into logic a special and a fully exact sign language, just as
is done in mathematics. This transforms logic into a purely formal manipulation of signs in which the content of these signs may be ignored, for the signs
and the rules for their operation give an exact description of logical inference.

Finally, Leibniz perceives, like Galileo before him, that 'necessary truths',
that is, logical or formal truths—truths that, as he puts it, hold in all possible
worlds—are different in kind from 'matters of fact' or 'contingent truths'. They
are different, that is, from sentences reporting experience. Leibniz thinks
that necessary truths can be reduced to implicit identities. On this point, too,
we shall take up where Leibniz has left off.

47. Leibniz, *Philosophische Schriften*, Band VII, 514.
48. Leibniz, *New Essays Concerning Human Understanding*, trans. A.G. Langley (La Salle, Ill.:
Open Court), Book IV, Chapter II.
49. "Logica mathematica sive mathesis universalis sive logistica," Leibniz, *Mathematische
Schriften*. Hrsg, von C.I. Gerhardt, Band VII (Halle 1863), 54; cf. H. Scholz, *Geschichte der Logik* (Berlin: Junker und Dünnhaupt, 1931), 51.

Chapter 5

Induction

In our previous investigations we saw how the search for invariances gives rise to a theory in which the regularities characterizing a given domain are presented in the form of basic statements that are as simple and as few as possible and from which other facts concerning the domain can be derived through logical inference. When the theory concerns some portion of reality, its basic statements, according to the Galilean conception of knowledge, are assumptions that—as Newton expressly points out—have not been given a general demonstration. They are instead 'probable', and will remain so, no matter how high this probability may be rendered by experience confirming the theory. In such cases inference is made from consequences to grounds, namely, from particular experiences to the general basic statements of the theory, which is not the way of logical proof. When something is 'empirically verified', as the phrase goes, it has not been shown to be *true*; it has been confirmed, that is, shown to be *probable*. Here we encounter a problem that concerns all theory formation, a problem that has occupied philosophers throughout centuries and is still being studied today.

It is evident that Galileo has hit upon something fundamental in his distinction between the way of demonstration and the way of discovery. The question is now this: Can the way of discovery, that is, the search for invariances, be subjected to a number of exact rules? In other words, can there be directions for scientific discovery giving a guarantee, if possible, that future experience will confirm, rather than refute, the assumptions or the basic statements of the theory? And if this should turn out to be impossible, could there at least be some rules for the estimation of the 'probability' of these assumptions, rules that might help us to avoid assumptions where this is low and to concern ourselves only with assumptions whose 'probability' is high?

This is the so-called scientific *problem of induction*. It has left its mark on modern English empiricism in particular, beginning with Francis Bacon, to whom must go the credit for its first formulation. We may call it the question of *'inductive logic'*: Is there, in addition to ordinary 'deductive logic', which comprises rules that we use to infer from the general to the particular, some sort of 'inductive logic' that would provide similar rules for how to infer generalizations from particular cases with at least some 'probability'? The best-known attempt to create this kind of 'inductive logic' is to be found in John Stuart Mill's extensive work, *A System of Logic, Ratiocinative and Inductive*, which came out in 1843.

To answer this big question, we wish to reduce its complexity somewhat by assuming that the theory we are about to consider involves no rationalization, all of its general statements being generalizations from experience. Why we make this assumption will become clearer later, when we consider the remarkable difficulties that are involved in the empirical verification of a rationalized theory.

The assumption we shall be making says, then, that the basic statements of our theory have been derived by a generalization from particular cases belonging to a given class to *all* cases in this class. This generalization from a finite number of particular cases to all cases of the relevant class, whose number has not been limited and may therefore be infinite, is what we shall here call *induction*. Thus, we shall ignore the trivial case in which the generalization concerns a finite number of cases, all of which are known to us; on the other hand, we shall also ignore so-called mathematical or complete induction, in which an inference is made from n to $n + 1$, something that is different from empirical or 'incomplete' induction. Our question, then, comes down to this. Suppose some statement, S, has been ascertained to be valid in a finite number of cases belonging to a class C and is then claimed to hold for all cases, possibly infinite in number, that belong to C. Can this generalization be made in a way that gives us some guarantee that future experience–that is, new instances of the class C–will not refute it? Or, at any rate, can we make it in a way that enables us to give an estimation of the 'probability' of this generalization within some limits? If all the ravens we have perceived so far have been black, can there be some guarantee, and under what conditions, that all ravens, including those that we shall meet in the future, are black? Or, can we estimate the 'probability' of this generalization?

Enumerative Induction

The question we shall consider first is, Can there be rules for how an inductive generalization itself is to be carried out, rules for *what should be generalized in a given case*? This has been the starting point in the attempts made so far to to create a special 'inductive logic'. A positive answer to this question would mean that the search itself for invariances, the 'way of discovery', could be regulated in such a way that—as Bacon puts it—there would not be much room left for "judiciousness and the power of the spirit." In this case, a theory could be discovered in principle in the same way as logical demonstration.

We shall first consider those apparently simple cases that are covered by *enumerative induction*, "inductio per enumerationem simplicem," also known as 'Aristotelian induction'; this latter name, though, has little justification, as Aristotle provides no unified theory of induction.

By 'enumerative induction' we mean elementary cases, such as our example of ravens. The idea, then, is this. Given a class C, we run through its known cases, $a, b, c, \ldots, n$, (always finite in number), see what they have in common without exception, and then generalize this to apply to all members of C. Bacon calls this kind of induction 'childish', 'res puerilis', since it gives no guarantee that contradictory cases or *negative instances* could not occur in the future; for example, that the next raven perceived after the nth could turn out to be white. We shall consider this in a little more detail with the help of a few examples.

Making use of calculations by Tycho Brahe, Kepler determined the orbit of the planet Mars. He tells us that he made close to twenty assumptions before he could discover a curve on which all observed points would lie with sufficient precision. (Recall the assumption made above that our theory involves no rationalization.) Kepler's generalization, the curve he had discovered, is an instance of 'enumerative induction'—and it is very far from being a mere 'res puerilis'. In cases like this, the gist of induction is to *figure out what is common to all observed instances of the class C*—in our example, to all observed points. This discovery is grounded in scientific imagination, whereas the generalization itself, once the discovery has been made, is a triviality. The very idea that this kind of scientific discovery could somehow be regulated is strange. For it seems that this kind of scientific discovery can be subjected to mechanical rules no more than the genius of an artist.

To illustrate the matter further, consider another example. Snellius discovers the law $\sin \alpha : \sin \beta = k$. Abstracting from the geometrical rationalization that is involved in this assumption, we have, again, an instance of enumerative induction. One studies a number of pairs of media, like air and water, etc., whence it is immediately observed that a light ray is refracted when it passes from one medium into another, and that the amount of refraction varies from case to case. The question is now asked: What law underlies this refraction? We are asking, in other words, what do these observed cases have in common, apart from the trivial feature that in every such case a light ray is refracted? Again, this is a matter where a creative scientific imagination is needed, and it is difficult to see how this could be controlled by simple rules.

Examples like these–and they could easily be multiplied–give rise to the following observation. The very first question we encounter once we set out to construct a so-called inductive logic, namely the question whether some rules can be specified for drawing a generalization in such a way that one could know in advance what one must generalize in given cases, receives a negative answer. It seems quite impossible to state any such rules.

How, then, did it ever occur to anyone to suppose that the search itself for invariances could be subjected to mechanical rules? No doubt, they came to this idea because they paid attention only to elementary–Aristotelian, so to speak–cases, in which some 'immediately perceivable' simple property is generalized so as to apply to an entire class, as was the case in our example of ravens. When we move from such property-generalizations–these really are 'res puerilis'–to cases in which a generalization is made over some relation, and what is searched for is thus a relational invariance, in these cases mere enumerative induction is far from childish. One cannot discover *the fact that is to be generalized* without scientific inventiveness.

Causal Induction

We shall next consider cases to which the term *causal induction* can be applied. These are cases where an inductive generalization has as its precondition or premise a general idea of lawfulness–the so-called causal principle–formulated in one way or another. The basic laws for such cases were formulated by Bacon. They were later taken up by Mill in his inductive logic, where he tried to give them detailed formulations. Let us suppose that every phenomenon has its 'cause'. Our goal, then, is to find out the cause of a given phenomenon. The following kind of case would seem to be the most promising. Imagine two situations, in one of which the phenomenon we are studying, F, occurs under certain circumstances, OPQ, while it does not occur in the other case, in which the circumstances are PQ. Now we reason as follows. Every phenomenon has its cause; therefore F, too, must have some cause. Since the only difference between the two circumstances is that O and F occur in the former, while both are absent in the latter, there must be a relation of cause and effect holding between O and F. This is known as Mill's method of difference, a rule that he himself regarded as the most important rule for experimental research. Here, even on the basis of a single, carefully performed experiment, we can formulate a general law that is derived logically under the assumption that the causal principle is valid. For example, sodium is placed in a spirit flame; when the light is examined, a yellow double-streak is observed in its spectrum. If performed carefully, a single such experiment is enough to show that the double-streak is caused by sodium, for no other change has occurred except that sodium was placed in a flame; and every phenomenon has a cause.

If this so-called method of difference has no other purpose than roughly to describe how, *in relatively advanced stages of research*, scientific experiments are conducted and how generalizations are based upon them, we have no objections against it. In fact, we can say that Mill's rules for experimental research give a rather fitting description of this kind of research, so much so that the famous chemist Liebig, on whose initiative Mill's logic was translated into German, could say that his own work was just a special application of Mill's rules.

It may seem, then, that in the case of causal induction, and supposing the validity of the causal principle, general rules could be given for how inductive generalizations ought to be pursued. On closer inspection, however, this would be a mistake. Putting aside questions about the content and validity of the causal principle, we shall show that even if we have no doubts about this principle, causal induction can be employed only when *certain further assumptions* are made. Even in the case of causal induction, these necessary assumptions render the supposed general rules largely fictitious.

Take a closer look at our previous example of spirit flame and sodium. Sodium is a known chemical element, defined by a number of characteristics: a specific atomic number, metallic nature, etc. Let these characteristics be *ABC*. What is the content, with respect to experience, of this statement: "sodium is a chemical element, whose characteristics are *ABC*"? Its content is this: when certain 'stuff' occurs whose characteristics are *ABC*, this 'stuff', whenever it occurs under certain constant circumstances, *OPQ*, has *identical* other effects and characteristics *FGH*. For if the causal principle is correct and if certain circumstances, *OPQ*, sometimes occurred together with phenomena *FGH* and sometimes with other phenomena, *KLM*, the difference between these phenomena would have to be a consequence of a different 'cause'. That is to say, *properties ABC alone do not suffice to single out a certain 'stuff'*, and these characteristics would have to be accompanied by a further characteristic, sometimes *D*, sometimes *E*, that is responsible for the different phenomena that occur under the circumstances *OPQ*. We can now see that in the case at hand, one of the key points about induction is the presupposition that the 'stuff' is a known *'element' that is supposed to be always the same*, that is, that the characteristics *ABC* suffice to determine the effects *FGH* under certain circumstances. If, instead of this stuff, we had placed in the flame some unknown stuff with characteristics *XYZ* that resulted in a certain spectral change, we would not infer that this stuff is always and necessarily the cause of the change, for we would not know whether the characteristics *XYZ* defined a chemically *determinate stuff* in the first place.

Similar considerations apply to all cases of causal inductions. Quite independently of the causal principle, induction can be employed only under certain conditions, namely when extensive earlier experience is taken to license the assumption that a number of particular causal, lawful effects are valid; such as those causal effects that characterize the chemical 'elements'.

We are victims of a kind of illusion when it appears that we could, indeed, make a reliable inductive generalization on the basis of a single experiment. These scientific generalizations are in fact based on the extensive earlier experiences; in our example, it rests on the multiplicity of experience that underlies the system of chemical elements. It is by no means sufficient to assume that the causal principle is valid; we need the further assumption that these lawful experiences occur in nature, like those we considered in our example.

We can see at the same time that *causal inductions are in fact always reducible to enumerative inductions*; and this independently of the fact that even the advocates of inductive logic agree that the causal principle, which is the premise underlying inductions of this kind and the conclusions they reach, are reducible to enumerative induction.

We have seen, however, that, in the case of enumerative induction, there cannot be any rules for inductive generalizations. Because causal inductions can be reduced to enumerative inductions, this conclusion applies to causal induction as well.

We should take notice of the following point, too. Earlier we assumed that under specific circumstances, OPQ, a change, FGH, is brought about through a certain factor that is defined by characteristics ABC, and then it was found out that the relation thus observed can be generalized only on the assumption that the characteristics ABC are sufficient to determine the change in question. Generalizations are based on the assumption that these characteristics are a reliable indicator of the presence of *identical* constant circumstances. But how do we know this? Again, we know only on the basis of earlier experience. Yet we must remember that the 'circumstances' under which a given phenomenon occurs always include, strictly speaking, an unlimited number of different characteristics. When we perform the experiment exhibiting the spectrum of sodium today and repeat it tomorrow, many changes will have occurred: heavenly bodies will occupy different positions, weather conditions will have changed, all kinds of objects will have been moved around, and so on. What, then, justified us in talking about *'same circumstances'*, OPQ, as soon as we have the spirit flame and other such experimental instruments available to us? Our earlier experience has convinced us that other characteristics pertaining to the 'circumstances' are irrelevant to the phenomenon under scrutiny and that the characteristics OPQ are sufficient to determine the result, provided the characteristics ABC are determinate in the sense explained above.

The following possibility, however, cannot be ruled out in principle: it could be that these so-called circumstances include some characteristic, R, which has not been identified, for example, because it has always been present in experience until now. This neglected R may nevertheless play a significant role in determining the relationship of cause and effect that is under scrutiny. For example, when a string is held taut and made to vibrate, we hear a sound in its vicinity. If, however, this occurs in a vacuum, no sound is heard because a characteristic that was present, namely the atmosphere surrounding the string, is now absent.[1] Which of these so-called circumstances under which a given phenomenon occurs are significant and which are insignificant is something that can be known only in their absence, when the effect of this absence on the phenomenon can be observed.

Newton formulated his General Law of Gravitation mainly on the basis of observations concerning the orbit of the Moon; he showed how Kepler's rules for planetary motion could be derived from the law together with the exception to these rules, which are consequences of disturbances in planetary motions caused by other planets. For more than two centuries the inverse square law was considered exactly valid, until a phenomenon was observed–the so-called perihelic shift of Mercury–that could not be derived from the Law of Gravitation in its Newtonian form without making certain more or less ad hoc assumptions. Mercury is close to the sun, that is, 'in a strong gravitation field', as the phrase goes, whereas the motion of other planets takes place in a relatively 'weak gravitation field'. One might therefore hypothesize that the inverse square law is valid with great accuracy only in certain specific circumstances, namely in a weak gravitation field, and that these circumstances were present in all those cases that were crucial for Newton. That these circumstances are relevant to the phenomenon under scrutiny is something that can be found out only when it occurs that they are absent and an exception to the law in question is observed.

Thus we reach the following conclusion. In the end, all inductive generalizations are reducible to so-called enumerative inductions. It is impossible, first of all, to state generally valid rules for what generalization ought to be made in a given case. As soon as one's concern is no longer elementary cases, finding out what generalization to make is a matter of scientific imagination, and this cannot be subjected to rules. On the other hand–and this is admitted more or less by everyone–if no guarantee can be given that, with respect to an enumerative induction, future experience will not reveal 'negative instances', then no such guarantee can be given for causal induction, either. This is because the latter is always reducible to the former, quite independently of what we may think about the so-called causal principle.

1. The example is from P.W. Bridgman's *The Logic of Modern Physics* (New York: The Macmillan Company, 1927), 84.

A theory is created through free invention regulated by the search for invariances, and this way of discovery cannot be marked out in advance. Only the 'way of demonstration' can be regulated.

Inductive 'Probability'

The question as to the possibility of inductive logic now takes this form: can we give a precise definition of the probability of so-called inductive generalizations and estimate it within certain limits in such a way that at least some rules could be formulated regarding what kinds of induction one ought to avoid and what kinds would be worthwhile?

In exact research, probability means the limit of relative frequency, a concept of which we have given a preliminary explanation. According to this conception, for example, to say that the probability of getting a six when a dice is tossed is 1/6 means this: when a fair dice is tossed, approximately one sixth of all tosses give a six, and the number of exceptions from this value will on average decrease as the number of tosses goes up. If we imagine the number of tosses increasing without limit, the relative frequency of tosses resulting in a six would converge precisely to 1/6, provided the number of exceptions continued, on average, to decrease. The central question in the philosophy of probability–one that has received an immense amount of attention during the past few decades–is this: Can we interpret each and every case of 'probability' (in science as well as prescientific thought) in ways that are analogous to this conception of relative frequency?

Consider the so-called probability of an inductive generalization. There is no doubt that we take some generalizations to be more likely than others. For instance, in our experience so far, it has always been the case that cloven-hoofed animals ruminate and vice versa. If, however, we consider what a biologist would say about this generalization (that it would apply to all future experience as well), we would see that it is not 'absolutely certain', for biologists are aware of analogous cases in which a similar relation has not been without exceptions.[2] A biologist would not consider the probability of this generalization to be the highest that he can conceive.

Next consider a contrary case, in which the probability of a generalization would seem to be as high as it could possibly be. In organic chemistry, 'homologous series' are series of compounds whose members differ from one another only because there is a constant increase in carbon- and hydrogen content from one member to the next. Thus, the physico-chemical properties of molecules change in a lawful manner with increase in molecular size. The

---

2. R. Hesse and F. Doflein, *Tierbau und Tierleben* I (Leipzig: J.G. Teubner, 1910), 44.

chemist now reasons as follows: "supposing a *gap* occurs in a homologous series, that is, supposing the increase in carbon- and hydrogen content between
two known members is greater than what a lawful change would presuppose,
this indicates the existence of a yet unknown compound. The chemical and
physical properties of this compound can be predicted with certainty."[3] This
means: a generalization made on the basis of established relations has in this
case a high probability.

Our question now is this: Is it possible to interpret probabilities of the
kind we have been discussing here as relative frequencies to which some numerical values could be assigned, at least within certain limits? Or else: does
'probability' here amount to no more that some vague 'reliability', of which
no exact definition or estimation can be given? Among contemporary logical
empiricists, Hans Reichenbach would seem to be the only prominent figure
defending the former possibility.[4] The overwhelming majority of philosophers
reject the idea that the so-called probability of inductive generalizations could
be given an exact definition, or that it could be estimated, even within certain
limits.

Relative Simplicity

We shall now consider a particular class of cases in which it might seem as
though one could speak of a greater of lesser probability, at least within certain limits. For this purpose, we shall define the concept 'relative simplicity'
and start with the following case. Let us suppose a number of observations
have been made and their results marked as dots in a suitable chosen coordinate system. (Imagine, for example, that we have made a number of determinations of location for heavenly bodies; or that we have been detecting changes in
some particular temperature and plotted the temperatures in the coordinate
system, say, once in every hour.) Thus we have a series of observation points,
and we draw through them a curve that is as simple as possible; hence we have
all the observation points adjusted on the curve with sufficient precision. Assuming again that we ignore all rationalization, this curve, which is as simple
as possible, will be an inductive generalization; after all, the curve assumes
what the course of the phenomena will be in between the observed points. Let
n be the total number of particular observation points, and let m be the total
number of randomly chosen observation points that is necessary and sufficient

3. Wallach, "Organische Chemie," in *Die Kulture der Gegenwart*, hrsg. von P. Hinneberg, Teil
III, Abt. III, Band 2 (Leipzig und Berlin: B.G. Teubner, 1913), 207.
4. H. Reichenbach, *Wahrscheinlichkeitslehre. Eine Untersuchung über die logischen und ma-
thematischen Grundlagen der Wahrscheinlichkeitsrechung* (Leiden: Sijthoff, 1935) (English
translation from the 2nd ed. as *The Theory of Probability: An Inquiry into the Logical and Mathematical Foundations of the Calculus of Probability*, trans. E.M. Hutten and M. Reichenbach

for the simple curve running through the points to be fully determined. If, for example, our curve is a straight line, $m = 2$, and if it is a circle, $m = 3$, etc. We then define the relative simplicity of a curve by the ratio m/n as follows: the curve and the corresponding generalization have *the greater relative simplicity, the smaller the ratio m/n is.*

It is evident that the relative simplicity of this curve stands in a direct relation to the so-called probability that we have assigned to it. Evidently, the smaller the ratio m/n, the greater is our confidence that the curve constitutes a faithful description of the course of the relevant phenomenon in the regions between the observation points. To see that this really is how we judge the matter, we only need to see that if $m/n = 1$–that is to say, if *each* of our observation points is necessary to determine the curve, so that we get another curve as soon as even one of the observation points is dropped–we consider the 'probability' of the curve to be $= 0$. We see at the same time that a curve that we consider to be probable need not be simple in the absolute sense, that is, in the sense in which, for example, a curve of second degree is simpler than a curve of third degree. In principle, we may make the curve as complicated as we wish, and yet it may possess a great relative simplicity and, hence, a great probability if only the ratio m/n is small; if, that is, the number of observation points, n, increases in the same proportion as m.

Now, it may seem that we could make a generalization from observations in this special case to cover an entire range of inductive generalizations, to wit, cases that are similar to our example of homologous series in chemistry. Consider one more example. In 1869 Dmitry Mendeleyev observed that when chemical elements are arranged according to their increasing atomic mass, the resulting series exhibits a periodic change in physico-chemical properties that is dependent upon the mass; the result is the so-called periodic table. Since there were gaps in the system, Mendeleyev predicted the existence of as yet unknown elements and described their probable physico-chemical properties. These 'prognoses' have since turned out to be correct with surprising accuracy. A theory like Mendeleyev's is, from a logical point of view, analogous with a curve possessing a great relative simplicity. What corresponds to observation points in Mendeleyev's theory are the known particular elements; what corresponds to m is the number of elements that is sufficient and necessary for the detection of the relevant lawfulness, namely, the dependence of physico-chemical properties on atomic masses, say, two 'periods'.

Thus it is possible to speak, quite generally, about the relative simplicity of a theory, which is directly proportionate to its 'probability'. The smaller the multiplicity of a theory–the smaller the number of its logically independent basic statements–in comparison to the data of experience that can be explained on its basis–in comparison, that is, to the number of different kinds of facts that can be derived from it–the greater is the relative simplicity of the theory. This would seem to agree with the fact that, in science, the probability of a theory is seen to increase greatly when it can be used to derive facts which are deemed unlikely in light of previous experience, but which nevertheless occur, as the theory predicts. In 1819, for example, Fresnel published his new theory of refraction of light. Poisson showed that if the theory was correct, bright spots should occur behind a small circle-shaped curtain that is perpendicular to a ray coming from a light source and situated on its axis. On the basis of experiments, Fresnel showed that this prediction, a consequence of his theory that many considered very unlikely, was in fact correct.[5]

There is no doubt, then, that we tend to think that the so-called probability of a theory is directly proportionate to its relative simplicity. If, now, we could show that in such cases probability can be given an exact definition and assigned a numerical value or range of values, then 'inductive logic' would in a sense be possible; admittedly, not in the sense that inductive discovery could be formalized, but in the sense that, for cases in which the relative simplicity of a theory can be defined, the 'probability' of generalizations drawn from the theory could be determined as well. Thus, inductive logic, insofar as there is such a thing, would amount to a calculus of probability. In so far as this leads us to a deductive branch of mathematics, we would arrive at the paradoxical result that what is logical in induction is in fact deduction.

This was how Leibniz saw the matter. In different connections, he emphasizes time and again that generalization from experience is in itself not a logical operation; it is something purely 'psychological'. As the ancient skeptics had done before him and as Hume would do after, he argued that it is grounded in memory and that in simple cases even animals use it, such as a dog that is scared of sticks because of its earlier experiences. Insofar as the inductive method is scientific, Leibniz thinks, it is an operation with the calculus of probability. The following example shows that Leibniz has in mind here what we have called relative simplicity. Imagine we have to encode a cryptogram, that is, a piece of text written in a secret code. If it is very short, there will not be enough facts (that is, the number of letters or figures will be too small) to identify its 'key', because it will allow of several interpretations. Typically, the longer the message becomes, the higher will be the probability of some particular interpretation, until, finally, the same 'key' can be identified in more than one way. If even a small part of the cryptogram is enough to provide an interpretation that fits its other parts as well, the probability of this interpretation is very high. Thus, let the multiplicity (length) of the part that suffices for the interpretation of the cryptogram be m, and let the multiplicity (length) of the entire text be n; then, in Leibniz's view, the ratio m/n, that is, the relative simplicity of the interpretation, determines its probability.[6]

5. P. Duhem, *La Théorie physique son objet et sa structure*, 2nd ed., 1914, 39. (English trans. by P. Wiener, *The Aim and Structure of Physical Theory* [Princeton: Princeton University Press, 1954].)
6. In his work, *La logique de Leibniz*, chap. V, VI, 176-92, Louis Couturat has given an exhaustive presentation of Leibniz's theory of probability.

Careful consideration is thus needed to see whether the 'probability' that is determined by the relative simplicity of a theory can be given an exact definition and estimation. For this purpose, we return to the case of a relatively simple curve. Let us suppose, then, that we have inserted in a coordinate system a number of observation points, $A, \ldots, N$, through which we can draw, say, a parabola with sufficient exactness. Of course, other curves can be drawn through these points as well, such as the wave-like curve in our figure. Both of these curves thus represent an assumption, consonant with actual experience, concerning the course of a certain phenomenon in the regions between the observation points. When we ask which of the two assumptions is more probable, it seems we could start reasoning in analogy with a certain line of

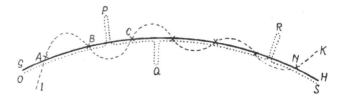

Figure 8

thought known as Bayes's Theorem in the calculus of probability and which once played an important role there. In this connection, it suffices to formulate its content as follows. Given a number of causes, one of which has brought about a certain effect, and each of which is equally possible in advance, the one that is the most probable is the one that is the likeliest to yield the effect. For example, let A and B be two dices, such that A is fair and, hence giving on average a six with the relative frequency of 1/6, whereas B is biased, giving on average a six with the relative frequency of 5/6. Given a series of tosses in which the relatively frequency approximates 1/6, but where it is not known which die, A or B, was used to produce the series, the probability that it was produced by dice A is much higher than the probability that it was produced by dice B. And in this case the meaning of 'probability' is, precisely, relative frequency in the following sense. Suppose we have a large number of series produced by both dice A and dice B; the majority of cases in which the relative frequency of sixes is 1/6, will then be produced by dice A, and only few of them with dice B; moreover, numerical values can be assigned to these relative frequencies and the corresponding probabilities.

We can now reason in a way that is analogous with the curves GH and IK in our example. Here the 'factual result' is the fact that the observation points $A, \ldots, N$ are located such that the curve GH, possessing a great relative simplicity, can be drawn through them with sufficient exactness. The other curve, IK, does not possess this property to the same degree, or else lacks it altogether. Let the former curve be determined by m, observation points and the latter by m_2 points, where $m_1 < m_2$. Hence, every class of observation points $A, \ldots, N$, the number of which is at least m_1, generates the curve GH, whereas the curve IK is only generated by classes with at least m_2 elements. Therefore, the assumption that the relevant phenomenon is represented by the curve GH yields the actual result in a greater number of cases than the assumption that it is represented by the curve IK; and the number of these cases is the greater, the smaller m_1 is in comparison to m_2, that is, the greater the relative simplicity of the curve GH is in comparison to that of the curve IK.

This kind of reasoning can be generalized so as to cover all those cases where the relative simplicity of a theory can be defined; and thus it seems as if Leibniz was correct in maintaining that 'inductive logic' exists in the sense that at least under certain conditions we could give an exact definition of the probability of a theory and measure it at least within certain limits.

This, however, is not the case. Closer inspection shows that the logical situation here is similar to what we found in the case of the so-called causal principle. For here, too, our reasoning is dependent upon certain implicit *additional conditions* that play an indispensable role in establishing the conclusion.[7]

Consider a curve of the form $OPQRS$ drawn through observation points, that is, a very irregular curve that is for the most part close to a parabola, but that deviates from it sharply in certain narrow regions between the observation points. If a curve of this kind is considered possible, our previous reasoning is no longer adequate. For if the observation points $A, \ldots, N$ were to change their positions in the interval GH in such a way that the curve OS deviated from a parabola only in certain narrow regions, the points constituting the curve OS would in most cases coincide with points on the parabola.

We see that in all these cases, the essence of inductive reasoning lies in the presupposition that the possibility of such strong deviations has been excluded; that the course of the relevant phenomenon, no matter what it may be in other respects, is always relatively regular, for example, in the sense that a mathematician has in mind when he speaks of analytic curves and their 'regularity'. In fact, we find precisely this presupposition in Leibniz.

But wherein lies its justification? From the standpoint of logical empiricism, it can have no other justification than previous experience. In this way we find ourselves returning to those relatively primitive enumerative inductions. Recall our examples from chemistry. The relevant theories are concerned with regions that vast experience has shown to be governed by certain relatively simple lawful patterns. When scientists create new theories in these regions, which are already subject to advanced scientific research, they may start from

---

7. This same conclusion is also reached by Hermann Weyl; see his *Philosophie der Mathematk und Naturwissenschaft* (Handbuch der Philosophie, Baumler und Schröter, 5), 116. (English translation as *Philosophy of Mathematics and Natural Science* [Princeton: Princeton University Press, 1949].)

the assumption that only theories that possess relative simplicity come into question. However, in the first place, this assumption has no basis other than 'brute empirical facts'. And, in the second place, no exact definition or estimation can be given of the 'probability' of this assumption; hence, neither can they be found for the 'probabilities' that we derive using the assumption.

Our general conclusion is that 'inductive logic' is impossible. The so-called probability, sometimes higher, sometimes lower, that we assign to inductive generalizations is purely 'psychological', a matter of vague 'reliability', and not an exact logico-mathematical property. *'The way of discovery', that is, the actual formulation of a theory, is something that falls outside the purview of logic*; logic is only concerned with the 'way of demonstration'.

Relative Simplicity and the Explanatory Value of a Theory

We must nevertheless point out one important positive result of our considerations. Admittedly, the relative simplicity of a theory is not a measure of its probability in any mathematical sense; and yet it is a property that is found in every good theory, for otherwise the theory cannot satisfy the requirement of invariance. To see this, let us recall, first of all, 'Occam's Razor', the principle that explanatory principles must not be multiplied beyond necessity. It is eminently natural to interpret this requirement as bearing on relative simplicity. Understood in this way, it can be expressed in the striking formulation that in our days has once been used by Einstein, a formulation that we have in fact already mentioned in passing:[8] an assumption has scientific value only to the extent that the multiplicity it contains (namely, the number of its logically independent basic statements) is smaller than the multiplicity of facts of experience that follow from it (namely, the number of distinct and logically mutually independent facts of experience that can be derived from it). The point of a scientific theory is, as we say, to *explain* some region. The word 'explain', however, can mean different things. The mythologizing primitive man explains thunder, saying that the Supreme God is riding his chariot over the firmament. He renders the phenomenon understandable to himself, trying to interpret it in light of familiar anthropomorphic events. When people sometimes argue that even scientific explanation is a matter of "reducing the unknown to the familiar," they are, to some extent, subscribing to this anthropomorphic conception. Some events are more familiar to us than others. For example, the push and pull of solid bodies are more familiar than electric phenomena, if only because we have a case in point in the movements of our own limbs. A

---

8. Einstein, "Physik," in *Kultur der Gegenwart*, 3. Teil, 3. Abt. 1. Band, 1915, 254. (English translation in *Collected Papers of Albert Einstein*, Vol. 4, *The Swiss Years, Writings 1912–14*, ed. A.J. Kox et al. [Princeton: Princeton University Press, 1995].)

contrary case, in a way, is found in intentional mental action, which may strike as more familiar than anything else, being, again, something in which we are ourselves constantly engaged. The atomists' mechanistic conception of nature as well as the Platonist-Aristotelian teleological conception are anthropomorphic to the extent that they draw upon explanatory principles that are, from a logical point of view, arbitrary, for they have been chosen purely on the basis of *familiarity*, and to the extent that they try to force the whole of nature into one or another of these frameworks, even though the overwhelming majority of natural phenomena can be said to be somewhere between these explanatory extremes. *Explanation in scientific sense is nothing else but logical derivation*, the derivation of the less general from the more general, independently of whether the explanatory principles are familiar or not. To explain experience is to find an 'economic description' for it. And now we can see that the relative simplicity of a theory is of great significance, because *the explanatory value of a theory is proportional to its relative simplicity*. A theory should satisfy the search for invariances, representing some domain in a way that is as simple and unified as possible. If a theory does not reduce the multiplicity of a domain but increases it, it can have no significance; on the other hand, it becomes the more significant, the more it reduces this multiplicity by revealing its underlying unity.

Justification of Induction

As for the general problem of induction, we arrive at the conclusion drawn by David Hume in his *Inquiry Concerning Human Understanding*. If we consider inductive generalizations from a logical point of view, thinking of them as a kind of reasoning, we come to see what Hume showed in detail, namely that this reasoning is possible only on the condition that 'the future is like the past', or that 'the course of nature is uniform'. And this precondition, it seems evident, cannot possibly be given a logical motivation. Since Kant's days, philosophers have searched for logically positive solutions to 'Hume's problem'– as Kant rightly calls it in the Introduction to *Prolegomena*. All such efforts have failed, a point on which the great majority of logical empiricists are in agreement. Some of these efforts to solve the problem will be mentioned in the following pages.

In accordance with the requirement of invariance–and not merely out of habit, as the ancient skeptics and Hume alike argued–we presuppose that the "course of nature is uniform," that is, that the invariances we have perceived so far continue to be valid in the future. However, we presuppose this in accordance with the requirement of empirical verification–the second basic ingredient in the Galilean conception of knowledge. For we accept, both generally and in particular cases, that future experience will decide whether it holds or not. We assume that in cases where the degree of invariance has been high so far, it will continue to be so in the future; and where it has been low, there we expect our future experience to confirm this, as well. If, then, our experience has recognized no exceptions to some relationship–say, that between being cloven-hoofed and being ruminant–but there have been exceptions in some analogical property or relationship, we make the generalization with less confidence than we do when analogous cases support our generalization. Such is the case with the examples from chemistry that we considered above. In the former case we readily talk about "empirical facts", even if they are very general. It is only in the latter cases that we speak about "laws of nature", and these different descriptions reflect the different degrees of "confidence" that we have in the corresponding generalizations.

Part II. Formal Truth of Theory

Chapter 6

Logical Truth

We move now from questions concerning the formation of scientific theories–
that is to say, from the phenomenology of theories–to questions having to do
with their validity–to *the logic of theories*. Here we enter the second main part
of our investigation, involving a heap of problems concerning the concept of
truth.

Mention has already been made of the insight, particularly clear in Leibniz's thought, that truth comes in two varieties; first, there are 'necessary
truths' that 'hold in all possible worlds', as Leibniz says. That is, they are *a
priori* or independent of experience and hold no matter what is the case; second, there are 'truths of fact', or empirical statements, which are *a posteriori*,
that is, dependent upon experience. The first we shall also call formal truths,
and the second material or empirical truths.

We have also mentioned the idea, clearly present even in Galileo's thinking, that logical inference is, as we shall call it, tautological. What this means
can be put in Leibniz's words: "A proof is nothing but a demonstration,
through the analysis of given concept . . . of what is covertly and, as it were,
virtually contained in these concepts." A proof proceeds by means of given
rules of inference, which constitute one important class of logical truths, such
as, "if *A* implies *B*, then not-*B* implies not-*A*."

These characterizations of logical truths are quite vague, however, and
are likely to be misunderstood. After all, we may ask, and with good reason,
what is really meant by this talk about what is 'covertly contained' in premises;

or what is meant when it is said that that something is 'implicitly' asserted in them, which is then 'made explicit' in the proof. In particular, such phrases are vulnerable to the psychologizing misunderstanding that logical 'tautology' implies psychological 'tautology', as if conclusions were no more than a repetition of what is *already in fact thought* in the premises. If this were so, all reasoning would be trivial, and not the series of psychological surprises that it often is. It is one of the notorious features of school logic that it is limited to consider such elementary cases—like Aristotelian syllogistic inferences—in which logical and psychological tautology do in fact coincide. For example, when we reason: "all men are mortal; Socrates is a man; therefore, Socrates is mortal," it may well be that our inference is a psychological tautology, as well. The conclusion that Socrates *qua* human being is mortal is not only 'logically included' in the premise 'all men are mortal' but may be included psychologically, too, in the sense that it happens to be thought in that premise. If we confine our attention to cases like these, we may well reach the conclusion, supported by Kant and his followers, that purely logical reasoning is something trivial and that, for example, mathematical reasoning, which is obviously not trivial, cannot be a case of purely logical reasoning.

We must therefore find a precise definition for what is meant by the 'tautological quality' of logical truth and logical reasoning. This will be our next undertaking, and here we shall make no further use of the misleading word 'tautology'.

Analytic and Synthetic Statements

Kant drew a distinction which he himself called "mighty" and "classical,"[1] one that we may use as our starting point, namely the distinction between *analytic* and *synthetic* judgments. As he himself points out, Hume had in fact already drawn the same distinction, though not for object-property judgments but rather for relational judgments.[2] Hume divided relations into two classes, analytic and synthetic relations—to use Kant's phrase—depending on whether or not the relevant relation was already determined through the objects that stand in that relation.[3] Equality would be an example of the former relation, spatial proximity of the latter. What this means can be explained as follows. A relational statement is analytic if it follows from the definitions of the meanings of relevant words; otherwise it is synthetic. "Purple is closer to red than it is to blue" is an analytic statement, because 'purple' means a certain color

1. Kant, *Prolegomena*, §3, §5.
2. Kant, *Critique of Pure Reason*, B792.
3. Hume, *Treatise of Human Nature*, Book I, Ch. 1, sec. 5.

between red and blue that is closer to red. "Cardinals wear purple robes" is synthetic in the sense that it does not follow from the concept of cardinal that he wears a robe of a particular color.

Starting from Aristotle's logic, Kant defines analyticity and syntheticity only for property-statements, that is, statements in which some property is ascribed to something or denied of it. Kant says: a judgment is analytic, if its predicate is "covertly contained" in the subject; otherwise it is synthetic. Regarding this definition, the following remarks should first be made.

Carnap seems to have been the first to notice a gap in Kant's division: it neglects the negations of analytic judgments.[4] Taking this oversight into account, we give the name "contradictory judgments" to sentences in which a predicate that is 'covertly contained' in the subject is denied of it. It follows, then, in the first place, that every property judgment is either analytic or synthetic or contradictory.

Second, we must explain what it means to say that a predicate is "covertly contained" in the subject. It means, we may agree, that an analytical sentence is one that follows from the meanings of the words in the sentence. That is, assuming these meanings can be given definitions, we may say that an analytical sentence is one that follows from such definitions alone.

Third, given this, we can free Kant's distinction from its Aristotelian limitation. As Hume already noticed, the corresponding distinction must be drawn for relational judgments, as well. Hence, independently of its kind, every sentence is either analytic or synthetic or contradictory.

Finally, we must notice that the analyticity of a sentence is a 'relative matter' in the sense that it depends upon the definitions of relevant concepts. One and the same word can be defined one way in one system and another way in another system. Kant agreed with the prevailing conception of his time when he held the judgment "every body is heavy" to be synthetic, for he thought that heaviness is not 'covertly contained' in the concept of body. A modern physicist might disagree. In what follows, the relativity of the distinction between analyticity and syntheticity turns out to be very significant.

Thus we arrive at the point where a precise logical analysis can be started. We put forth the following question: Can all logical and mathematical truths—in general, all formal truths—be construed as analytical sentences, that is, sentences that follow from definitions alone? To answer this question, we must examine three concepts, namely, the concepts 'sentence', 'follow', and 'definition'. We start with the last of these concepts.[5]

---

4. R. Carnap, *The Logical Syntax of Language*, trans. A. Smeaton (Paterson, NJ: Littlefield, Adams & Co., 1959), 39. (Originally published in German as *Logische Syntax de Sprache*, Schriften zur wissenschaftlichen Weltauffassung, Band 8 [Wien: Verlag von Julius Springer, 1934], 36.)
5. Cf. here Carnap, *Logical Syntax*, 23–25 (21–24 in the German original).

Definition

First of all, we distinguish between so-called *implicit* and so-called *explicit* definitions. We have already mentioned that when a theory is highly developed, that is, when it possesses as great a generality as possible, it becomes a so-called axiomatic system, the basic concepts of which are in fact variables and not constants. This implies that these basic concepts can be assigned any meaning that satisfies the axioms. Thus, for example, in axiomatic geometry, 'point', 'straight line', and 'congruence', etc., represent any objects and relations to which the axioms apply. In this case we say, then, that the basic concepts are implicitly defined by the axioms.

We put aside these 'implicit definitions' when we consider the concept of analytic sentence; for they are definitions in an improper sense only. After all, they do not fix the meaning of a phrase except within the often quite loose limits of an axiom system. And even this they accomplish only through one another, so that the elimination of the relevant signs is not possible. This will come up again later.

We shall next consider so-called explicit definitions. There are two main types. Suppose we define a word or a sign, X; suppose, that is, that we give an exact expression of the meaning of a certain X with the help of some other words or signs. This can be accomplished in two ways. With the help of a defining equation $X = YZ$ we state which combination of signs can be used to replace the definiendum, X. Here it is presupposed that the meaning of the combination YZ is known, and the defining equation is then used to stipulate that the meaning of X shall be the same as the meaning of YZ. Or, the definition can be established by a defining equation that states which sentence or group of sentences in which X does not occur can be used to replace a sentence in which X does occur, so that both sentences mean the same, but the meaning of X is not specified. In the former case we speak of explicit definitions in a stricter sense. This class includes, for example, Aristotelian definitions in which something is defined through a 'specific difference' and 'genus proximum'. A non-Aristotelian example of explicit definition in this stricter sense would be the definition of number 2 through the equation $2 = 1 + 1$.

The second of these two cases are known as '*use definitions*'. Definitions in exact logic–logistic–are mostly of this kind. Thus, for example, identity, '$a = b$' can be given an explicit definition by laying down that '$a = b$' is to mean the same as the following sentence: "if a has a property F, whatever property this may be, then b, too, has this property." In a case like this, then, we do not define the identity sign '$=$' itself but state through a definition how a sentence in which the sign occurs can be replaced by another–in this case by a certain 'if-then' sentence–in which the given sign does not occur.

Explicit definitions possess a property that is logically and in particular epistemologically quite significant; they are, at the same time, *elimination rules.* They state how a given sign can be eliminated by replacing the sign or a sentence in which the sign occurs by a combination of signs that defines the original sign, or in the latter case, by a sentence in which the original sign does not occur. In fact, explicit definitions are nothing but appropriate, economical abbreviations.

Let us suppose we have been given a set of sentences, S_1, in which there occurs a class of explicitly defined signs, *ABC*. Let us first consider a case in which the relevant definitions are explicit in the stricter sense of the word. In this case we can 'translate' S_1 into another set of sentences, S_2, in which *ABC* have been replaced by defining expressions.[6] This 'translation' is then *word-by-word*: signs occurring in S_1 correspond one by one to signs occurring in S_2, though not *vice versa*. If, on the other hand, the signs belonging to S_1 have been given through use definitions, and if S_1 is translated into S_2, in which *ABC* do not occur, the translation takes place not word-by-word but *sentence-by-sentence*, that is, the correspondence occurs only at the level of complete sentences.

Of course, both of these cases may occur in translations in the usual sense of the word, that is, when a text is translated from one natural language into another. These circumstances, too, are of considerable epistemological importance, as we shall see in due course.

There are, however, definitions that do not permit the elimination of defined concepts in every case. So-called *recursive definitions*, which are widely used in arithmetic and have begun to be applied more and more in logic, too, are of this kind. For example, the well-known arithmetical function $n! = F(n) = 1 \times 2 \times \ldots \times n$ can be given a recursive definition by means of the following two equations:

$$F(1) = 1$$

$$F(n + 1) = F(n) \times (n + 1)$$

This kind of definition provides an instruction for determining the value of the function $F(n)$ if n is some definite integer, any integer; in this process the defined sign $F(n)$ itself gets eliminated. For, according to the latter equation, $F(n)$ can be replaced by the expression $F(n\text{-}1) \times n$, and when we continue in this way, recursively, from each number to its predecessor, we finally arrive at number 1, for which the value is determined by the former equation, and the sign $F(n)$ has disappeared. But if n is not a determinate number but rather a number-variable representing any number, the recursively defined sign cannot be eliminated.[7]

---

6. For the notion of translation, see Carnap, *Logical Syntax*, 222–27 (165–70 in the German original).
7. Carnap, *Logical Syntax*, 25 (23 in the German original).

This case, too, will be important for us later in our epistemological investigations. We must take note: we cannot in advance exclude the possibility that there exist definitions, other than recursive, that do not permit a general elimination of defined signs. This is sufficient about definitions.

Again, when we say, "a sentence is analytic when it follows from definitions alone," we mean by definition here only explicit, recursive, or other such *proper definitions*; these are definitions that either generally or at least in some particular cases permit the elimination of defined signs. What we say, then, does not apply to improper or implicit definitions.

Next we must next consider the concepts 'sentence' and 'follow'. Here the word 'follow' has the meaning that it does when we say that this or that sentence follows logically from such and such a class of sentences. Neither this concept nor the concept 'sentence' can be adequately explained without considering some points in the elements of logistic.

Propositional Calculus

Modern exact logic or 'logistic' was developed gradually in the course of the previous century. Here we present its elements in a form that is nowadays often called 'classical' (why such a phrase is used we shall see later); this is the form it has, for example, in the systems of Russell[8] and Hilbert.[9]

Exact logic starts from the so-called *propositional calculus*, which constitutes the basis for the entire system. Historically speaking, this calculus has its origin in the Stoic doctrine of hypothetical and disjunctive judgments and inferences, whereas the Aristotelian doctrine concerning so-called categorical judgments and inferences falls outside its purview.[10]

A remarkable proof of the Greek logical acumen is found in the fact that even the ancients Stoics interpreted hypothetical or "if-then" sentences in the same way as they are interpreted today, without exception, in the systems of logic known as 'classical'.[11]

Let us consider the proposition, "if there will be lightning tomorrow, there will be thunder." This proposition is, of course, true if there will be lightning and thunder tomorrow; equally evidently, it is false, if there will be lightning tomorrow but not any thunder. But what should we say about the two remaining cases, namely, the possibilities that there will be neither lightning nor thunder tomorrow, or that there will be thunder but no lightning? The Stoics answered that the proposition must be considered true in both of

8. Whitehead and Russell, *Principia Mathematica*, Vol. I–III; 2nd ed. 1925–27.
9. D. Hilbert and P. Bernays, *Die Grundlagen der Mathematik*, I (Berlin: Springer, 1934).
10. See, e.g., H. Scholz, *Geschichte der Logik*, 1931.
11. Sextus Empiricus, *Outlines of Pyrrhonism*, Against the Grammarians, VIII, 113.

these cases, too. For one may say: suppose, in a given situation, a proposition, 'P', would not turn out to be false; then, if every proposition is either true or false, 'P' must be considered true in the said case. Let 'P' be the proposition "if there will be lightning tomorrow, there will be thunder". 'P' will not be false, if there will not be any lightning and thunder tomorrow; nor will it be false, if there will be thunder tomorrow but not lightning. In these cases, too, therefore, the proposition is true. The Stoics applied exactly analogous reasoning to propositions with 'or'. For example, the proposition "there will be lightning or thunder tomorrow" is true in every case except when there will be neither lightning nor thunder tomorrow. Thus, in the case at hand, 'or' is the so-called 'inclusive or' and not 'either-or'.

This interpretation can be supported by a different kind of consideration. Let us suppose we make the following assertion today: "If there will be lightning tomorrow, there will be thunder," and let us suppose that tomorrow there will indeed be lightning and thunder. Once we have learned this much, we no longer say, "If there was lightning today, there was thunder." Rather, we say: "Today there was lightning and thunder." Accordingly, if we make today the following assertion: "Tomorrow there will be lightning or thunder," and there will be, say, lightning tomorrow but no thunder, then, as soon as we have learned this much, we no longer say: "Today there was lightning or thunder," but will say: "Tomorrow there was lightning." This shows that the natural language words 'if-then' and 'or' have a 'subjective' connotation, insofar as they express the notion that certain circumstances remain purely hypothetical for the speaker. Once these hypotheses have been replaced by known facts, they are no longer used. When somebody says, for example, "if A, then B" he simultaneously delivers the information that it is not yet know to him whether A will occur or not. As soon as A has occurred, or failed to occur, and this fact has become known, the word 'if' will no longer be used. Of course, this kind of connotation, describing, as it does, the particular situation of a particular speaker, is inappropriate in logic; hence we cannot use such words as 'if-then' and 'or' with their natural meanings.

Of these natural language words, 'if-then' and 'or', we replace the former with the so-called *implication*, which we may represent by the sign '→', and the latter with the so-called *disjunction*, which we may represent by the sign 'v'.[12] This does not mean that we could not read '$A → B$' as "If A, then B", or '$A ∨ B$' as "A or B"; but we must bear in mind that such translations are inaccurate. We shall take the formulae "$A → B$" and "$A ∨ B$" as our starting-point here. The signs 'A', 'B', 'C', . . . etc. are known as *sentential variables* that represent arbitrary sentences; for now we presuppose that the concept

12. The symbolism that we will be using is taken over, with minor adjustments, from Hilbert and Bernays; it follows the symbolism used in O. Ketonen, "Todistusteorian periaatteet" (*Ajatus*, IX, 1938); the following presentation makes use of Ketonen's excellent treatise on a number of points.

'sentence' has been made determinate. The formulae we shall consider are kind of unambiguous logical functions, so-called *truth functions*. What this means is this: when unique truth-values are assigned to variables 'A', 'B', 'C', . . ., that is, when they are replaced by sentences that are either true or false, the formulas '$A \rightarrow B$' and '$A \vee B$' receive a unique truth-value, 'true' or 'false'. The former formula is true in every case except when we substitute some true sentence for 'A' and some false sentence for 'B'; the latter sentence is true in every case except when we substitute a false sentence for both 'A' and 'B'. We introduce two further truth-functions: "not-A", which we shall represent as '$\sim A$', and "A and B", which we shall represent as '$A \& B$'. The former we call the *negation* of A; the latter we call the *conjunction* of A and B. We can then formulate the following so-called truth-value table, which shows how the truth of a logical function is dependent upon the truth-values of its variables. We shall use 'α' to denote truth and 'β' to denote falsity.

Variable A	Negation A	Variables A	B	Implication $A \rightarrow B$	Disjunction $A \vee B$	Conjunction $A \& B$
α	β	α	α	α	α	α
β	α	α	β	β	α	β
		β	α	α	α	β
		β	β	α	β	β

If two truth functions have the same values no matter what values are assigned to their variables, we say that they are logically equivalent. Thus the truth-value table shows us, for example, that

$$\text{`}\sim A \rightarrow B\text{'} = \text{`}\sim (\sim A \& \sim B)\text{'} = \text{`}A \vee B\text{'}.$$

These equations are important, for they show how certain truth-functions can be given explicit definitions by means of one another. If, for instance, we let '$\sim$' and '$\vee$' be our basic signs, implication and disjunction can be defined by their means. Further, we define *equivalence*: '$A \leftrightarrow B$' = '$(A \rightarrow B) \& (B \rightarrow A)$', which can be read, "'$A$' is true if, and only if, 'B' is true." The truth-value table shows us that 'A' and 'B' possess the same truth-value, and hence that either both are true or both are false, if and only if '$A \rightarrow B$' and '$B \rightarrow A$' are both true. Similarly we may define, for example, "exclusive or" or "either-or" by means of the formula '$A \leftrightarrow \sim B$'.

There are three kinds of truth-functions: those that receive the value 'true' no matter what truth-values are assigned to variables; those that receive the value 'false' no matter what truth-values are assigned to variables; and those that receive the value 'true' for some values and the value 'false' for others. The first kind we call identically true formulae.[13] Wittgenstein, to whom

13. D. Hilbert and W. Ackermann, *Grundzüge der theoretischen Logik*, 1928, 2nd ed. (English edition as *Principles of Mathematical Logic*, trans. L.M. Hammond, G.G. Leckie, F. Steinhardt,

in fact goes the credit for inventing the method of truth tables, used to call them 'tautologies'.[14] The second kind we call identically false formulae. To the third kind–the most important, in fact–we do not assign any name here.

Let us apply the truth-table method to a formula like '$(A \rightarrow B) \rightarrow (\sim B \rightarrow \sim A)$', "if B follows from A, $\sim A$ follows from $\sim B$" (this is known as 'contraposition'):

A	B	$(A \rightarrow B)$	$\rightarrow$	$(\sim B \rightarrow \sim A)$
α	α	α	α	α
α	β	β	α	β
β	α	α	α	α
β	β	α	α	α

We note that the formula receives the value 'true' no matter values are given to its variables. Similarly, we note, for example, that

'A → A', or the 'law of identity',

'A ∨ ~A', or the 'law of excluded middle', and

'~(A & ~A)', or the 'law of (non-)contradiction',

are identically true formulae in propositional calculus. In the same way, for example, '$[A \& (A \rightarrow B) \rightarrow B]$', or 'modus ponens', and '$[(A \rightarrow B) \& (B \rightarrow C)] \rightarrow (A \rightarrow C)$', or the rule of chain inference, are identically true formulae. '$A \& \sim A$' is an example of a formula that is identically false.

In this way the formulae of propositional calculus give a precise expression to the so-called 'laws of thought' of school logic, that is, logical truths, insofar as these can be stated using no other resources than sentential variables and the truth-functions determined above.

The identically true formulas of propositional calculus, when they are given content via interpretation, constitute therefore our first group of rules for logical inference. Suppose we are given a theory in which sentences 'A', 'B', 'C', . . . occur, and suppose further that one of the axioms of the theory is '$A \rightarrow B$' and another one '$B \rightarrow C$'. Then we can apply the rule of chain inference and infer '$A \rightarrow C$'. Or let 'A' be one of our axioms; if we have succeeded in showing '$A \rightarrow B$', we can apply the rule *modus ponens* and infer 'B'.

The following far-reaching questions arise here. How can we derive all necessary identically true formulae? Given a formula of propositional calculus, how can we show whether it is identically true or not?

ed. and with notes by R.E. Luce. New York: Chelsea Pub. Co., 1950).
14. L. Wittgenstein, *Logisch-philosophische Abhandlung*, Ostwald's Annalen der Naturphilosophie (1921). Wittgenstein's work is better known in its German-English edition, *Tractatus Logico Philosophicus* (London: Kegan Paul, 1922).

One way to try to solve these questions is the *axiomatic method*. In this case, we act in accordance with the general principles of theory formation and formulate the propositional calculus in the form of an axiomatic system. We select a small number of simple and logically independent formulae that are identically true; these are the basic sentences of the system or the axioms of propositional calculus. From these we derive other formulae, using *modus ponens* and the rule of substitution. The latter rule is based on the idea that the sentential variables 'A', 'B', 'C', ... represent some sentences–any sentences– and hence other sentences–any sentences–can be substituted for them; an identically true formula receives the value 'true' no matter what truth-values are given to its variables, and therefore we can put any sentences whatsoever– true or false–in place of these variables without changing the identical truth of the formula.

Here we must define the concept 'sentence'. Putting aside all issues of principle concerning this concept, we restrict our attention to the following. In propositional calculus, a 'sentence' (or 'formula') is any of the following: a sentential variable, a truth-function of these variables (negation, disjunction, implication, conjunction, or equivalence), or, finally, any combination result- ing from a substitution of truth-functions for sentential variables in truth- functions; for all occurrences of a given sentential variable in a formula can be replaced by a sentence in the sense we have just defined.

What identically true formulae are selected as axioms is largely a matter of arbitrary decision; for insofar as we give them interpretations, they are all formulae for rules that we in fact use for logical inference. In the same way, it is in principle arbitrary what formulae are selected as rules of inference and what as axioms. Considered as an axiom, *modus ponens*, for instance, is a particular logical formula; considered as a rule of inference, it is this formula together with a material interpretation assigned to it. In such a case, identically true sentences are divided into a number of axioms and theorems provable from these axioms, together with rules of inference, exactly as in other axiomatic systems. Here we must note that axioms, too, are not only identically true, but *provable sentences* as well; for given an identically true formula '$A \to A$', any axiom can be substituted for 'A', and then the axiom can be proved. We should therefore observe that in a logical system even the axioms are consequences; that is, they are consequences of themselves.

Several axiomatic propositional calculi have been formulated. Here we shall only mention two.[15]

The first system:

$$A \to (\sim A \to B)$$

$$(\sim A \to A) \to A$$

15. Both systems have been formulated by Łukasiewicz; see, e.g., Hilbert and Bernays, *Grundla- gen der Mathematik*, 70–72.

$(A \to B) \to [(B \to C) \to (A \to C)];$

The second system:

$A \to (B \to A)$

$(\sim A \to \sim B) \to (B \to A)$

$[A \to (B \to C)] \to [(A \to B) \to (A \to C)].$

The first axiom of the first system may be stated as follows: "if A is true, B follows from not-A"; that is to say, if it is known that some sentence, 'A' is true, then its negation, which is a false sentence, implies a sentence 'B', no matter what sentence 'B' is; which means that a *false sentence implies every sentence*. The first axiom of the second system may be stated thus: "If A is true, then B, where B is any sentence, implies A"; that is to say, a *true sentence is implied by every sentence*.

At first sight, these two claims may strike us as rather paradoxical. This appearance can be dispelled, however, once we recall that the meaning of implication is not exactly what we are accustomed to attaching to the words "if-then". In fact, these properties of implication are only apparently paradoxical.[16]

Consistency

Both of these axiom systems possess a number of important properties. First, both can be shown to be consistent; secondly, they can be shown to be sufficient, that is, complete; thirdly, the axioms of both systems can be shown to be logically independent from one another. If possible, every axiom system ought to be shown to be consistent, that is, such that no sentence of the form 'A & $\sim A$' can be derived in it. We shall presently explain why this is necessary.

In principle, consistency proofs are of two different kinds. First, a proof of this kind can be given by showing that the relevant system is isomorphic with some other system the consistency of which we take as given; whence it follows that the first system must be consistent. Since the systems are isomorphic descriptions of one another, a contradiction, if it occurs in one system, must occur in the other system as well. In this way, for example, Euclidean geometry can be shown to be consistent by giving it an arithmetical interpretation in analytic geometry, in which case arithmetic is supposed to be consistent.[17]

---

16. For further consideration of this issue, see B. Russell, *Introduction to Mathematical Philosophy* (London: George Allen & Unwin, 1919) 153.
17. D. Hilbert, *Foundations of Geometry.* Authorized translation by E.J. Townsend (La Salle, Ill.: Open Court Publishing Company. 1950), §9. (Originally published in German as *Grundlagen der Geometrie* [Leipzig: Teubner, 1899, 7th edition, 1930].)

Another method, which is the only one that can be applied to logical and arithmetical axiom systems, is to make it evident that a formula of the form '*A* & ~*A*' cannot be derived from the axioms by means of rules of inference. In his large-scale consistency proofs, Hilbert has shown, firstly, how this proof can be carried out without being caught in a circle; for this is exactly what seems to be the threat here, insofar as one is trying to prove that logic consistent by means of logic.

Let us draw a distinction between *logic* and '*metalogic*'. The first is now understood as a completely formal manipulation, in accordance with a determinate set of rules, of written formulae, the meaning of which is ignored. In this way logic becomes completely formalized, as in Leibniz's program. Metalogic, in turn, consists in an investigation of the properties and relations of these sets of concrete formulae. In this way, the relationship between logic and metalogic is similar to that between the game of chess and its theory, for example. Just as it can be shown in the theory of chess, for example, that if the rules of the game are followed correctly, then certain pieces cannot occupy squares of the same color, so too, it can be shown, with respect to favorable cases in logic—and similarly in arithmetic—that one cannot arrive at a formula of the form '*A* & ~*A*', if the formulae that constitute the starting-point are manipulated in accordance with logical 'game-rules'.

In propositional calculus this proof is exceedingly simple.[18] First, it is established using the truth-table method that the formulae constituting the starting-point—that is, axioms—are identically true sentences. Next, it is shown that insofar as we use rules of inference, we can only get from identically true formulae to identically true formulae. For, first, the rule of substitution can only yield such formulae, because an identically true sentence is a formula the truth-value of which is true no matter what values its variables possess. Secondly, as is shown by the truth-value table for implication, the rule of inference '$[A \,\&\, (A \to B)] \to B$' is such that if '*A*' and '$A \to B$' are true, then '*B*' has the same truth-value as '*A*', namely 'true'; and also that when '*A*' and '$A \to B$' are identically true, '*B*', too, is identically true. Thus, in propositional calculus there cannot occur a formula of the form '*A* & ~*A*', which is identically false.

The distinction between logic and metalogic is among the most important results of modern logic. It corresponds, approximately, to the distinction that we must draw between the so-called *object language* and the so-called *syntax language*, or language in which the object language is studied.[19] As our present task will not allow us to pursue this distinction in any depth, we shall only make the following point to clarify these terms. When logic is completely formalized and meanings are abstracted away, the study of logic is transformed into a kind of logical syntax; it explains, precisely, such concepts as those that are central to our purposes, like the concepts 'analytic' and 'true'. These con-

---

18. Hilbert and Bernays, *Grundlagen der Mathematik*, 73.
19. Carnap, *Logical Syntax of Language*.

cepts are not a part of logic itself–of the object language–but belong to meta-logic, or logical syntax. Starting from this basis, Alfred Tarski has given the first precise definition of the concept of truth that is consistent and suffices at least for certain simple cases.[20] It is remarkable because, among other things, it applies, within certain limits, to formal as well as material truths. These results, however, can only be presented using a much more complex logical apparatus than what we can develop here.

Returning now to the propositional calculus, the following question arises: Why is consistency a necessary property of all axiom systems? The answer is very simple. From a sentence of the form 'A & $\sim A$', any sentence can be derived that can be formed within the system.[21] A false sentence implies every sentence, and, therefore, 'A & $\sim A$' implies 'B', no matter what sentence 'B' is. The point can also be seen in this way. Above we considered the formula '$A \rightarrow (\sim A \rightarrow B)$'. If, then, we can prove both 'A' and '$\sim A$', we can apply *modus ponens* twice and prove 'B' no matter what sentence 'B' is. Thus, if a theory contains a contradiction, this is a catastrophe that destroys everything, for in that case anything can be proved.

The Character of Logical Axioms

Like any other logical system, propositional calculus contains a number of undefined basic signs, so-called logical constants; these represent in an exact form the meanings of certain concepts of the natural logic. The number of these basic signs (as well as the number of axioms in which they occur) can be made smaller than what was done above, but there must always be some. We shall now consider the following point. Materially speaking, we must, of course, demand that every concept that we use is fully determinate. Corresponding to this, there is the formal requirement that every concept must be used in accordance with some fixed rules. Each explicit definition is there, precisely, to give a rule of use for such a sign. What are we now to say of the basic logical concepts and the "logical constants" representing them? How are they determined?–In the case of the propositional calculus, they could be the following, for instance: 'sentential variable', 'implication' and 'negation'. With respect to content, these concepts, too, must have a fully determinate meaning; and speaking formally, there must be determinate rules for their use.

20. A. Tarski, *The Concept of Truth in Formalized Languages*. In A. Tarski, *Logic, Semantics, Metamathematics* (Oxford: Oxford University Press, 1956). Polish original published in 1931; German translation as "Der Wahrheitsbegriff in den Formalisierten Sprachen," *Studia philosophica*, I (Lemberg, 1935).
21. Hilbert and Bernays, *Grundlagen der Mathematik*, 86.

They cannot be given explicit definitions. After all, in this kind of definition it is presupposed that there are known signs by means of which the definition can be formulated. It is clear, therefore, that not *all* logical constants can be defined while staying within the realm of logic itself. We take it to be equally evident that they cannot be defined, say, by starting from empirical concepts. Here it may suffice to point out that in nature we never experience anything 'negative' or 'disjunctive'; therefore it is inconceivable that negation or disjunction, say, could be defined by means of some empirical concepts. How, then, are these concepts determined?

One question is whether logical constants could be *implicitly defined* through logical axioms in the way that, for example, geometrical axioms define geometrical concepts. If this were so, it would have to be possible to give different interpretations, for instance, to axiom systems in propositional calculus, just as we can give, say, an arithmetical interpretation to a system of geometry. It might seem that this could be done. For example, let R be a class of objects, $A, B, C, \ldots$ which we call 'regions'; let negation, '$\sim A$', stand for the region of R that remains when A is removed from it; and let '$A \rightarrow B$' mean the same as 'region A is within area B'. When this interpretation is developed further, we see that there is a correspondence between the structure of the propositional calculus and that of the class C.[22] Here we see a kind of isomorphism that is basically the same as that which Euler noted some two hundred years ago, to wit, that the rules of Aristotelian syllogisms can be represented by geometrical figures.

Nevertheless, we readily see that attempts to construe logic as an axiomatic system in which basic concepts are implicitly defined through axioms are rather ill-conceived. Let us suppose that the structure of the above class R is described by basic sentences that correspond to the axioms of propositional calculus. In this description, one is bound to use some basic logical concepts. Consider, for example, the formula '$[(A \rightarrow B)\ \&\ (B \rightarrow C)] \rightarrow (A \rightarrow C)$'. In accordance with the interpretation indicated above, we read this as follows: "if region A is within region B, and region B is within region C, then, region A is within region C"; here certain logical constants are used. If propositional calculus were an axiomatic system like geometry, we should have to find an interpretation for it in which logical constants are used *consistently* only in accordance with this interpretation. This, however, seems impossible, and thus the attempt to construe basic logical concepts as being implicitly defined by axioms falls through.

To answer our question we consider more closely the rule of inference '$[A\ \&\ (A \rightarrow B)] \rightarrow B$'. We see that it expresses a condition under which the implication signs it contains can be eliminated; to wit, when 'A' and '$A \rightarrow B$' are true. Or we consider the formula '$(\sim A \rightarrow A) \rightarrow A$'. It expresses a condition un-

22. O. Huntington, "The Method of Postulates," *Philosophy of Science* 4, no. 4, (1937): 482-95.

der which the negation sign it contains can be eliminated; to wit, when '$\sim A$' implies 'A'. We can see that even though the axioms of propositional calculus are not implicit definitions of the basic concepts that occur in them, let alone explicit definitions, there nevertheless is a sense in which they *determine these concepts*; speaking formally, they give *instructions for the use of certain signs*. The most concrete indication of this is the fact that these axioms permit the elimination of certain signs just as do definitions under certain specific conditions. Materially speaking, axioms and rules of inference are consequences of the meanings of basic concepts, and are, in this sense, analytic sentences. For example, given the meanings of the words 'true' and 'if-then', it is always the case–'in all possible worlds', no matter how things are–that if 'A' is true and if 'B' follows from 'A', then 'B' is true. If we succeed in finding an exact and *formal* characterization for this insight, we have come a long way in our attempt to interpret logical truths as analytic sentences.

Decidability

Above we asked how we can derive all identically true sentences that we need and how we can decide whether a formula of propositional calculus is identically true or not. So far we have considered the axiomatic method, which is, historically speaking, the first method that was introduced to answer these questions. Concerning this, though, we must make the following remark: we can never know that all the rules of inference that turn out to be necessary, provided they can be represented as sentences in the propositional calculus, have in fact been proved. Furthermore, the resolution of the problem of whether a given formula is identically true or not will be dependent upon whether we succeed in finding a proof for it. It is for this reason that the method of truth-tables, invented by Wittgenstein, is so important; it enables us to show, for every formula of propositional calculus and without a proof, whether it is identically true or not. Another step forward in the same direction is the observation made by Hilbert that by means of certain methods all formulae of propositional calculus, be they identically true or not, can be reduced to so-called *normal forms*.[23]

Here we shall only mention the so-called conjunctive normal form. A formula is said to be in this form when it is a conjunction of certain disjunctions, where the sentential variables in each disjunct have been negated at most once. Thus, for instance, the formula '$(A \lor \sim A \lor C)\ \&\ (B \lor \sim B \lor D)$' is a conjunctive normal form, and for that matter, an identically true one. It is the conjunctive normal form of the formula '$[\sim A \to (A \to C)]\ \&\ [\sim B \to (B \to D)]$'. When we have transformed a formula into this form, we can readily see whether it is

23. Hilbert and Ackermann, *Grundzüge der theoretischen Logik*, 10.

identically true or not; a conjunction is identically true only when each of its conjuncts is identically true, and a disjunction is identically true as soon as it contains at least one pair of sentences of which one is the negation of the other.

Here we cannot go about showing *how* each formula of propositional calculus can be transformed into a conjunctive normal form. But we can make it intelligible *that* every formula must be capable of such transformation; for in a conjunctive normal form there occurs only a conjunction and a disjunction and, in addition to these, at least when the formula is identically true, a negation. But we know that these suffice for the definition of all other truth functions, and thus we can understand that every given formula can be transformed into a normal form by means of operations in which identical truth is retained. And hence, with respect to every formula of propositional calculus, we can resolve the question of whether it is identically true or not. This question, which arises for every logical system, is known as the *decision problem*. Its content varies slightly from one logical system to another. Propositional calculus is remarkable in the following respect: in it one cannot raise any question about the identical truth of a given formula that could not be given a complete solution by a finite number of relevant operations.

It is one of the remarkable achievements of exact logic that it is possible to identify the precise point where this general decidability reaches its limit, a point, that is, where questions can be raised within a given system that cannot be resolved by means of previously given rules and even questions that are provably quite undecidable.[24] It is a matter of far-reaching consequences that this is also the point where the transition from logic to arithmetic takes place.

Finally, we should indicate one important general question that is raised as much in propositional calculus as it is in every logical system, namely the question of *completeness*.[25] Here the question is whether a given system is complete in the sense that every sentence of this system that is 'true' in a certain specifiable sense—in propositional calculus, every identically true sentence—can be proved from the axioms. It can be shown, for instance, that both of the axiom systems we presented above are complete in this sense. Propositional calculus, however, is complete also in the following sense: if a formula that is not identically true is added to the axioms of propositional calculus, every formula can be proved. We show this with the help of the following example, which can be easily generalized. Let formula '$A \lor B$', which is not identically true, be our axiom. By substitution we get '$A \lor A$', and from there 'A'. Substituting again, we get a formula like '$B \ \& \ {\sim}B$', is a contradiction, from which anything follows.

24. K. Gödel, "On formally undecidable propositions of *Principia Mathematica* and related systems, I", in Shanker, ed., *Gödel's Theorem in Focus*, 1988. (Originally published in German as "Über formal unentscheidbare Sätze der Principia Mathematica und verwandter Systeme," *Monatshefte für Mathematik und Physik*, 38, 1931.); Cf. Carnap, *Logical Syntax*, 131–34 (93–95 in the German original).
25. Hilbert and Ackermann, *Grundzüge der theoretischen Logik,* 33; Hilbert and Bernays, *Grundlagen der Mathematik,* 66, 86, 94.

Predicate Calculus

The identically true sentences of propositional calculus suffice for the representation of only some of the rules of inference that are actually used; in these rules sentences are treated as unanalyzed wholes, as in the hypothetical and disjunctive inferences in school logic. However, as soon as we come to ordinary categorical syllogisms–that is, to the rules for proper Aristotelian inferences–we find rules that cannot be represented in propositional calculus because these inferences depend upon the *constituents* of sentences. This is the case with such inferences as "Everything is perishable; therefore something is perishable".

Formally, this means that sentential variables and their truth-functions are not sufficient. In addition to these, we must introduce so-called *individual variables* 'a', 'b', 'c',... 'x', 'y', 'z', ... representing some objects or 'elements' as they are also called. Then we have not only sentential variables but combinations of signs of the form '$A(a, ...)$'. Signs 'A', 'B', 'C',..., followed by individual variables, we call *predicate variables*. They represent some properties or relations. Thus we read '$A(a)$' as "a has the property A", and '$B(a, b, ..., n)$' may be read "$a, b, ..., n$ stand in the relation B". In the former case, the formula stands for a property judgment; in the latter case it stands for a relational judgment. In the former case, the letter 'A' is called a '*unary predicate*' and in the latter case we call 'B' an n-place or n-ary predicate, where n expresses the number of individual variables associated with B.

This, however, is not yet enough. Suppose we want to negate a sentence of the form '$A(a)$'. We see that we cannot yet distinguish between the following two possibilities: 'every a is non-A' and 'not every a is A'.[26] Or, to use the language of school logic, we cannot yet, by means of the resources introduced so far, distinguish between the contradictory and contrary opposites of a sentence. For this purpose we introduce the so-called *operators*, of which there are two in standard predicate calculus: 'all'-operator '(x)' and 'existence-operator' '(Ex)'. Variables occurring in a formula of the form '$A(a, ...)$' are said to be free, and when they are individual variables, we designate them with letters $a, b, c, ...$ from the beginning of alphabet. Variables occurring in a formula of the form '$(x) A(x, ...)$' or '$(Ex) A(x, ...)$' are said to be bound; these bound individual variables we designate with letters $x, y, z, ...$ from the end of alphabet. A formula of the form '$(x) A(x)$' may be read, 'for every object x, A'; a formula of the form '$(x) (Ey) B(x, y)$' may be read, "for any x, there is an object y such that x and y stand to each other in the relation B." Similarly, for example, '$\sim (x) A(x)$' may be read, 'it is not the case that every x is A'; and '$(Ex) \sim B(x)$' may be read, 'there is an x such that it is not B'.

---

26. Hilbert and Bernays, *Grundlagen der Mathematik*, 94.

Here we encounter a number of new issues with far-reaching consequences. We must give rules of use for our operators; or, materially speaking, we must clarify the exact meaning of the concepts 'all' and 'some'. Moreover, we need to redefine the concept "sentence" and find an analogue in this so-called predicate calculus introduced here for the notion of identically true sentence with which we operated in propositional calculus.

Sentence

We begin with the concept 'sentence'. Every predicate 'A', 'B', 'C', ... possesses what is known as a *value-range*; materially speaking, this is the class of objects to which this predicate can be "meaningfully" applied, i.e., in such a way that the result is a true or false sentence. For instance, the value-range of the predicate 'red' is constituted by colored objects; "snow is red" is a sentence, though it may be false. A group of words is a sentence in the *grammatical sense* as soon as it has a subject and a predicate; exceptions to this rule—there are always exceptions to grammatical rules—are irrelevant here. In this sense, strings of words such as "a human is an opposite" and "between red and blue there is penal code" are sentences, but *they are not sentences in the logical sense*. They have no content and make no assertion; they are "meaningless," neither true nor false. For example, the predicate 'opposite' presupposes a relation to which it is applied, either truly or falsely, but 'human' is not a relation. 'Between' is a relation that presupposes that its terms are logically of the same type, but 'red' and 'blue', on the one hand, and penal code, on the other, are logically of an altogether different type.

These issues are clarified in what is called the *logistic theory of types*.[27] It shows, among other things, that there are great many strings of words, particularly common in metaphysical philosophy, which are in fact not sentences in the logical sense. For instance, the sentence "every object demands to be acknowledged"—the basic thesis of a contemporary metaphysician—is not a sentence at all, because the predicate 'demands to be acknowledged' requires a certain specific kind of object and cannot be applied to 'every object'.

The gist of the logistic theory of types is to be found precisely in the insight that every predicate has a certain 'value-range'. If this principle is ignored, we can go about composing combinations of words with the appearance of a sentence that grammar and school logic deem acceptable but which lead to contradictions and are 'meaningless' and lacking in content. The best-known are the so-called logical paradoxes that are similar to Greek sophisms. Consider the well-known 'Epimenides': the Cretan Epimenides argues that all Cretans

27. The theory was introduced by Russell; see Whiteheand and Russell, *Principia Mathematica*, Vol. I, 37–65; B. Russell, *Introduction to Mathematical Philosophy*, ch. 13.

are liars. This implies that Epimenides, too, was lying when he made his assertion, and that Cretans are not always liars. If, then, his statement is true, it is false. The problem is solved by noting that this sophism is not a sentence in the logical sense because it breaches the logical requirement that the object language in which some subject matter (say, what Cretans assert) is discussed must be kept separate from the syntax language, which is concerned with assertions made in this object language. What is important here is that a great many theses in metaphysical philosophy are in this way logically erroneous and amount to nothing but 'pseudo-statements'. We shall return to this point later on.

Keeping in mind these issues, we shall now provide a definition for 'sentence' in the predicate calculus. Our task is greatly simplified if we assume that our individual variables always indicate objects that belong to the same logical type; that is, that they always indicate, for instance, only material objects or numbers. In that case only predicate variables $A, B, C, \ldots$ are logically of different types, as some of them may indicate properties and others, relations.

'*Sentences*' include, first, the formulae of predicate calculus in the sense explained above; second, they include those combinations of signs that can be derived from the formulae of propositional calculus by substituting sentential variables for predicate variables together with their associated variables '$A(a,\ldots)$'; finally, they include those combinations of signs that can be similarly derived by replacing sentential variables by combinations of the form '$(x) A(x,\ldots)$' or '$(Ex) A(x,\ldots)$', where these combinations may contain one or more operators with their associated bound variables. To avoid ambiguity, we must stipulate that, in a given sentence, a variable for a formula can be replaced by a sentence of the form '$(x) A(x,\ldots)$' or '$(Ex) A(x,\ldots)$' only if x does not occur as bound in the original formula. For example, the string $(x) [A \lor (x) B(x)]$ is not a sentence. Predicate variables may be bound in accordance with principles similar to those that concern individual variables. If '$F(a)$' is a sentence, '$(F) F(a)$' and '$(EF) F(a)$' are sentences, too; of these, the former may be read, "for any of those properties the value-range of which includes a, a has this property."

We can now formulate substitution rules for predicate calculus by extending the corresponding rule for propositional calculus so that it becomes possible to include the sentences of predicate calculus as defined above. Thus, first, individual variables may be replaced by other individual variables or, also, by constants designating definite individuals, if these are recognized. This applies to free variables. The corresponding procedure that is applied to bound variables is relettering, when this is needed, whence we replace the formula '$(x) A(x, \ldots)$' by the formula '$(y) A(y, \ldots)$' provided y does not occur bound in the first formula. Considering the content of these two formulas, we can see that they mean exactly the same thing. Further, variables for formulae may be replaced by predicate variables and predicate variables may be replaced by other predicate variables; here it must be noticed that if '$A(a, \ldots)$' is a predicate, then '$\sim A(a, \ldots)$', too, is a predicate. Notice here, however, that predicates may be of different logical types. The ensuing restriction is one that we formulate in the following "liberal" fashion: the replacement of a predicate '$A(a, b, \ldots)$' by another predicate is forbidden only if the latter contains fewer individual variables than the former. For example, relation predicates with more two or more places must not be replaced by unary property predicates. And, finally, variables for formula may be replaced by formulae of the form '$(x) A(x, \ldots)$' or $(Ex) A(x, \ldots)$ or '$(F) F(a)$' or '$(EF) F(a)$'.

In all these substitution rules, when a sign is replaced by another one, the latter is substituted for each occurrence of the former in a formula.

Similarly, we extend the second rule of inference in propositional calculus, *modus ponens*, in such a way that it includes all sentences of predicate calculus in the sense we have just defined.

'All' and 'Some'

How should the rules of inference for operators be formulated; or, semantically speaking, how should the concepts 'all' and 'some' be interpreted? Here we reach a critical point in exact logic, a kind of crossroads.[28]

We assume, first, that we consider some finite class of objects, that is, a class of which we can enumerate the elements by the numerals $1, 2, \ldots, n$, where 'n' signifies a definite natural number. Let *all* these objects possess the property 'A'. Thus we have '$A(1) \& A(2) \& \ldots \& A(n)$'. We use the slightly shorter notation '$A_1 \& A_2 \& \ldots \& A_n$'. We can then lay down the following definition:

$$'A_1 \& A_2 \& \ldots \& A_n' = '(x) A(x)'.$$

Similarly, if *some* among the given objects have the property 'A', we can lay down the following definition:

$$'A_1 \vee A_2 \vee \ldots \vee A_n' = '(Ex) A(x)'.$$

We notice further–still assuming we are concerned with a finite number of n elements–that one of these operators can be defined by the other; for example:

$$'(x) A(x)' = '\sim (Ex) \sim A(x)'.$$

Let us assume, further, that the following holds of these n elements: '$(A \rightarrow B_1) \& (A \rightarrow B_2) \& \ldots \& (A \rightarrow B_n)$'. Then, by propositional calculus we have:

$$A \rightarrow (B_1 \& B_2 \& \ldots \& B_n).$$

We use the shorter notation '$A \rightarrow B(a)$', which we read: "from A it follows that a has the property B, where a may be any object belonging to the relevant class."

28. The development given here follows that of Hilbert and Bernays, *Grundlagen der Mathematik*, 100-106.

Given the above definition for the all-operator, we also have: '$A \to (x) B(x)$'. Thus we have the following formula:

(α) $[A \to B(a)] \to [A \to (x) B(x)]$.

If, on the other hand, and still assuming we are concerned with a finite domain of n elements, the following holds: '$(B_1 \to A)$ & $(B_2 \to A)$ & ... & $(B_n \to A)$', then by propositional calculus, '$(B_1 \& B_2 \& ... \& B_n) \to A$', which, when the above shorthand notation is applied to it, yields '$B(a) \to A$'. But here again we have, by propositional calculus: '$(B_1 \to A)$ ∨ $(B_2 \to A)$ ∨ ... ∨ $(B_n \to A)$'. Thus we have '$(B_1 \vee B_2 \vee ... \vee B_n) \to A$'; given the above definition of the existence-operator, this is the same as '$(Ex) B(x) \to A$'. Summing up all of this, we have the following formula:

(β) $[B(a) \to A] \to [(Ex) B(x) \to A]$

Similarly, when we consider only finite domains, by propositional calculus and applying the shorthand notations introduced above, we get the following formulae:

(a) $(x) A(x) \to A(a)$

(b) $A(a) \to (Ex) A(x)$.

For the purpose of the following development, we take notice of these four formulae, (α), (β), (a) and (b). They have one remarkable property: *They are satisfied in every finite domain*, that is, *they are 'identical in the finite'*.[29] This means: As far as finite domains are concerned, operators can be explicitly defined with the help of propositional calculus; the all-operator by means of a certain conjunction and the existence-operator by means of a certain disjunction. If, then, in the given formulae, (α), (β), (a) and (b), these signs are replaced by the defining conjunctions and disjunctions, and the variables occurring in them by some individual names, the result is an identically true formula of propositional calculus. We say of every formula of predicate calculus which is transformed in this way, through substitutions, into an identical formula of propositional calculus that it is satisfied in a finite domain; or that it is identical in the finite, namely if it is satisfied in *every* domain of n elements, where n is any natural number.

Let us suppose we are concerned with a domain of two elements. In that case the formula '$(x) A(x) \to A(a)$' is transformed into

'$[(A_1 \& A_2) \to A_1]$ & $[(A_1 \& A_2) \to A_2]$',

which is an identically true formula of propositional calculus. Similarly, the formula '$A(a) \to (Ex) A(x)$' is transformed into

'$[A_1 \to (A_1 \vee A_2)]$ & $[A_2 \to (A_1 \vee A_2)]$',

which is, similarly, identically true.

29. Hilbert and Bernays, *Grundlagen der Mathematik*, 121.

We also take notice of the following important point. If we consider how the notations '$(x) A(x)$' and '$A(a)$' have been introduced, it may look as if these two mean the same. Incidentally, we may here add that these two formulae are formally equivalent ('*deduktionsgleich*'), which means: whenever one can be derived, the other can be derived, as well. It by no means follows from this, however, that we could write '$A(a) \rightarrow (x) A(x)$', for this formula is not identical in the finite. It is identical only in a domain of one element, where it is transformed into '$A_1 \rightarrow A_1$'; but it is no longer identical in a domain of two elements, for there we have:

$$'[A_1 \rightarrow (A_1 \& A_2)] \& [A_2 \rightarrow (A_1 \& A_2)]',$$

which is not an identically true formula. The important difference between the formulas '$A(a)$' and '$(x) A(x)$' is made clearer by considering their meaning. Let our formula be '$(x) A(x) \rightarrow B$'. This means, 'if every x has the property A, then B'. Let our formula be '$A(a) \rightarrow B$'. This means, 'If any object a, no matter which, has the property A, then B'. In the latter case, B follows already on the condition that *some* of the given objects has the property A.

Materially speaking, these investigations amount to a logical analysis of the concepts 'all' and 'some', applied to cases where the relevant domain is finite. In this case the concepts 'all' and 'some' may be considered entirely unproblematic. They can be given explicit definitions and the rules of use for the corresponding operators, (α), (β), (a) and (b), are shorthand for known rules in propositional calculus.

Things change completely, however, if we allow for an infinite domain of elements. For the time being, we shall not define the concept 'infinite' but will rest content with this intuitive conception, so to speak—one that leads us to assert, for instance, that every moment of time is followed by another or that every natural number is followed by another natural number. Then the question arises whether our new axioms, (α), (β), (a) and (b), are 'correct' in this case, too. At first sight, it may well seem that we need not hesitate to affirm that they are. Looking closer, however, we see that the concepts 'all' and 'some' entangle us in deep difficulties when we allow for an infinite domain of objects.

In the case of a *finite* domain, again, 'all' signifies a certain conjunction and 'some' signifies a certain disjunction. If we now generalize this interpretation so as to cover an *infinite* domain, we would have to construe 'all' as an infinite conjunction and 'some' as an infinite disjunction. But is this legitimate? Conjunction is a kind of logical product and disjunction is a kind of logical sum. From mathematics we know that there are important differences between finite and infinite sums. Thus, certain infinite series are convergent if their terms are ordered in a particular way, and divergent if their terms are ordered in a different way. It is by no means obvious that it is legitimate to speak about infinite conjunctions and disjunctions.

Supposing we allow for an infinite domain, axioms (a), (b), (α) and (β) look even more suspicious when we consider their consequences. We are now familiar with the axioms and rules of inference of the predicate calculus, so we can draw these consequences. From the formulas (a) and (b) we derive, using the rule of chain inference

(1) $(x) A(x) \rightarrow (Ex) A(x)$

Substituting into the formula, we get $\sim A(a) \rightarrow (Ex) \sim A(x)$, and from this by contraposition (and taking into account the equivalence $\sim\sim A \leftrightarrow A$)

$\sim (Ex) \sim A(x) \rightarrow A(a)$,

and from this, in accordance with formula (a)

$\sim (Ex) \sim A(x) \rightarrow (x) A(x)$,

and applying contraposition again,

(2) $\sim (x) A(x) \rightarrow (Ex) \sim A(x)$.

By contraposition, formula (a) yields

$\sim A(a) \rightarrow \sim (x) A(x)$,

and from this we get in accordance with formula (β)

(3) $(Ex) \sim A(x) \rightarrow \sim (x) A(x)$.

By the definition of equivalence, formulae (2) and (3) yield

(4) $\sim (x) A(x) \leftrightarrow (Ex) \sim A(x)$.

In this way we have given a proof of the Law of the Excluded Middle in the form it has in the predicate calculus. Let us be clear about what formula (4) means by giving it an interpretation: "if it is not the case that every x is A, there is at least one x such that it is not-A, and *vice versa*." We now give separate interpretations of this sentence for a finite and infinite domain of elements. Applied to a finite domain, this formula becomes an identically true formula of propositional calculus, and is to that extent self-evident. If, for example, it is not the case that all objects lying on the table are made of metal, then there must be at least one object among them that is made of some other material than metal. This object can be found by searching for it among the n objects on the table, where n can be any natural number. But let us now suppose that the number of the objects is infinite. In that case it could happen that no matter how many objects we check for the property, we fail to find one, because it need not be among the first n objects, where n can be any natural number. Regarding the content of the formula, then, it is meaningful to say that the sentence expressing the Law of the Excluded Middle, although self-evident as long as we apply it to a finite domain, is doubtful in an infinite domain. For in that case we can say: We have not two but rather three 'possibilities'. Suppose we have somehow succeeded in showing the formula '$\sim (x) A(x)$' to be correct. This is the "first possibility." Now it may happen that we also succeed in finding an x that is not-A. This is the second 'possibility', the case in which we show: '(Ex) ~ A(x)'. But it may happen that there is no way we can find an x that would be ~ A. That is the third 'possibility', that is, a case in which we can show '~ $(x) A(x)$' but not '(Ex) ~ $A(x)$'.

We shall not explore this line of thought further.[30] What has been said here suffices to show that the axioms (a), (b), (α) and (β) of the predicate calculus are not unproblematic.

To resolve the problem, we turn to a consistency proof. For while the generalization of these formulae from a finite to an infinite domain is not without doubts, we may set these doubts aside if we can show that the predicate calculus is nevertheless consistent.

We must therefore carry out a *consistency proof for predicate calculus*. This proof, too, is relatively simple, though not quite as simple as the analogous proof for propositional calculus. The basic idea is as follows. Suppose that some proof in the predicate calculus, for instance the proof of the Law of the Excluded Middle given above, leads to a contradiction; that is, that the last sentence in the proof is of the form 'A & ~A'. In that case, this contradiction should turn up even when all the formulas that were used in the proof, including the starting formulas, are interpreted for any finite domain. For in that case the formulae (a), (b), (α) and (β) are replaced by certain conjunctions and disjunctions in the way we explained above and free variables by names denoting objects, with the result that all the formulae in the proof are transformed into identically true formulae of propositional calculus. The original proof is still a proof, but now it is a proof in propositional calculus. If the final formula was of the form 'A & ~A', it will be so even after the interpretation has been carried out. But propositional calculus has been shown to be consistent. Hence, there can be no proof in predicate calculus that ends with a formula of the form 'A & ~A'.[31]

To ward off a misunderstanding, we should remark that the consistency proof indicated here is of course not in itself enough to prove that the concept of the infinite is consistent; after all, we have not yet even defined that concept. What has been shown is that certain operators—or, in terms of content, the concepts 'all' and 'some'—can be used in accordance with given rules inde-

---

30. This line of thought underlies the so-called "intuitionistic" mathematics and the "finitistic" attitude within the so-called "formalist" mathematics. For the "intuitionistic" conception, see, for example, A. Heyting, "Mathematische Grundlagenforschung." *Intuitionismus, Beweistheorie, Ergebnisse der Mathematik und ihrer Grenzgebiete*, II. 4. (1934). For the "formalist" conception and the "finitistic attitude", see, for example, D. Hilbert, "Über das Unendliche," *Mathematische Annalen*, Bd. 95 (1926) 161-90. (English translation as "On the Infinite," in J. van Heijenoort, ed., *From Frege to Gödel: A Source Book in Mathematical Logic* (Harvard: Harvard University Press, 1967), 367-92.
31. The proof outlined here conveys something of the detailed execution that we cannot undertake here. See Hilbert and Bernays, *Grundlagen der Mathematik*, 122, 185.

pendently of the domain of objects to which they may be applied. If this domain is infinite, it has to be given a separate definition and shown to be consistent.

Completeness and Decidability

Propositional calculus is complete in the sense that, given suitable axioms, all identically true formulae can be derived. In predicate calculus, one of the counterparts of an identically true formula is a formula that is identical in the infinite. Now, can all finitely identical formulae of predicate calculus be derived from the axioms (a), (b), (α) and (β) together with the axioms of propositional calculus? That is to say, are all formulae that are identical in the finite provable and, in that sense, 'correct' sentences? The answer to this question leads us to some significant new issues.

First, we extend predicate calculus by introducing a new binary predicate, the sign for which is '=' and which we interpret as identity. We have already used this sign in definitions, but considered in that way it belongs to metalogic or logical syntax. Now we are introducing the sign into logic itself, that is, into the object language.

This can be done, first, through an explicit definition like this:[32]

$$\text{`}a = b\text{'} = \text{`}(F)[F(a) \rightarrow F(b)]\text{'}.$$

Or, it can be done by defining identity implicitly through two axioms for identity.[33] These are as follows:

$$I_1 \; a = a$$

$$I_2 \; (a = b) \rightarrow [A(a) \rightarrow A(b)]$$

If the first approach is chosen, the axioms for identity can be derived in predicate calculus from its definition. The second approach is supported by the consideration that it allows the sign '=' to be given any interpretation whatsoever that satisfies the axioms, for instance, arithmetic equality. The sentence '~ ($a = b$)' we shall abbreviate as '$a \neq b$'. The definition of sentence as well as the rules of substitution that we gave for predicate calculus will be extended to cover these new notations.

Now we can define the concept 'immediate successor'. It is a two-place predicate that we shall write as '$S(a,b)$'. This formula reads, "the immediate successor of a is b." We say that '$S(a,b)$' holds if and only if the following condition is fulfilled:[34]

32. This is how it is done in Russell's system: *Principia Mathematica*, Vol. I, *13.
33. This is Hilbert's approach; see Hilbert and Bernays, *Grundlagen der Mathematik*, 165.
34. Hilbert and Ackermann, *Grundzüge der theoretischen Logik*, 63–65.

(ER) (x) (Ey) $\{R(x,y)$ & (z) $[R(x,z) \rightarrow (y=z)]\}$.

This condition says: "There exists some relation R such that no matter what individual x is, there exists some y, to which x stands in the relation R; moreover, every z to which x stands in the relation R is identical with y." That is, if 'S(a,b)' holds, every a has a unique b corresponding to it. In that case we write '$b = a'$', which we read: 'b is the immediate successor of a'. a' is therefore a function of a in the mathematical sense, defined through the condition given above, and can be substituted for an individual variable.

The formula '(x) (Ey) $(x = y)$' can be derived from the axioms for identity in the predicate calculus. This can be seen easily even without a proof.[35] For as soon as the concept 'immediate successor' has been defined, it follows from this definition with the help of the axioms for identity that there is an immediate successor; for identity, '$a = a$', is precisely that kind of relation 'R' which fulfills the condition given in the definition. For every a there is a unique b, namely a itself. Hence the formula '(x) (Ey) $(x = y)$' is trivial as long as we have not, by means of new axioms, excluded the possibility that $a' = a$. This exclusion we accomplish through the following two axioms, which cannot be derived from the axioms we have acknowledged so far:

A_1 (Ex) (y) $(x \neq y')$

A_2 (x) (y) $[(x' \neq y') \rightarrow (x = y)]$

Interpreting these axioms, we see that if we give the name the 'natural numbers' to the value-range of the predicate 'immediate successor', these axioms become *arithmetical axioms*. In that case, the former axiom says that there is some natural number x such that no matter what number y is, x is not its immediate successor. We use the sign '1' for this number. Then A_1 says that '1' is not the immediate successor of any number, and using a free variable we can write axiom A_1 as '$1 \neq a'$'. Formula A_2 in turn says that no matter which natural number x and y may be, if their immediate successors are the same, then the numbers themselves are the same.

Let us now consider some domain consisting of two elements and assume that the axioms A_1 and A_2 hold for it. If this is the case, then, first, the condition '$1 \neq a'$' must be satisfied. We assume that this is the case and we shall give the name '1' to that element with respect to which the condition is satisfied. To the other element we give the name '2'. There are no other elements. Now we recall that the formula '(x) (Ey) $(x = y)$' is provable. Hence every element has its immediate successor. Thus, '1', too, has an immediate successor. It cannot be '1' itself, because, according to axiom A_1, '1' is not the successor of any element. Hence, the successor of '1' is another element, '2'. But what is the successor of '2'? Given A_1, it cannot be '1'. But it cannot be '2', either, for in that case '1' and '2' would have the same successor, namely '2'. But it follows from A_2 that

35. Concerning the proof, see Hilbert and Bernays, *Grundlagen der Mathematik*, 216.

if x and y have identical successors, x and y themselves are identical. In that case, '1' and '2' would be identical, and therefore, because '2' is the successor of '1', '1', which is identical with '2', would also be the successor of '1', which is against axiom A_1. This implies that axioms A_1 and A_2 cannot both be satisfied in a domain of two elements. Observing how this proof was carried out, we see then that this applies to every domain of n elements, where n can be any natural number. If we form a conjunction from formulae A_1 and A_2, we get the formula 'A_1 & A_2', which is not identical in the finite, and which, indeed, is not satisfied in any finite domain. In other words, the said formula, when applied to any finite domain, receives the value 'false'. Hence, conversely, the negation of this formula, '$\sim (A_1$ & $A_2)$', when applied to any finite domain, receives the value 'true'; that is, the formula '$\sim (A_1$ & $A_2)$' *is identical in the finite*.[36]

The significance of this result lies in the question that was raised above, namely, whether predicate calculus is complete in the sense that every formula that is identical in the finite can be proved from the axioms of propositional and predicate calculi. Our answer is negative. Predicate calculus is not complete in this sense. (But it is complete in another sense, though we shall not consider this point here.[37])

Now we make the following observation. Suppose that predicate calculus were complete in the sense that we could prove in it any formula whatsoever that is identical in the finite; in that case, for example, we could prove the above formula '$\sim (A_1$ & $A_2)$' and, hence, the equivalent formula '$\sim A_1 \vee \sim A_2$'. Therefore we could prove that either both of these arithmetical axioms A_1 and A_2 or at least one of them is false. In that case, arithmetic would be impossible. In a sense, then, we can say that the possibility of arithmetic presupposes the incompleteness of predicate calculus in the sense explained above.

We call 'monadic' that fragment of predicate calculus in which only one-place predicates are used. A slightly more complicated proof—one that we cannot consider here[38]—shows that monadic predicate calculus is complete in the sense explained above; hence every formula that is identical in the finite and contains only one-place predicates is provable from our axioms. For every monadic formula can be reduced to a normal form that is analogous to the normal forms of propositional calculus, and from this fact it follows, according to propositional calculus, that every formula that is identical in the infinite is provable. Hence, also, monadic predicate calculus is *fully decidable* in analogy with the full decidability of propositional calculus. That is, every question regarding the provability of any monadic formula can be given a complete

36. Cf. Hilbert and Bernays, *Grundlagen der Mathematik* I, 123.
37. K. Gödel, "Die Volständigkeit der Axiome des logischen Funktionenkalküls," *Monatshefte für Mathematik und Physik*, Bd. 37 (1930). (English translation as "The completeness of the axioms of the functional calculus of logic," in van Heijenoort, ed., 1967, 582-91.
38. Hilbert and Bernays, *Grundlagen der Mathematik*, 190-95.

answer by means of a certain procedure. To that extent, monadic predicate calculus, like propositional calculus, is in a sense trivial.

These results, which we merely mention here, are far-reaching. For when we give a formal description of the logical structure of the series of natural numbers, it is necessary to introduce a two-place predicate–for instance, the predicate 'immediate successor'–as we did above. It is precisely at this juncture of logical development, in which the formation of arithmetical concepts becomes possible, that the formulae of the predicate calculus cease to be *generally* decidable.[39] At this juncture, in other words, logic becomes a field of unpredictable possibilities, one that provides endless material for new discoveries in spite of the fact that all these possibilities are fully determined by logical and arithmetical axioms in which they are already 'implicitly contained', to use the old phrase.

At the concrete level, these observations are connected to the following circumstance. Consider the formula '$(x) (Ex) R(x, y)$' and take the relation 'R' to be 'is smaller than'. Now, if the value-range of 'R' is interpreted as the natural numbers, the formula may be read: "let x be any natural number, there is a number y such that x is smaller than y," that is, "every number is followed by a number that is greater." If in this formula we switch the operators, we get the formula '$(Ey) (x) R(x, y)$', the meaning of which under this interpretation is: "there is a number y such that no matter which number x is, x is smaller than y," that is, "there exists a greatest number"–something that contradicts the axioms of arithmetic. The point is that when we consider predicates with two or more places, the *order of operators* is crucial, unless they are all either 'all'- or 'some'-operators.[40] This circumstance is connected to the fact that the calculus of binary predicates is not generally decidable.

General Implication

The implication of propositional calculus, '$A \rightarrow B$', we call singular implication. The implication of predicate calculus, which is of the form '$(x) [A(x) \rightarrow B(x)]$', we call general implication. Singular implication '$A \rightarrow B$' is equivalent with the formula '$\sim (A \ \& \sim B)$'. Accordingly, general implication '$(x) [A(x) \rightarrow B(x)]$' is equivalent with the formula

'$\sim (Ex) [A(x) \ \& \sim B(x)]$'.[41]

Just as the former is true in every case except when 'A' is true and 'B' is false, so the latter is true in every case except when there is an x which is A but is not

39. Cf. Hilbert and Bernays, *Grundlagen der Mathematik*, 144.
40. Hilbert and Ackermann, *Grundzüge der theoretischen Logik*, 49–50.
41. For the formal proof of this equivalence, see Whitehead and Russell, *Principia Mathematica*, Vol. I, theorem 10.51 (2nd ed., 149).

B. Thus, general implication is true not only in the normal case where every x that is A is also B, but also when no x is A, whether or not some x is B. Here 'true' and 'false' mean *empirical* truth and empirical falsity, respectively, as we are now concerned with formulae that are not identically true or identical in the finite, but formulae for empirical sentences. For instance, let the predicate 'A' stand for 'lightning' and predicate 'B' for 'thunder'. Then we may read the formula '$(x)\ [A(x) \to B(x)]$' as "whenever there is lightning, there is thunder." Thus we can see that general implication is the formula for a general empirical sentence, in particular for sentences expressing laws of nature.

Here, however, we must observe carefully that the 'if-then' that occurs in natural language is not the same thing as implication; indeed, the case of general implication makes this flagrantly obvious. We illustrate the point with the following humorous story, based on an actual event.

A well-known scientist, Mr. R, had died. A colleague of his, Mr. N, was writing an obituary, which included the following line: "I haven't found a single observation by Mr. R that did not contain an error." When N was called to account for this glaring statement and asked whether he had reviewed any of R's observations, he answered "No", adding: "Since I didn't check any of his observations, I couldn't find any errors, either. Hence, I'm justified in arguing that every observation made by R that I have checked is erroneous." His critics took N's reply as a sophism with which he tried to talk his way out of an embarrassing situation. But what had N claimed from a formal and logical point of view? Let 'x' be 'an observation made by R', let '$N(x)$' be 'an observation checked by N' and let 'Mistake (x)' be 'an observation made by R that is erroneous'. We then have the general implication, '$(x)\ [N(x) \to$ Mistake $(x)]$'. This implication is true as soon as no x is N, that is, as soon as N has not checked any of R's observations, regardless of whether they are erroneous or not. So if we assume the normal interpretation of implication, N's claim, despite the protests of his critics, was in fact true.

This illustrates how general implication differs from 'if-then'-sentences. In 'if-then' sentences, we always imply that there are cases for which $A(x)$ holds; that is, in our example, that N did check at least one observation by R and spotted some error in every case that he reviewed. This must also be taken into account when it is said that general implication is the formula for sentences stating laws of nature. In using some such sentence as "if there is lightning, there is thunder" we imply that we know at least some cases where there has been lightning and that in each of these there has been thunder, as well. A general 'if-then' -sentence, when translated into the language of logic, should therefore be written as:

'$(Ex)\ A(x)\ \&\ (x)\ [A(x) \to B(x)]$'.

In other words, general implication is the formula for a general empirical statement, provided that there occurs at least one instance of $A(x)$; provided, that is, that the antecedent of the implication is not empty. A general implication fulfilling this condition, formally expressed by this formula, is one we shall call an *existential implication*. This kind of formula is the formal expression that we use for general empirical sentences and, in particular, for sentences expressing laws of nature.

For another illustration, imagine someone saying, "Whenever the Man in the Moon shows up, there will be a flood on the Earth." We do not say that the connection asserted here is a law of nature; we might even add that the sentence is false because the 'Man in the Moon' has never shown up. If, however, we translate this sentence into the language of logistic, using normal general implication, we get a true sentence precisely because the 'Man in the Moon' has never shown up. This sentence must therefore be interpreted as an existential implication, which, when understood in this way, is false.

In the third and final part of our investigation, when we turn to consider questions belonging to what is known as theory of knowledge, that is, questions belonging to the empirical applications of logic, we must be careful to avoid this kind of mistake.

The 'Relativity' of Logical Truths

We have now reached a point where we can address questions relating to the concept of logical truth. It will be useful for our investigations, however, if we first consider one matter of principle.

As we have mentioned, the analyticity or syntheticity of a sentence is a 'relative matter' that depends on how certain concepts have been defined.[42] We say that a sentence is analytic insofar as it follows solely from definitions. Therefore, a given sentence can be analytic in one system, while in another system, in which certain concepts have been defined differently, it can be nonanalytic. Insofar as logical truths are analytical sentences, they become relative truths, in a sense. There is not just one logic; there are many logics–even, in principle, indefinitely many logics, depending in particular on how we interpret the concepts 'true' (similarly 'false') and 'all' (similarly 'some'). Here we are not committing ourselves to some vague 'skepticism'; this is a simple consequence of the fact that these words can be, and in fact often are, understood in different ways. Since logical axioms are there precisely to interpret the meanings of these and other logical constants–formally speaking, to give rules for their use–axioms vary from system to system. For this reason, we can

---

42. Hempel makes useful remarks on this issue in his accessible essay, "Le problème de la vérité," *Theoria* (1937): 206–46. (English translation in C.G. Hempel, *Selected Philosophical Essays*, ed. R. Jeffrey [Cambridge: Cambridge University Press, 2000], 35–74.)

speak about logical truth only relative to some determinate 'language' or, semantically speaking, relative to some determinate system of logical concepts.

Modern research has in fact developed several different systems of logic.
First of all, this allows us to reject an assumption found in what is today known
as 'classical' logic, namely, that there are only two truth-values, true and false.
For we can say, as for instance Reichenbach has,[43] that once we take into account the empirical application of logic, it is more appropriate to assume that
truth-values constitute a continuous series from 1 = truth to 0 = falsity. If, for
instance, an archer says he can hit the bull's-eye, we can say meaningfully that
the truth of his statement depends upon the distance of a shot from the centre.
If 'truth' is interpreted in this way (and similarly for 'falsity'), there occurs, of
course, a corresponding change in truth-functions, with the two truth-values
of classical logic being seen as a highly rationalized special case.

Here we can do no more than indicate the possibility of this kind of multi-
valued logic.[44] But we shall investigate a little more closely the so-called *intuitionistic logic* that was established by Brouwer and formalized by Heyting.[45]
This logic has its starting-point in the problems concerning the concepts
'all' and 'some' that we have already considered. The advocates of this line of
thought argue that the law of excluded middle is unproblematically valid only
within the finite domain, whereas in the infinite domain we have to distinguish not between two but between three 'possibilities'. If, then, we start, for
example, from the sentence '~ $(x) A(x)$', these three 'possibilities' are: first,
it may be that this sentence has been proved true by indicating some '~ $A(x)$';
second, it may be false; third, it may be that is cannot be false–such as when
there exists some general procedure to show '~ $(x) A(x)$'–but no instance of '~
$A(x)$' has been indicated and it nevertheless remains unproven.

This kind of intuitionistic logic constitutes a coherent system that differs from classical logic even at the level of propositional calculus. We shall
give a few examples. Here we should, in fact, use new primitive signs because
their meanings differ from those in classical propositional calculus. Keeping
this reservation in mind, however, we may continue to use signs that we are
already familiar with. Let, then, 'α' stand for 'truth', 'β' for 'falsity' and γ' for
the truth-value of a sentence that 'cannot be false but remains unproven'. We
then have the following truth tables for intuitionistic propositional calculus:

43. H. Reichenbach, *Wahrscheinlichkeitslehre*. Leiden: A.W. Sijthoff's Uitgeversmaatschappij
N. V. 1935, §76. (§70 in the English translation, H. Reichenbach, *The Theory of Probability*,
trans. E.H. Hutten and M. Reichenbach. Second edition [Berkeley and Los Angeles: University
of California Press, 1949].)
44. For more details, see, e.g., C.I. Lewis and H. Langford, *Symbolic Logic* (London: Century,
1932), ch. VII.
45. A. Heyting, *Die formalen Regeln der intuitionistichen Logik*, Sitzungsberichte der. pr. Akad.
D. Wiss Phys.-Math. Klasse, 1930.

~	α	β	γ
	β	α	β

→	α	β	γ
α	α	α	α
β	β	α	β
γ	γ	α	α

&	α	β	γ
α	α	β	γ
β	β	β	β
γ	γ	β	γ

v	α	β	γ
α	α	α	α
β	α	β	γ
γ	α	γ	γ

In these tables, the first argument of the functions 'A & B', 'A → B' and 'A v B' can be found in the uppermost row and the second argument can be found in the column on the left. From the tables one can see that the sentence for the excluded middle 'A v ~A' does not always receive the value 'α', for if 'A' has the value 'γ', the table for negation shows that '$\sim A$' receives the value 'β'. If 'A' receives the value 'γ' and '$\sim A$', therefore, the value 'β', the table for disjunction shows that '$A \vee \sim A$' receives the values 'γ'.

Which one is correct, classical or intuitionistic propositional calculus?– This is an improper question. Logical axioms express the meanings of logical constants. When axioms are different, this shows that basic concepts have been given different interpretations. We cannot ask which interpretation is correct, because it is a matter of arbitrary decision which meaning we give to a sign.[46]

Here is another illustration of this issue from predicate calculus. The following formulae, for instance, are classically provable, but cannot be proved in intuitionistic predicate calculus:

$$\sim (x)\,A(x) \rightarrow (Ex) \sim A(x) \qquad\qquad \sim (x) \sim A(x) \rightarrow (Ex)\,A(x)$$

$$\sim (Ex) \sim A(x) \rightarrow (x)\,A(x) \qquad\qquad \sim (Ex)\,A(x) \rightarrow (x) \sim A(x)$$

The difference between the two calculi depends upon how we interpret 'all' and 'some'. In terms of semantics, since the classical predicate calculus can be proved to be consistent, it is considered legitimate in this system to give the relevant signs a meaning that is independent of the question concerning the finitude or infinitude of the relevant domain. Thus, for instance, these formulae are accepted independently of the character of this domain, whereas in intuitionistic logic they are accepted only in the case the domain is finite.

We cannot ask which of these conceptions is correct, because the two systems use a different 'language' and it is a matter of arbitrary decision which kind of 'language' one wants to use.

The Concept of 'Logical Truth'

Here we reach the end of our investigation of logistic. Our goal was to determine how we should understand analytical sentences. We gave the following definition: a sentence is analytical if it follows from mere definitions. To clarify what is really involved in this statement, we began with an investigation of the concept 'definition' and the concept 'sentence'. Our most recent accomplishment has been an analysis of the concept 'follows from'. For when we say: "a set of sentences, S_2, follows logically from a set of sentences S_1," this means: S_2 can be derived from S_1 through logical inference. Hence, insofar as logic is a theory of rules of inference, it is a theory of the concept of 'follows from'. It is

46. Lewis and Langford, *Symbolic Logic*, 212.
47. Carnap, *Logical Syntax*, 27 (25 in the German original). As for its content, the definition of "analytical sentence" that we have given in the text is the same as Carnap's (39, 182; 36, 135 in the German original), but we have simplified it as much as one can without compromising its perspicuity.

remarkable that this simple but far-reaching fact has only been clearly seen in our times by Carnap.[47]

Thus we are now in a position to explicitly define the concept 'follows from'. We say that a set of sentences, S_2, follows from a set of sentences, S_1, if the former has been derived from the latter by means of some rules of inference. Each of the rules of inference that we apply in a given case defines the concept 'follows from' for this case, and the disjunction of all rules of inference gives a general definition for the concept 'follows from'. *In this sense* every rule of inference is a definition. Given $A \rightarrow A$, when a particular logical axiom is substituted for 'A'–this axiom being what a rule of inference becomes when it is given content–this axiom implies itself. Thus it follows from itself, that is, from a certain rule of inference. Hence, rules of inference, that is, *logical truths, are consequences of definitions and are, therefore, analytical sentences.*

This result is nothing but a precise formulation of what was shown above, to wit, that rules of inference are rules of use for logical constants; or, speaking in terms of semantic content, these rules determine the meanings of certain basic logical concepts. From this it follows, furthermore, that all logical truths are 'relative' in the sense explained above. We can say that each of them presupposes a certain logical co-ordinate system, that is, a certain system of concepts the meaning of which they determine.

Chapter 7

Mathematical Truth

Now that the first main group of formal truths has received sufficient elucidation we can turn to the second main group, the group of formal sentences that we call mathematical truths. They will be our next focus, and here we limit ourselves to mathematical statements belonging to the arithmetic of integers or elementary geometry. Our goal is to find out what is meant when it is asserted, for example, that $2 + 2 = 4$ is true or that it is true that the sum of the angles of a triangle is two right angles.

The Concept of 'Infinite'

There is a very apt saying: "Mathematics is the logic of the infinite." We move from general logic to mathematics when we assume, through the axioms of arithmetic, that there is an infinite class of individuals or an infinite domain of elements.[1] These axioms define the concept of the infinite that we shall now consider.

As a matter of historical fact, Aristotle has had an immense influence on questions regarding the infinite, one that may exceed his influence on any other question. Aristotle's conception of the infinite, very clearly set out in his

---

1. Hilbert and Ackermann, *Principles of Mathematical Logic*, 71.

Physics,[2] was dominant until the second half of the nineteenth century. The core idea is that one can speak consistently only about the so-called potential infinite but not about the actual infinite. The former means a constantly increasing finite quantity, whereas the latter is a quantity that is greater than all finite quantities. Aristotle thought, for instance, that the set of natural numbers is potentially infinite, because there is no greatest or last natural number. On the other hand, he and his followers did not believe that one could speak about the actually infinite multitude of natural numbers. This conception, they thought, was contradictory.

To see Aristotle's reasons for this view, assume as a given logical axiom that a whole is always greater than its proper part, where 'proper part' means a part of a given quantity that results when something is subtracted from that quantity. For example, the series of prime numbers is a proper part of the series of natural numbers. Now imagine that there exists some actually infinite quantity. We then reason as follows. Either its parts are already infinite or it consists of infinitely many finite parts. If the parts of an infinite whole are themselves infinite, the whole would not be greater than its proper part. If, on the other hand, an actually infinite quantity consisted of infinitely many finite parts, the phrase 'infinitely many' would come to mean 'infinite number', but there are no such numbers.

This Aristotelian conception reappeared throughout most of the modern era. For example, when we turn to Galileo and Leibniz, we find the following line of thought. There is a one-to-one correspondence between the series of natural numbers and the series of square numbers:

1, 2, 3, 4 . . .

1, 4, 9, 16 . . .

If, then, one could speak of the number of natural numbers, one would have to conclude, given the correspondence, that the number of square numbers equals the number of natural numbers, but this is impossible, for the former are but a tiny fraction of the latter. Aristotelian influence can also be detected in Kant's famous 'antinomies of the infinite'. Talk of the infinite is but a manner of speaking, a *façon de parler*, said Gauss, the famous mathematician, among others.

It was not until Cantor and Dedekind that the weak point in this reasoning was exposed.[3] As long as we are concerned with finite quantities, the claim that a whole is greater than its proper part is an analytical sentence. It does not follow from this, however, that it would apply to infinite quantities as well. On the contrary, we can use the negation of this claim to define the actual infinite;

2. Aristotle, *Physics*, 204. Cf. H. Scholz, "Warum haben die Griechen die Irrationalzahlen nicht aufgebaut?" *Kant-Studien 33* (1928), 35–72.
3. See, for example, A. Fraenkel, *Einleitung in die Mengenlehre* (Berlin: Julius Teubner Verlag. 1919 [third ed. 1928]); Russell, *Introduction to Mathematical Philosophy*, ch. 8.

that is to say, we may call *'infinite'* *a quantity that is not always greater than its proper part.* If we can show that this definition does not lead to a contradiction, we have thereby shown that the concept of actual infinity is flawless and, therefore, legitimate. In that case we can, for instance, speak about the infinite set of natural numbers. We define the 'equinumerosity' of two classes using the notion of one-to-one correspondence of their elements. For example, the one-to-one correspondence between natural numbers and square numbers shows that there are 'as many' of both kinds. Since the latter set is a proper part of the former, the number of natural numbers, as well as the number of square numbers is infinite. As Cantor was the first to demonstrate, this idea can be developed further to yield an infinite series of ever greater 'infinite numbers'.

Definition of the Natural Number Series

Here we need a precise definition of the concept of 'infinite', and this we find in the axioms of arithmetic. The point of such axioms is to describe the structure of the natural number series through a number of basic statements that are sufficient for the purpose, independent of one another as well as consistent. We all possess a natural conception of this structure. The series of natural numbers includes, to begin with, a first number, which is not the successor of any number. Secondly, every number has an immediate successor, and hence the series has no last member; similarly, each number, except for the first one, has an immediate predecessor. This, however, is not yet enough. For instance, the series

$$-1, -1/2, -1/4, -1/8,\ldots 1/8, 1/4, 1/2, 1, 2, 3, \ldots$$

satisfies both of these conditions, but it is not yet isomorphic with the series of natural numbers. It differs from that series through the fact, among others, that it has a subset, namely the series of positive fractions contained in it, which has no first member. Natural numbers, on the other hand, are characterized by the fact that not only the series as a whole but each of its subclasses has a first member; and hence, for any sentence, S, that is true of some number, there is always a smallest number of which it is true. Assuming the validity of the law of the excluded middle, this so-called *principle of the smallest number*[4] is logically equivalent with the *principle of mathematical or complete induction*, an inference that is used constantly in mathematical proofs. This principle states that if the first number possesses a certain property, F, and if, given that any determinate natural number n possesses that property, its immediate successor possesses the property, too, then n has this property, where n is any

---

4. Hilbert and Bernays, *Grundlagen der Mathematik*, I, 284, 286.

determinate natural number. That is, all natural numbers have the property F. This so-called *inference from n to n + 1* is at work when, for example, the rules for elementary calculating operations are shown to be generally valid. Using logistic notation, we may write down the formula for complete induction as follows:

$$\{F(1) \ \& \ (n) \ [F(n) \rightarrow F(n')]\} \rightarrow (n) \ F(n).$$

First, we must make it clear that the so-called principle of the smallest number and the axiom of complete induction are logically equivalent, assuming classical sentential and predicate calculus as well as the two arithmetical axioms mentioned above: 'there is a first number' and 'every number has an immediate successor and, also, every number, except the first, has an immediate predecessor.'

We assume, then, that the following has been proved: number 1 has the property F, and if n has it, n' has it, too. Now we wish to show, using the principle of the smallest number, first, that in this case number n has property F, where n is any natural number. For if there were a number c such that $\sim F(c)$, there would have to be, among those numbers for which this is true, a smallest number, b, such that $\sim F(b)$, in which case $b \neq 1$, since $F(1)$. Let the immediate predecessor of b be a. It follows from our assumptions that $F(a)$. But since we are supposing that '$F(a) \rightarrow F(a')$' has been proved and '$F(a)$' is true, it follows that '$F(a')$' = '$F(b)$' is true. Thus we are led to a contradiction. Hence, the assumption leading to this conclusion must be erroneous, namely that even though $F(1)$ and $(n)[F(n) \rightarrow F(n')]$ have been proved, there nevertheless is some number c such that $\sim F(c)$; therefore, all numbers n must have the property F. It is relatively easy to show, conversely, that if the axiom of complete induction is assumed, the principle of the smallest number can be proved. Next we set out an axiom system for arithmetic as follows:

$M_1 \ \ 1 \neq a'$

$M_2 \ \ (a' = b') \leftrightarrow (a = b)$

$M_3 \ \ \{F(1) \ \& \ (n) \ [F(n) \rightarrow F(n')]\} \rightarrow (n) \ F(n).$

Regarding these axioms,[5] we should note that we have already given definitions of the concepts '1' and 'immediate successor' in our investigation of predicate calculus. Thus '1' is that number x, assuming there is one, that satisfies the condition '$(Ex) \ (y) \ (x \neq y')$'. The requirement that every number has an immediate successor need not be stated as a separate axiom; for, as we have shown above, the sentence '$(x)(Ey)(x' = y)$' can be derived from the axioms of identity. Axiom M_2 is usually given a weaker formulation '$(a' = b') \rightarrow (a = $

---

5. The chosen axioms are very nearly the same as those that are given by Hilbert and Bernays; see *Grundlagen der Mathematik*, 220, 273.

b)'. For the converse implication of this formula, '$(a = b) \rightarrow (a' = b')$', can be derived from the axioms of identity in the calculus of predicates.[6] We shall not prove this here. We will simply take M_2 as our second axiom. It says that if the immediate successors of *a* and *b* are the same, then *a* and *b* are the same, too, and conversely. Finally, axiom M_3 is the formula for complete induction, which is equivalent with the principle of the smallest number.

The axioms A_1 and A_2 that we gave for predicate calculus are contained in our axioms M_1-M_3. Since the former are not identical in the finite, neither are the latter.

These axioms, then, constitute a definition of an infinite domain of elements. But this is not all that has been given. What has been given is a definition of a *certain determinate kind* of infinite domain of elements, namely, a definition of the natural number series. And therefore we say: we call 'natural numbers' those numbers that satisfy the conditions laid down in axioms M_1-M_3.

We must note that it is only through these axioms that the concept 'natural number' is introduced into logic. True, we have already made use of this concept; for we have spoken about a domain of *n* elements, where *n* might be, for instance, the number 2. But this was always a matter of interpreting some formal formula, that is, of applying the formula to some domain of elements, as is done, for instance, in investigating satisfiability or consistency. These investigations are not part of logic itself or of an *object language*; they belong to metalogic or syntax language, which studies logic. There is therefore no circularity involved, even though it is only at this point that we give a definition of natural numbers in our object language; indeed, here there is as little circularity as there would be, say, in using the identity symbol in definitions before the relation of identity itself has been defined as a logical relation.

Our next task ought to consist in showing that the given definition of natural number series is consistent, that is, that no formula of the form 'A & $\sim A$' can be derived from the axioms M_1-M_3 using acknowledged logical axioms and rules of inference. Unlike similar proofs in predicate and sentential calculus, this proof is so complicated that it is well beyond our present concerns, and we must rest content with an affirmation that the proof has been carried out in full, thanks to the investigations carried out in the Hilbertian School.[7] The basic idea here is the same as it was in the consistency proofs discussed above. Assume there is a proof leading to a contradiction. The proof is then transformed, through certain operations, into a form in which it retains its character as a proof, but appears now as a proof in sentential calculus. Since sentential calculus is consistent, there can be no such proof.

---

6. Hilbert and Bernays, *Grundlagen der Mathematik*, 189, 220.
7. Hilbert and Bernays, *Grundlagen der Mathematik*, 209, 286; Ketonen, "Todistusteorian periaatteet," 77–108.

We must notice that this proof does not yet imply that the whole of arithmetic would have been proved consistent; in arithmetic we must add rules defining calculating operations as well as definitions for positive and negative integers, rational and irrational numbers, and these should, of course, be shown to be consistent, if possible.

This consistency proof is of tremendous importance philosophically, because in it we have at last an *irrevocable refutation of the Aristotelian conception that the concept of actual infinity is contradictory.*

The Relation of Arithmetic to Logic

Here we shall assume that all definitions have been given that are necessary for the development of arithmetic–starting with definitions for sum and product. We then ask: What is the logical character of the arithmetical sentences that have been derived logically from these assumptions, be these sentences particular equations for numbers, like 2 + 2 = 4, or general arithmetical statements, like the statement, already proved by Euclid, that there are infinitely many prime numbers (that is, numbers divisible only by themselves and 1)?

We have shown earlier that there is a sense in which logical axioms (rules of inference) are definitions; namely, they define the concept 'follows from'. Last, it was shown that the conjunction of arithmetical axioms M_1 & M_2 & M_3 is a definition, namely a definition of the natural number series. Our question above can then be given the following answer: *Arithmetical sentences are analytic, for they can be derived from mere definitions.* Like the sentences of logic, they are, therefore, *a priori*, independent of all experience. Quite independently of facts, it is always the case that 2 + 2 = 4. Materially speaking, this follows from the meaning of natural numbers and their sum; and formally speaking, it follows from definitions, which are laid down as need be.

Here we remind ourselves of Leibniz's claim that mathematics is nothing but a 'special development of logic'. Some among the present-day advocates of logistic–Russell, for instance–have adopted this view without any reservations. On this view, mathematics is nothing but a branch in the tree of logic, though it is such a huge branch that it renders the tree itself almost invisible.[8] Let us now consider this question in more detail, confining our considerations to arithmetic. Our question, then, is this: What is the relation of arithmetic to logic? This question divides into two sub-questions.[9] First, what is the relation of arithmetical concepts to logical concepts? Can the former be defined in

8. Russell, *Introduction to Mathematical Philosophy*, ch. 18.
9. F. Waismann, *Einführung in das mathematische Denken. Die Begriffsbildung der modernen Mathematik* (Wien: Gerold and Co., 1936), 56.

terms of the latter? Secondly, what is the relation of arithmetical axioms to the axioms of logic? Can the former be derived from the latter?

The answer to the latter question is definitely 'no'. For arithmetic to be possible, we need not only logical axioms but a few additional assumptions that have not been given logical proofs. In Russell's system there are no less than three such axioms.[10] There is a clear difference between logical and arithmetical axioms in that the former are rules of inference whereas the latter are axioms of existence in which the assumption of an infinite domain of objects has been made. The former are identical in the finite, whereas the latter are not. For this reason it is difficult to accept the strict logistic interpretation of mathematics, according to which mathematics is no more than a branch of logic.

On the other hand, the answer to the first of these questions is affirmative. Arithmetical concepts, starting with the concept of natural number, can be defined by means of logical concepts, as we have done above. Psychological empiricists have often argued as though number concepts were just exceedingly general empirical concepts and arithmetical statements exceedingly general statements reporting experience. What has been said here makes it clear that this is not correct. Arithmetical statements are analytic and therefore independent of experience. Being *a priori*, they make no claims about experience and do not have any empirical content.

Furthermore, this implies, contrary to empiricism, that arithmetical concepts are not formed from experience through a step-by-step process of abstraction. Let us consider, for instance, number 1. Frege wisely asks,

> What is it, in fact, that we are supposed to abstract from, in order to get, for example, from the moon to the number 1? By abstraction we do indeed get certain concepts, viz. satellite of the earth, satellite of a planet, non-self-luminous heavenly body, heavenly body, body, object. But in this series 1 is not to be met with; for it is no concept that the moon could fall under.[11]

It is to be observed that it is precisely here, with respect to the question of the relation of mathematical concepts and statements to empirical concepts and statements, that we find a striking difference between the logical and psychological types of empiricism.

10. See for instance Russell, *Introduction to Mathematical Philosophy*, chapters 12 and 13.
11. G. Frege, *Grundlagen der Arithmetik: eine logisch mathematische Untersuchung über den Begriff der Zahl* (Breslau: Verlag von W. Koebner, 1884), §44. (English translation as *Foundations of Arithmetic: a logico-mathematical inquiry into the concept of number*. Translated by J. L. Austin. Second revised edition [Evanston: Northwestern University Press, 1980].)

Axiomatic and Analytic Interpretation of Arithmetic

This interpretation of arithmetic is one that we would like to call its *analytic interpretation*, with a view to the fact that the axioms of arithmetic have here been construed as explicit definitions. In fact, there is another possible interpretation, to some extent different from the one that we have been considering so far. Sentences M_1-M_3 can also be understood as an axiom system containing variables called natural numbers and constituting their *implicit* definition. This interpretation differs from the earlier one in the following respects. Here we do not regard 'natural numbers' as any kinds of constants; we take them to be variables, which can be given any content whatsoever, as long as it satisfies the axioms. Hence, further, sentences such as '2 + 2 = 4' or the statement that there is an infinite number of primes are not analytic sentences, for there are no explicit definitions of which they would be consequences. If we modify the axiom system so as to turn it into a different system, we get new sentences to replace the familiar ones. If this kind of interpretation is adopted, arithmetical assertions are no longer statements like "2 + 2 = 4"; they become statements like "from such and such axioms it follows that 2 + 2 = 4." In a different axiom system it might happen, for example, that $2 + 2 \neq 4$. We see immediately that in the case of geometry this kind of *axiomatic interpretation*, as we would like to call it, is a natural one. Now we must consider the question of whether a similar axiomatic interpretation of arithmetic is possible, analogous to the natural interpretation of geometry.

We must be clear, then, as to how this kind of interpretation changes the character of arithmetical sentences. Let 'M_k' stand for the conjunction of arithmetical axioms and 'T' for arithmetical theorems. Every arithmetical sentence now assumes the form 'T follows from M_k'. These sentences do not include the axioms, and we do not assert anything about their truth. Arithmetical sentences are now instances of certain 'consequence-facts', that is, they are instances of rules of inference, viz. of logical axioms. For we get arithmetical sentences from certain logical sentences simply by certain substitutions.

Thus we can see: Even when arithmetic is understood as an axiomatic system, which gives no more than implicit definitions of variables called 'natural numbers', arithmetical sentences turn out to be analytic sentences. Given this, we may put aside the question as to which of the two interpretations of arithmetic should be given priority; after all, the main point is the same in both cases. Nevertheless, we wish to consider what can be said in support of the axiomatic interpretation of arithmetic as well as against it.

In *favor* of the axiomatic interpretation, considering how we understand natural numbers in our everyday *practices*, both pre-scientific and scientific, we see immediately that axioms M_1-M_3, in the sense they are commonly used, do not yet supply a full determination of natural numbers. No matter what things we are considering, be they line segments or consecutive generations of human beings, as long as they satisfy arithmetical axioms–that is, as long as they constitute a 'progression', which is isomorphic to the natural number series, having a first member, and an immediate successor for each member, except for the first one, and with each subset possessing a first member–these things, no matter what they are, will be the 'natural numbers', according to our definition. This, however, is not how we interpret these concepts in our daily lives. In our actual practices–a point which Frege was probably the first to make and which has then been given a detailed development in Russell's hands[12]–natural numbers are classes of certain classes or–what comes to the same, as there is a property corresponding to every class–properties of properties. We say, for instance, "the Earth has one satellite, viz. the moon," "human beings have two eyes," "the Apostles were twelve." What is involved in this kind of talk? The number 1 is not a property of the moon; it is a property of the property of the moon that the moon is the only satellite of the earth, which means that the moon can be put to a one-to-one correspondence with every other object that is 'the only one'. '12' is not a property of the Apostles; it is a property of the fact that the apostles can be put into a one-to-one correspondence with every group of class of things of which there are exactly one dozen, for instance, the group whose members include our ten fingers and two eyes. It is precisely this correspondence that we set up every time we 'count', that is, every time we enumerate the elements of some set using the numerals 1, 2, 3, . . ., n. Also, when we say that the Earth has no more than one satellite, we count the number of its moons and get the result that this number is 1. In the same way, when we say that the Earth has no self-luminous satellite, we count the number of self-luminous satellites of the Earth and get the result that their number is 0.

In all of these cases we put the members of some class–of which there may be 0–into a one-to-one-correspondence with the members of some other class. The latter may be our own fingers and toes or certain sounds we utter, namely numerals. If the correspondence is one-to-one, we say that there are as many members in each of these classes, or that they are *equinumerous*. This kind of counting can be carried out only if our classes are finite. But infinite multitudes, too, can be equinumerous, even though they cannot be counted. The number of males and females may be finite or it may be infinite; if monogamy is the strict rule, the classes of husbands and wives are equinumerous. In this case correspondence is set up not by counting but through a rule, a rule that establishes that there is exactly one wife for every husband.[13] The correspondence that holds between classes yields *cardinal numbers* in the sense in which they are commonly used. To begin with, we may define, using nothing but familiar logical concepts, the concepts '1', '2', '3', . . .

---

12. See Frege, *Grundlagen der Arithmetik*; Russell, *Introduction to Mathematical Philosophy*.
13. This example is Russell's; see *Introduction to Mathematical Philosophy*, 15.

as certain classes of classes,[14] the members (classes) of which we then put into a one-to-one correspondence with one another:

'0(F)' = '~ (Ex) F(x)',

that is, if there is no object possessing the property F, we say that the number of these objects is 0. Hence: the class the members of which are F belongs to the class that is the number 0. Similarly:

'1(F)' = '(Ex) {F(x) & (y) [F(y) → (x = y)]},

that is, if there is an object possessing the property F, and every other object y that is F is identical with x, we say that there is one x. In the same way we define, for instance, the cardinal number 2: If x and y are distinct objects which possess the property F, and if every object z which is F is identical with x or y, we say that the number of the objects x and y is 2.

In this way we arrive at the following result. If the axiomatic interpretation of arithmetic is presupposed, the axiom system of arithmetic may be realized in several domains that are mutually isomorphic but differ in their respective contents. One of the models for the arithmetical axiom system thus obtained is particularly noteworthy, namely the domain the elements of which are classes of classes or properties of properties. For in this model the elements are precisely the natural concepts of cardinal numbers. Furthermore, insofar as their series satisfies the axioms M_1-M_3, we get the series of *ordinal numbers*.

It is to be observed that we can give no logical proof that there 'exist' any other classes besides the 0-class and the unit-class. We get the former if in the definition of '0' we replace '$F(x)$' by the negation of identity '$x \neq x$', and the latter we get if in the definition of '1' we replace '$F(x)$' by identity '$x = x$'.[15]

Against the Axiomatic Interpretation of arithmetic the following point may be pressed. We must distinguish between arithmetic as a theory and arithmetic in practice, or between so-called pure and applied arithmetic. The latter we use when we determine empirical multiplicities; for instance, we use it already in ordinary calculation. We say that at some particular moment there were, for instance, 7 + 5 objects lying on the table. An empirical calculation is a procedure that always takes some time. It presupposes that the objects one is counting remain the same during the calculation, and nothing disappears or comes into being during the process. In many cases it is presupposed, furthermore, that the counted objects are preserved independently of their local grouping. Considered as an empirical procedure, addition may involve a local grouping of objects, for instance, when the objects on the table are sorted out into two groups of 7 and 5 objects, respectively, which are then brought

14. Whitehead and Russell, *Principia Mathematica*, Vol. I, Part II, section A; Hilbert and Ackermann, *Principles of Mathematical Logic*, 109.
15. Whitehead and Russell, *Principia Mathematica*, *25, *52.

together to constitute just one group. Of course, it does not follow from the axioms of arithmetic that a group of 7 objects and a group of 5 objects, when brought together, yield a group of 12 objects, insofar as this presupposes that the relevant objects are preserved at least throughout the counting process and independently of their grouping. This statement is by no means *a priori* and analytic; it presupposes certain laws of nature, to wit, that certain objects, in particular certain solid objects, are relatively stable. What is remarkable about this is the following point. When we apply arithmetic to experience, we do not consider it possible that arithmetic could be falsified by some experience; hence, in fact, in its applications arithmetic retains its analytic and *a priori* character.

Let us now imagine that the objects on the table are drops of quicksilver in motion. We wish to count their number. First we get the result $7 + 5 = 11$, while the second try yields the result $7 + 5 = 13$. What do we say about such results? One possibility that we do not even consider is to change the axiom system for arithmetic in such a way that one or other of these results could be derived from it. Rather we say either that we have made a mistake in calculation or else that the empirical conditions of counting have not been fulfilled. Perhaps the quicksilver drops were not preserved, but some of them merged together or split up. We remain firmly committed to our old arithmetic of natural numbers, and when some of its applications return results contradicting arithmetic, we do not say that the mistake lies in arithmetic; we say that in the given situation the application is not possible in the relevant respect. Just as the statement "all bodies are extended" is true independently of what is the case, because we do not *call* something a body unless it is extended, so also, the statement "$7 + 5 = 12$" is valid, no matter how things stand, because it assumes the form of a definition. No empirical experiment can confute this statement; should experience yield an apparent exception, we immediately set about invalidating it, explaining that *since the result was arithmetically erroneous, the objects at hand were not units in the arithmetical sense,* just like finding a nondimensional "thing" would not undermine the statement "all bodies are extended," but merely show that the 'thing' in question was not really a body.

This shows that the application of arithmetic is logically speaking quite peculiar. We apply the terminology of 'unit' and other 'natural numbers' only to those objects of nature whose behavior agrees with the axioms of arithmetic when they are manipulated in some way or other that is familiar from arithmetic. It follows from this that there can be no experience contradicting arithmetic. An interpretation of arithmetic in the way of geometry, that is, as an axiomatic system that gives no more than implicit definitions of certain variables called 'natural numbers', though logically possible, does not comply with the actual use to which we put arithmetic. This becomes quite clear as we move on to consider geometrical truths, in which case we come to see how marked the difference is between applying arithmetic and applying geometry to experience.

Before considering this issue, however, we make note of the following points. The ancient giant Antaeus was strong only when he remained in contact with Mother Earth. Heracles could beat him by lifting him off the ground and holding him aloft. In the same way, even the most abstract creations of human thought, insofar as they are fruitful, retain a connection, as it were through a hidden umbilical cord, to the fertile ground of experience. If the question is asked, "Why is arithmetic the way it is?" the answer turns out to be, at the end, that the decisive factor is the secret influence of experiential practice. This is why it is appropriate to raise the axiom system of arithmetic to the status of *a priori* truth, that is, into a definition that we hold to irrespective of the course of experience; this system has an empirical application that is so wide and so natural that it is appropriate to give the system a generality that is even greater than that of an ordinary axiomatic system, namely the generality of an analytic system, and then its validity becomes independent of experience, even when it is applied to it.

As we mentioned above, the axiomatic interpretation of arithmetic is supported by the fact that axioms M_1-M_3 do not suffice to determine the natural numbers in the sense in which they are commonly used. In response to this, though, it must be pointed out that in fact no objects of experience fully satisfy the axiom system of arithmetic. After all, this presupposes an infinite domain of elements, but we may consider it evident that in our experience we nowhere encounter anything infinite. Our experience is finite through and through, with respect to both the great and the small. But we do possess a natural conception of infinite space and time; after every moment, quite independently of what ordinal number it has, we expect a next moment. For this reason even the sphere of empirical elementary concepts, concepts like 'red', 'adjacent', 'simultaneous', is potentially infinite insofar as there is no limit to how many objects we may encounter that fall under such concepts. This being so, it is appropriate to create, through rationalization, a series of natural numbers, which is actually infinite, a series that will be sufficient for any finite quantity that we may find in our experience.

But this implies at the same time that the only models that fully satisfy the axiom system of arithmetic are formal systems themselves. And then it must be said that there are a great many such models; in fact there is an infinity of models that, though they are isomorphic with one another, are distinct in their respective contents. Even within arithmetic we find infinitely many, such as the series of odd or prime numbers that satisfy the axioms of arithmetic. An important result by the Norwegian logician Skolem finds that no finite number of axioms is sufficient if all models that satisfy the axiom system of arithmetic are to be not only isomorphic to the natural number series but also identical in content with it.[16] In this sense, no finite axiom system can give a complete definition of the concept 'natural number'. And for this reason the axiomatic interpretation of arithmetic is appropriate, too.

16. Th. Skolem, *Über einige Grundlagenfragen der Mathematik* (Norske Vid. Akad. Skrifter I, Mat. Kl., 1929).

One final remark: natural numbers are in fact one of the most remarkable discoveries of the human spirit, so much so that it is scarcely surprising that Kronecker, one of the most eminent mathematicians of the last century, should have said: "God created the natural numbers; all the rest is the work of man."

Sentences of Geometry

We move on now to geometrical sentences. We shall investigate Euclidean elementary geometry. As is customary today, we shall take it as an axiomatic system that implicitly defines certain thing- and relational variables, namely the so-called points, straight lines, and planes, as well as certain basic relations holding between them. Naturally, if one so wishes, one may write down these axioms in the form that logistic gives them, using besides logical constants nothing but variables $x, y, z, \ldots A, B, C. \ldots$ When points x, y, z lie on the same straight line, we may regard this as a relationship between x, y and z and write $S(x, y, z)$, $T(x, y, z)$, etc. Then, for example, the following two axioms, "Through any two points, there is exactly one straight line," and "There are at least three points not situated on the same straight line" would be written as:

$$(x) \, (y) \, (ES) \, \{S(x, y) \, \& \, (T) \, [T(x, y) \rightarrow (S = T)]\}$$

$$(Ex) \, (Ey) \, (Ez) \, [\sim S(x, y, z)].$$

Were the entire axiom system of Euclidean geometry to be completely formalized in this way, we would then encounter the very same problem that we met in connection with the arithmetical axiom system. True, in contemporary mathematics the axiomatic interpretation of geometry is prevalent, but from the standpoint of logic there is another interpretation, to wit, the analytic one, which is equally permissible. We wish to present the latter interpretation as well, in particular because it has had some very eminent advocates.

In this case, then, the axiom system of Euclidean geometry, which we write as 'G_k', is an explicit definition. It defines an object that we call a 'Euclidean space'. This object consists of so-called points, straight lines, and so on between which there are certain relationships. These objects and relations, too, can be given explicit definitions in the following manner: We call 'points' objects $x, y, z, \ldots$, fulfilling the following conditions (1), $\ldots$, (n), when we include among the conditions all axioms featuring variables x, y, z. We give similar definitions of straight lines, congruity, etc. In this way the entire Euclidean system becomes an analytic system; its axioms are explicit definitions and its theorems, arrived at by inference from these axioms, become analytic sentences, too. For instance, the statement that the sum of the angles in a triangle is two straight lines is a 'necessary truth' and independent of experience because it has the character of a definition—like, for example, the statement that 7 + 5 = 12. There can be no triangle the angle-sum of which is more than, or less than, two straight lines, because we do not *call* such a figure a 'triangle'. Further, the application of geometry becomes similar to arithmetic; applied geometry says nothing about experience because there can be no experience refuting it just as there can be no experience refuting arithmetic. It is conceivable that suitably chosen natural objects and events, like solid bodies and, for example, light rays in a vacuum, should conform approximately, or even quite precisely, to the rules of Euclidean geometry. But if they do not, that does not mean that Euclidean geometry would be empirically incorrect; it means, just as in similar applications of arithmetic, that the conditions for applying Euclidean geometry have not been fulfilled. As in arithmetic, this kind of interpretation can be carried out consistently for geometry.

The fact that mathematicians of the past hundred years have developed other provably consistent systems of geometry–in particular so-called non-Euclidean geometries–in no way undermines the analytic interpretation of Euclidean geometry.[17] As it is usually understood, 'non-Euclidean' geometry means that, independently of how many dimensions are assumed in it, certain Euclidean axioms–in particular the parallel axiom–have been replaced by different axioms, for instance by the assumption that through a point lying outside a given straight line there passes infinitely many straight lines parallel to it. Note that insofar as we interpret Euclidean geometry as an analytical system in this way, as a system in which points, straight lines, and so on have been given explicit definitions, it is misleading to call the elements of non-Euclidean geometry "points" and "straight lines," etc. The basic concepts in these systems are different, so meanings, too, differ from those we find in Euclidean geometry.

The following points speak *for* the analytic interpretation of Euclidean geometry. First, of all geometries with a given number of dimensions, it is the simplest in the definite sense in which, for example, a first-degree curve is simpler than a second-degree curve. Mathematically, this can be seen in the following facts. In Euclidean geometry, the so-called curvature of space = 0. Only in this space are there different congruent figures. Only in this space is the sum of the angles of a triangle the same, namely two straight lines, independently of the triangle's size. This being the case, Euclidean geometry exhibits *higher invariance* than other geometries comparable to it. Second, certain physical objects and events–suitably chosen solid bodies and light-rays in a vacuum–conform so closely to the rules of Euclidean geometry that it may be appropriate here to adopt an attitude similar to arithmetic: we turn it into an analytic system that is independent of experience. This may be regarded as an

17. Accessible introductions to the basics of Euclidean geometry can be found, e.g., in R. Bonola and H. Liebmann, *Die nichteuklidische Geometrie* (Leipzig, Berlin: B.G. Teubner, 1919); H. de Vries, *Die vierte Dimension.* Wissenschaft und Hypothese, XXIX. Translated into German from the second Dutch Edition by R. Struik (Leipzig, Berlin: B.G. Teubner, 1926).

appropriate policy given the benefits that accrue to this kind of geometry and the generality and naturalness of its application.

In our century, this view has been defended by an influential figure, the remarkable mathematician and philosopher Henri Poincaré, whose name we have all the more reason to mention, as he has been philosophically one of the most important predecessors of logical empiricism.[18]

Today, however, a different view of the matter is quite generally accepted not only by physicists and mathematicians but also by philosophers advocating logical empiricism. The analytic interpretation of geometry is, indeed, formally possible, but weighty considerations can be brought against it and, in turn, in favor of the alternative interpretation. It turns out to be appropriate to interpret geometry in such a way that applied geometry becomes an empirical science of 'physical geometry' constituted by synthetic sentences that describe the structure of 'physical space' and thus make determinate statements about reality. Here, first of all, we must use appropriate conventions to assign some empirical content to the variables occurring in the axiom system. For instance, we give the name 'straight lines' to light rays in a vacuum and 'points' to their points of intersection and we choose some solid body as the unit of measurement, and so on. Next we find out whether or not physical objects and events conform sufficiently closely to the rules of our chosen geometry. When certain stipulations have been laid down, we go on to see how experience replies to the question: "What is the geometry of 'physical space'?" This does not mean, "What is the geometry of a physical vacuum?" It means this: given certain conventions, does the behavior of solid bodies, light rays, and other natural objects and events conform to the rules of Euclidean geometry? The greater simplicity of Euclidean geometry in comparison with other geometries is not the decisive factor here, for the assumption that the geometry of so-called physical space is non-Euclidean in one way or another is admittedly less simple than the Euclidean hypothesis. Nevertheless, adopting the non-Euclidean hypothesis may render the *total system of laws of nature* simpler, and this may in the end be the appropriate way to achieve greater invariance.

Now, the search for the highest possible invariance is the guiding thread for all scientific inquiry. Taking this into account, we must give priority to the axiomatic interpretation over the analytic one. It is precisely this search for maximal invariance that is the reason why in Einstein's so-called general theory of relativity physical space is assumed to be non-Euclidean.

The two interpretations sketched above and the exchange of ideas between them is a topic that we need not explore any further here, for the result that is most important for us is the same: either way, the sentences of geometry are

---

18. H. Poincaré, *La Science et l'Hypothese* (Paris: E. Flammarion, 1902); *La Valeur de la Science* (Paris: E. Flammarion, 1905); *Science et Méthode* (Paris: E. Flammarion, 1908). (English translations of all three volumes appear in H. Poincaré, *The Foundations of Science*. Authorized translation by G.B. Halsted [New York and Garrison, N.Y.: Science Press, 1913].)

analytic sentences. We have already indicated that this will be the case if we choose the analytic interpretation. From this axiomatic standpoint, the logical situation is as follows. What we really assert in, say, Euclidean geometry is not that the sum of the angles in a triangle is two straight lines, or that there are exactly five regular solids; if we change our axioms, the theorems corresponding to these statements may well be different. The truths of geometry, therefore, are of the form "T follows from G_k," where G_k is the relevant axiom system and T is a theorem derived from axioms by rules of inference. However, as we pointed out in dealing with arithmetic, this statement is one we get as a special case from some logical axiom, viz. a rule of inference, via appropriate substitutions; therefore, it is an analytic sentence.

In every mathematical system we could carry out an investigation analogous to what we have here done for arithmetic and geometry. In each case the result would be the same. Every truth of theoretical or 'pure' mathematics is an analytic statement and, as such, will be independent of experience or *a priori*. This is perfectly compatible with the psychological fact that the origin of axiomatized mathematical theories is to be sought, in the last analysis, in empirical application.

The First Two Basic Theses of Logical Empiricism

Thus we arrive at a result with far-reaching consequences for epistemology. The following *meta-logical statements: "sentence S is analytic" and "sentence S is a priori"* are equivalent. This is the first main result of our investigations so far, and it is *the first main thesis of logical empiricism*. All advocates of this philosophy are in agreement on this point. Let us first consider what this thesis implies and, secondly, how certain counter-arguments may be resisted.

We call a sentence 'a priori' when it is independent of experience, when it is 'true' no matter what experiences we may have. Our claim is then that every sentence that is *a priori* is analytic and, naturally, *vice versa*. In fact, this already follows from the fact that in the context at hand the word 'true' means formal truth, viz. *analyticity* and nothing else. Everything that is analytic has the character of a definition in the sense explained above, that is, the character of a convention. We set up certain conventions and adhere to them strictly; this is the answer to the question of how there can be sentences which are "necessary truths" holding in "all possible worlds."

Thus, a sentence that is *a priori* is formally true, or true independently of all experience, and has therefore no consequences for experience. Here we lay down a definition that will be of importance in the third part of our investigations: *Given a set of sentences, S_1, its factual content is the set of empirical sentences, S_2, that follows logically from S_1.*[19] On the basis of this definition, to say

---

19. The concept of factual content we have defined here corresponds approximately, but not com-

that *a priori* sentences are analytic is to say that they possess no factual content. The second main thesis of logical empiricism, for which we shall be giving reasons here, is as follows: *Every sentence concerning reality must possess a determinate factual content, that is, it must have some definite consequences with respect to experience.* This second main thesis, then, does not concern analytic sentences, that is, logical and mathematical truths, since these are not concerned with reality; that is the business of their applications. But with the notion of application we move to a new area.

Kant's Doctrine of Synthetic A Priori Statements

If these arguments are correct, it will be logically impossible that there should be true statements that are independent of experience and yet nonanalytic. This, though, is a claim that certain famous philosophical schools have advanced; above all, this view was endorsed by Kant. As is well known, the question that constitutes the starting-point for his 'Critique of Pure Reason' is, "How are synthetic *and a priori* statements possible?" That is, how can there exist statements which are both independent of experience and nonanalytic?

In order to assess Kant's doctrine, it is helpful to start with his belief that *a priori* statements are not only independent of experience by definition; they also possess the further characteristic that, psychologically, they are understood as necessary or apodictic and thus claim greater generality than empirical statements. What Kant means by this can be illuminated by the following example. A heavy body released from a hand has always fallen to ground, but it is easy to imagine that next time this will not happen. When, on the other hand, we assert in accordance with our natural conception of space that a straight line is the shortest distance between two points, we feel that this claim is necessary, that it *could* not be otherwise.

Consider this latter example by Kant a little more closely. To begin, note that our natural conception of space, the logical structure of which is represented by axiomatic Euclidean geometry, is not equivalent in its content with this formal system. In our natural conception, the basic concepts have definite perceptual content, though it may be difficult to express this content. Points, so to speak, have a point-like quality, and circles have a circle-like quality, and so on. As we have seen, on the other hand, the basic concepts of an axiomatic geometry are variables having no perceptual content. This must be taken into account when our natural conception of space leads us to say, for example, that a straight line is necessarily the shortest distance between two points. To find out whether this sentence is analytic or synthetic–whether it follows from the

---

pletely, to Carnap's concept of "Gehalt" or "content"; see Carnap, *Logical Syntax*, 42, 175 (38 and 128 in the original German).

meanings of words–we must consider what meanings 'straight line' and 'short-est' possess on our natural conception of space. The result would be something like, "A straight line is a line through which we can set up a surface known as a plane. A plane is a surface which divides space into two fully symmetrical halves, whereas a straight line divides a plane passing through it into two fully symmetrical halves." But our thought here involves several of the axioms of Euclidean geometry from which it follows logically that a straight line is the shortest distance between two points. Therefore, there is no doubt that the psychological necessity or apodicticity that seems to belong to these sentences is nothing but an expression of the logical necessity involved in this latter sentence; that *psychological apodicticity is nothing but a correlate of logical necessity*, as Reichenbach, who has studied these questions in detail, has very aptly remarked.[20] This implies that the sentence, in the form licensed by our natural conception of space, is an analytic sentence, from whence derives its necessity.

But Kant dissents. A statement of this kind, he says, is not analytic but synthetic. He even argues that mathematical statements are "without exception synthetic."[21] Thus he is in sharp disagreement with Leibniz, for example. How did Kant reach this remarkable conclusion?

To begin with, Kant had a very narrow, Aristotelian conception of logical proof. When he discusses the topic, he has only trivial syllogisms in mind. He thinks that a logical proof consists in nothing but an analysis of subject- and predicate-concepts and that the concluding sentence states something that is 'covertly contained' in them. This description can be applied to such inferences as "If every man is mortal, then, also, Socrates, being a man, is mortal." But this Aristotelian conception is seen to be insufficient as soon as we begin to consider the proof, say, of a simple arithmetical equation like 7 + 5 = 12. Kant thinks that this kind of equation, too, is synthetic, for it supposedly does not follow from the sum of 7 and 5 that the sum should be 12. Leibniz had already shown, however, how such equations work. Consider Leibniz's example '2 + 2 = 4'.[22] If we wish to prove this sentence, we must first, of course, define the relevant numbers, for instance in this way:

$$1 + 1 = 2, 2 + 1 = 3, 3 + 1 = 4.$$

From these defining equations we get, using the law of association for addition $(a + b) + c = a + (b + c)$, which is provable, and by repeated substitutions

$$2 + 2 = 2 + (1 + 1) = (2 + 1) + 1 = 3 + 1 = 4.$$

20. H. Reichenbach, *Philosophie der Raum-Zeit-Lehre* (1928), 56. (*The Philosophy of Space and Time*, Engl. translation by M. Reichenbach and J. Freund [New York: Dover Publications, 1958].)
21. Kant, *Critique of Pure Reason*, 2nd edition, 14.
22. Leibniz, *New Essays on Human Understanding*, Bk. IV, Ch. 7, §10.

In the same way we can prove that $7 + 5 = 12$ is an analytic statement. But Kant, by contrast, thinks that mathematical proof is something essentially different from logical proof. He argues that mathematical proof requires "constructing the objects corresponding to mathematical concepts"[23] in the 'pure intuitions' of time and space, from which we can, independently of experience, gather knowledge concerning the relevant objects–knowledge, that is, which is not contained in their concepts. Because the concept of 'pure intuition' is not defined, however, this talk is no more than unclear metaphysics. What Kant seems to be thinking about in such passages are our natural perceptions of time and space; what these dictate to us, he supposes, must be unconditionally correct 'for all possible experience'.

Here we meet Kant's second stumbling block: he has failed to take notice of the *problem of application.*[24] He has not sufficiently taken into account that the word 'space' can be used with several different meanings.[25] In the first place, it can be used to denote that natural conception of space which we all possess and which, as Kant seems to have realized, is not just a simple copy of perceptual (for instance, visual) space, as the empiricists used to think. But this conception implicitly involves rationalization, as indicated for example by our way of saying that spaces are infinitely great and infinitely small when, on the other hand, our perceptual space is finite in every respect. The blue dome of the sky appears to be a finite, not an infinite, distance away. Between two perceived spots one can never discern more than some finite number of spots. In this way, we already have two meanings of 'space'. Moreover, we must distinguish the mathematical or formal space of axiomatic geometry, to which arithmetic content, for instance, can be assigned. Yet another thing is the physical space of solid bodies and other objects of experience. A physical triangle may be constituted by three light-rays on a plane intersecting each other at different points, for example, and only physical measurement can decide whether the sum of their angles is two straight lines.

What, then, could Kant mean by saying that Euclid's geometry is "*a priori* valid for all possible experience?" It means nothing as long as we continue to ignore the problem of application. Taking this into account, it is clear that Kant cannot mean the *a priori* validity or formal truth of an analytic sentence; for here the question does not concern analytic but synthetic sentences. Kant seems to have thought that the dictates of our natural conception of space have some factual content, viz. some consequences for our experience. This cannot be so, however, until the concepts of geometry have been given some empirical–for instance, physical–content. But then these statements are no longer analytic and *a priori*; they become synthetic and *a posteriori* statements, which are either confirmed or refuted by experience.

23. Kant, *Critique of Pure Reason,* 2nd edition, 741 seq.
24. Reichenbach, *Philosophie der Raum-Zeit-Lehre*, §13.
25. Carnap, *Der Raum*, in: *Kant-Studien*, Ergänzungsheft, n. 56 (1922).

We see, then, that Kant's basic question, "How are synthetic *a priori* statements possible?" is a mistake because there are no such statements. Only analytic sentences are *a priori* and *vice versa*. Synthetic sentences are *a posteriori*, dependent upon experience. It is to such sentences that we turn next when we move on to consider what empirical truth is.

Part III. Empirical Truth of Theory

Chapter 8

The Principle of Testability

Turning now to the question of empirical truth, it would be natural first to define the concept of 'empirical truth'. We have already mentioned that Tarski has formulated an explicit definition of a concept of truth that defines, within certain limits, both formal and material or empirical truth in the same way.[1] The starting-point here is the discovery that 'true' (and, similarly, "false") are metalogical or syntactic predicates, that is, that what are 'true' and 'false' are not states of affairs but statements which make assertions about these states. The statement 'it is raining now' is true if it is raining now. Statement S is true when and only when things are as statement S says they are. Hence we may say that there is something right in the time-honored 'correspondence theory of truth'. There are, however, considerable difficulties in the way of an exact formulation, and these cannot be resolved until we have at our disposal a logistic apparatus much more sophisticated than the one we have developed above. We must therefore rest content with the inexact conception of truth that can be gleaned from the above remarks.

This, however, is in fact quite sufficient for our purposes. The main question here is, provided we know what empirical truth is, how do we know *whether* a sentence asserting something about reality–*a factual sentence*, to use a

---

1. A. Tarski, "Der Wahrheitsbegriff in den formalisierten Sprachen," *Studia philosophica*, I (1936), 261-405. (English translation as 'The Concept of Truth in Formalized Languages', in Tarski, *Logic, Semantics, Metamathematics*, ed. J. Corcoran [Indianapolis: Hackett Publishing Company, 1983], 152-278.)

shorter phrase–is true or false? Suppose we answer by saying that those factual sentences are true which have been shown to be true, viz. have been verified; and those factual sentences are false which have been shown to be false, that is, have been falsified. Our question then re-emerges in a new form: Are there some factual sentences that have been verified and how has this verification been carried out? In other words, our main question concerns empirical validation or *verification* and empirical refutation or *falsification*.[2]

Problem Setting

The difficulties we will face here are rather intricate. The correct procedure would seem to be that one shows one's hand, so to speak. By this I mean that we must be quite clear as to the point of the following investigations. This is the task that we shall take up first.

We have already mentioned the first two main theses of logical empiricism; all advocates of this philosophy are in agreement upon them. The first was that all *a priori* sentences are analytic; in negative terms–and this formulation is directed specifically against Kant–there are no sentences that are both synthetic and *a priori*. The second main thesis was that every factual sentence must have some determinate consequences with respect to experience; or, what comes to the same, every statement concerning reality must have a determinate factual content. All empiricists share this view, be their empiricism psychological or logical; as we shall see later, though, we must here add a clarification to make our principle both accurate and generally valid.

In a way, this principle was already stated by Aristotle. The rationalist Leibniz gave it a particularly memorable formulation–it is precisely this principle that imposed significant limits on his rationalism. We remember Leibniz's pertinent remark that if two theories have exactly the same empirical consequences, there is no factual but at most a psychological difference between them, namely, in so far as one attaches different thoughts to them. In accordance with this, we wish to say that two sets of sentences, S_1 and S_2, *have the same content* or are *equipollent–'gehaltgleich'* in German–if the set, S_3, of empirical sentences that are their consequences is the same.[3]

Modern psychological empiricists have time and again stated this main thesis underlying all empiricism, but their formulations have often been less successful than Leibniz's. The reason for this is the well-known fact that for them the question concerning the psychological origin of our knowledge and

2. Carnap, "Wahrheit und Bewährung," *Actes de Congrès international de philosophie scientifique* (Paris, 1936). (English translation as "Truth and Confirmation," H. Feigl and W. Sellars eds., *Readings in Philosophical Analysis* [New York: Appleton-Century-Crofts, Inc., 1949], 119-27).
3. Cf. here Carnap, *Logical Syntax*, 42, 176 (38 and 129 in the German original).

the question concerning its logical validity have been brought together in a misleading manner. This happens, for example, in Locke's famous statement, "In experience all our knowledge is founded; and from that it ultimately derives itself." In the following considerations our primary target is to establish the main thesis of all empiricism, what we shall call (for reasons to be explained below) *the principle of testability* (*Prüfbarkeitsthese* in German).[4]

The point has already been made that this principle–which empiricists have been insisting upon in one formulation or another–has not been given a clear and conclusive justification prior to logical empiricism in our time. As a rule, we find psychological empiricists appealing to the point that since knowing is, as they say, a matter of copying experience, its validity, too, is decided by experience. Here, though, we must point out, first, that the reason cited is valid only with severe restrictions, and second, that it does not prove what one wants to prove, because, among other things, it fails to draw a clear distinction between formal and empirical (factual) knowledge. For the time being, therefore, we shall settle for the following formulation: *From every statement concerning reality there must follow a determinate set of empirical sentences; this set constitutes the factual content of the statement.*

Two points require special attention. First, we must consider the concept of 'empirical sentence'. Naturally it must be given as precise a definition as possible. We shall see that the definition can be devised in different ways, giving the principle of testability slightly different meaning in each case. Second, we should note the phrase that from every factual sentence there *must* follow some empirical sentences. This manner of expression implies that the second main thesis is construed as logically necessary and, therefore, analytic. As we see it, then, the principle of testability follows from the concept of factual sentence. A sentence that does not satisfy this requirement but is meant to be factual is logically faulty. This, too, is something that we shall have to establish.

It is easy to see the far-reaching consequences of this proof. For instance, sentences belonging to so-called metaphysics in its various forms often fail to satisfy the principle of testability. They are therefore logically faulty, and in this way logical empiricism shows not that this so-called metaphysics is merely rather unfruitful while otherwise containing nothing illegitimate, but rather that it is, logically speaking, a complete error. There is no knowledge of reality apart from so-called ordinary scientific knowledge, including our prescientific everyday knowledge; and all of this is founded upon experience.

At the same time, however, we wish to investigate the *third main thesis of logical empiricism*, which has not won general acceptance as the other two have. This thesis says that *every theory concerning reality must be translatable into the 'language of experience'*, that is, must be capable of being transformed

4. Carnap, "Über Protokollsätze," *Erkenntnis* 3 (1932), 215–28. K. Popper, *The Logic of Scientific Discovery* (1935). Carnap, "Testability and Meaning," *Philosophy of Science* 3 (1936), 419–71; 4 (1937), 1–40.

into an equivalent form in which there occur, besides logical constants, only empirical predicates. Here, of course, we must determine what such predicates are.

Here we recall from our earlier discussion of definitions that 'translation' may come in different varieties. If it only makes use of explicit definitions in the stricter sense of the term, the result is a 'word-by-word' translation. If, in addition, one makes use of use-definitions, one gets a 'sentence-by-sentence' translation. We shall see, furthermore, that there may be 'translations' that are even 'freer' than sentence-by-sentence translations. This case occurs when a rationalized theory is translated into the language of experience.

The third, controversial main thesis of logical empiricism has often been maintained together with an additional conception, even though the connection between them, being no more than psychological and historical, is not logically necessary. The principle of testability says no more than that every factual sentence must have some consequences with respect to experience. It does *not* imply that every factual sentence should be capable of a definitive verification or falsification. On the contrary, our first task will be to show that there is in fact not a single factual sentence of which it could be shown in the strict sense that it is true or false. A sentence of this kind can only be confirmed or disconfirmed to a greater or lesser degree by experience. And yet many empiricists, including many logical empiricists, have thought that every factual sentence should have to be able 'in principle' to be verified or falsified completely. Rejection of this additional 'positivistic requirement'—one that is too radical, as we shall see—is characteristic of the final stage in the development of logical empiricism.

The Verification and Falsification of a 'Factual Sentence'

Radical psychological empiricists—David Hume, for instance—have apparently thought that all factual knowledge must be capable of being 'translated into the language of experience', even in the strictest 'word-by-word' manner. Let us consider, for example, the following passage from his *Inquiry*:

> Complex ideas may, perhaps, be well known by definition, which is nothing but an enumeration of those parts or simple ideas, that compose them. But when we have pushed up definitions to the most simple ideas, and find still more ambiguity and obscurity; what resources are we then possessed of? By what invention can we throw light upon these ideas, and render them altogether precise and determinate to our intellectual view? Produce the impressions or original sentiments, from which the ideas are copied.[5]

5. D. Hume, *An Enquiry Concerning Human Understanding*, sec. VII, Part I.

Hume seems to think–to put the point in modern terms–that all empirical concepts have been formed from some 'original sentiments' with the help of explicit definitions. For this reason it must be possible to translate every statement about reality back into the language of 'original sentiments' using substitutions grounded in explicit definitions.

When logical empiricism reached its present stage of development in the 1920s, the strongest impetus came from *Tractatus Logico-Philosophicus*, a work by the brilliant Wittgenstein, which gained repute gradually in the beginning of the decade and has since exercised remarkable influence. Wittgenstein and his followers–in particular Schlick, the intellectual father of the so-called Vienna Circle–were radical positivists in the following sense. They gave the principle of testability a very strict formulation, demanding that every factual sentence must in principle be capable of complete verification or falsification. At the same time, they also thought that every factual sentence must be capable of translation, in the strictest sense, into the 'language of experience'. The following quotation from a paper by Schlick dealing with these issues indicates their line of thought:

But when do I understand a proposition? When I know the meaning of the words that occur in it? This can be explained by definitions. But in the definitions new words occur, whose meaning I also have to know in turn. The business of defining cannot go on indefinitely, so eventually we come to words whose meaning cannot again be described in propositions; it has to be pointed out directly; the meaning of the word must ultimately be *shown*, it has to be *given*. This takes place through an act of pointing or showing, and what is shown must be given, since otherwise it cannot be pointed out to me. In order, therefore, to find the meaning of a proposition, we have to transform it by introduction of successive definitions, until finally only such words appear in it as can no longer be defined, but whose meanings can only be indicated indirectly. The criterion for the truth or falsity of the proposition then consists in this, that under specific conditions (stated in the definitions) certain data are, or are not, present. Once this is established, I have established everything that the proposition was talking about, and hence I know its meaning. If I am *not* capable, in principle, of verifying a proposition, that is, if I have absolutely no knowledge of how I should go about it, what I would have to do, in order to ascertain its truth or falsity, then I obviously have no idea at all of what the proposition is actually saying; for then I would be in no position to interpret the proposition, in proceeding, by means of the definitions, from its wording to possible data, since insofar as I *am* in a position to do this, I can also, by this very fact, point out the road to verification in principle.[6]

6. M. Schlick, "Positivismus und Realismus" *Erkenntnis* 3 (1932), 1-31. (English translation

The quotation shows that its author makes two assumptions. First, he assumes that the logical foundation for all knowledge of reality is to be found in certain observational sentences whose predicates like 'red' and 'adjacent' cannot be defined but can only be 'shown' (to borrow a phrase from the quotation). Second, he assumes that all other empirical concepts are to be derived from these observational concepts by explicit definitions. From this he concludes, as did Hume, that every factual statement must be capable of being translated back into the language of such observational predicates; that is, that they can be transformed into an equivalent form involving, besides logical constants, only these predicates. And he also concludes that a statement must be capable of being verified or falsified in principle, as the resulting translation presents those experiential situations in which a statement is either verified or turns out to be false.

This was the radical view of so-called logistic neopositivism, the first phase in the development of logical empiricism.[7] Now, we must first show why this view has been almost universally given up and why the requirement of testability has been replaced by the less stringent principle of testability.

In discussions concerning testability, we must begin by stating what is meant by 'experiential sentences'. The two most important interpretations are these.

φ-language

By 'experiential sentences' one may mean, first, statements about those perceptual phenomena, of any kind whatsoever, that occur at a given moment of time, that is, sentences like "this looks red," "this, which feels hard, tastes sweet," or "after a sound there is pain," and so on. Such observation sentences are singular, positive, and categorical; that is, they assert something about something *particular* (not general), they are *affirmative* (not negative) they are *unconditional* (not conditional, viz. hypothetical or disjunctive). We call their predicates phenomenal predicates, in short *φ-predicates*, and the language which contains only φ-predicates, when logical constants like implication have been excluded, we call phenomenal or φ-language. These φ-

as "Positivism and Realism." In M. Schlick, *Philosophical Papers*, Vol. II (1925-1936), ed.H. Mulder and B.F.B. van de Velde-Schlick, trans. P. Heath, Vienna Circle Collection, vol. 11 (Dordrecht: D. Reidel Publishing Company, 1979), 259-84.
7. Concerning logistic neo-positivism, see my essay *Der logistische Neupositivismus. Eine kritische Studie.* Turun yliopiston julkaisuja, B 13, 1930. (Translated into English as "Logistic Neopositivism. A Critical Study." In E. Kaila, *Reality and Experience*).

predicates include words representing not only so-called sense qualities but also, for instance, feelings or any other contents of experience. The number of φ-predicates occurring in observation sentences is always finite; for we can distinguish no more than a finite number of different shades of color, shapes, pains, etc. A sufficiently comprehensive dictionary would include all possible such φ-predicates. Like other predicates, these φ-predicates are general; they, too, represent *general concepts*.

We call the meaning of a representing word a 'concept'. A word is a symbol or a sign for a *factual meaning*, and this must be distinguished from the *meaning-experience* that we have when we understand a word we hear or see. Factual meaning and meaning-experience are two distinct things. Meaning-experience is simultaneous with the word; it is a particular, private content of consciousness. Factual meaning may be general or particular, real or unreal, past or future. Here we shall be concerned only with factual meaning.

As we pointed out, the meanings of φ-predicates, too, are general. The extension of a concept like, for example, 'red' or 'adjacent' is even potentially infinite, insofar as there is no limit to the number of things falling under this concept.

Here we should recall Aristotle's view that knowledge can be had only of that which is general, as well as the reason given for this view, namely, that definitions can be given only of what is general, because the meanings of the defining words could not be understood otherwise. Appropriately understood, this view is correct. Let us suppose a sound is heard here at this moment. Of course, we can give it a name, say, 'stub'. But suppose the meaning of this word remains entirely private or singular, so that it means only the sound heard a moment ago and not, for instance, the class of sounds similar to the one that was heard a moment ago; in that case, everyone admits, the sentence "x is a stub" conveys no *knowledge*. The meaning of so-called proper names, like 'Socrates' or 'the Earth', is by no means private in this sense. They contain a great deal that is general, if only because they name things that persist in time.

All knowledge concerns invariances of some kind or other. A minimal requirement that a series of signs must fulfill to qualify as a sentence representing something is that it represents some similarity holding between different things. (Incidentally, this feature, like all human knowledge, has a deep basis in certain biological facts. Life can be preserved only if it possible to respond to the unlimited multiplicity of phenomena by a rather limited set of different reactions.[8])

We recall, further, an argument that was directed against Aristotle's view that all knowledge concerns what is general, viz. invariances. The counter argument ran that, according to this view, in all our knowledge–at any rate in all our ordinary scientific knowledge–we only reach what is common to several things. So if a thing possessed a feature that is something absolutely unique to

8. See Mach, *Knowledge and Error*, 93.

it, it would remain beyond our reach, or else could be captured only with the help of some special, mystical knowledge. We respond by pointing out that if there occurs something that is so absolutely individual and unique–and that, of course, may very well be the case–it can be named just like any feature that the thing in question has in common with others.[9] When we assert of a thing a predicate that applies to other things as well, we have done no more than *name* something. In this case, however, we have named an unlimited class of things, namely, all those things to which the predicate can be applied. But now we have a case of *knowledge*, because we have *found an invariance and assigned a name to it*. This is the only difference between the two cases. The counterargument is based on the prescientific conception of human knowledge, according to which when we know something we, as it were, come to possess a quality, when, in fact, knowledge is just a matter of representation–a representation of invariances. It may be psychologically worthwhile to possess ideas or other such meaning-experiences sharing content with the objects of knowledge; indeed, sometimes this may be a practical necessity. However, as far as the character and truth of knowledge goes, this is quite immaterial; there need not be any qualitative similarity between a representation and the object represented. We ask someone whether he recognizes the smell of lilac. The person may reply 'yes' and with good reason, even if he possesses no impression of the smell of lilac; namely, insofar as he can correctly use the relevant expression– for instance, to pick out the smell that is most like the smell of lilac. We are to keep in mind, then, that even the most primitive φ-predicates are general, indeed, even unlimited in their extensions.

ƒ-language

From the phenomenal language or φ-language we must now distinguish the physical language, or *ƒ-language*. This speaks about bodies and events occurring in physical space. Here we are not yet thinking of physics in the scientific sense; we are thinking of the 'naïve' physics that we constantly use in our everyday life, when we make such statements as "this thing is a piece of chalk" or "tree burns in fire," and so on.

Now we must note that a considerable number of our words are ambiguous in that they possess a φ-meaning as well as an ƒ-meaning. Such words are, for example, the names of colors, the names of shapes, words like 'motion', 'space', 'to see', 'to perceive', etc. With such words, we must distinguish between these two meanings. 'Red' may mean a present shade of color, but it may also mean a certain 'physical' color, when, for instance, we say that a certain stamp is

9. Cf. Carnap, "Erwiderung auf die vorstehenden Ausätze von E. Zilsel und K. Duncker," in *Erkenntnis* 3 (1932/1933): 181.

red in spite of the fact that it looks grey in strong green lighting. The word 'straight' may mean the impression of straightness, but it may also mean measured straightness, a physical property that may be meant even in the presence of something that looks bent. The word 'motion' may mean the impression of movement, but it may also mean measured physical motion. These f-meanings are so predominant in ordinary use that it sometimes takes considerable effort before we manage to capture the φ-meaning. Here is an example. We say that we 'see objects', say for instance, a matchbox. We say that this object is 'non-transparent' because we cannot say without opening the box what the matches are like that are contained in it. In this case the word 'see' has been used in its f-sense, the sense in which we must all *learn to 'see'*, just as we must learn to read, since in such cases we must learn to see certain occurrences as signs of physical objects and events. On the other hand, when we use the word in its φ-sense, the interior of that visible 'matchbox' is something experienced just as its exterior is. But what we experience in the φ-sense is not what we would perceive, were we to open the box; it is the impression we have of a portion of visual space, which is delineated by the surfaces of a given visual object and of whose dimensions at least we can state something. There are no openings or holes in perceptual space. Perceived colored surfaces are not limits of perceptual space; they are figures occurring in that space. The interior of the *visual* object that we call a matchbox is perceived in the same sense that we perceive, for instance, a distance lacking color and other such 'sense qualities'. Here, too, dimensionality is very nearly all we can state about what we perceive.[10]

If this sounds odd, it is only because under normal conditions our attitudes and reactions are dictated by the reifying or physical orientation which, because it is so important to us, makes us speak most of the time the language of naïve physics; after all, most phenomena are significant for us only insofar as they are signs of some particular physical fact.

Of particular importance is the distinction between phenomenal or perceptual space and physical space. The former is ego-centered, as we always experience ourselves as its centre, whereas physical space is not. Phenomenal space contains a great many visual objects that have no physical counterparts, such as the perceived dome of the sky. We experience it in dreams as well as when awake, and so on.

Our starting-point was the question: What can we mean by 'experiential sentences'? We now see that there are two major possibilities. We mean either the singular perceptual sentences of a φ-language; in which case, then, perception sentences are singular sentences concerning perceptions and other experiences reported by a subject as he experiences them. The other possibility is to say that experiential sentences are singular statements belonging to

10. Cf. here my essay "Über das System der Wirklichkeitsbegriffe," *Acta Philosophica Fennica* 2 (1936). (English translation as "On the System of the Concepts of Reality," in E. Kaila, *Reality and Experience*, 59-125).

an *f*-language in which the subject makes assertions about the properties or relations of physical objects and events appearing to him at the moment of assertion.[11]

Why the Requirement of Full Decidability Cannot Be Applied to Factual Sentences

Let us assume, first, that our experiential sentences are sentences of an *f*-language; later on we shall consider the possibility of choosing *φ*-sentences as our experiential sentences. With respect to both of these possibilities, we wish to show why full decidability, that is, actual verification or falsification, cannot be applied to factual sentences, and hence that testability is all that we can require.

With *f*-sentences as our experiential sentences, we must first consider some points that Karl Popper, one of the younger advocates of logical empiricism, has brought to a wider attention.[12] He has shown with special clarity that a general sentence of the form '$(x) A(x, . . .)$' cannot be verified, although it may be capable of falsification. In the case of empirical sentences, verification must always take place, as we say, *extensionally*, that is, by running through the particular cases. This cannot be done *intensionally*, that is, through a logical proof. This is evident insofar as general factual sentences have been formed by generalizing from experience. No matter have many instances we have checked of those that belong within the sphere of the generalization in question, even if 'A' should occur in each of them, there of course always remains the possibility that '$\sim A(c)$' might occur on some later occasion. On the other hand, a sentence of the form '$(Ex) A(x, . . .)$' cannot be falsified, although we might succeed in verifying it. The latter possibility materializes as soon as we find some case in which '$A(c)$' occurs, but no matter how many cases we have run through in which '$\sim A(c)$' has occurred, this does not mean we would not, on some later occasion, find a case in which '$A(c)$' occurs; therefore, a sentence of the form '$(Ex) A(x, . . .)$' cannot be falsified. Now, from this it follows that a factual sentence of the form '$(x)(Ey) A(x, y. . .)$' can be neither verified nor falsified.[13] The following would be an example of this kind of sentence: "given a temperature, no matter how high, there is always a higher temperature". This sentence cannot be verified, insofar as it is a general sentence, but it cannot be falsified, either, for even if a finite sample of temperatures did not yield any *y* such that '$A(x, y. . .)$', this would not yet show that we could not find one among the infinity of cases that we have not checked. The general undecidability of

---

11. Concerning these two possibilities, cf. Carnaps's two essays, "Über Protokollsätze" and "Testability and Meaning."
12. Popper, *The Logic of Scientific Discovery*; see in particular p. 70.

such sentences is important because the sentences of rationalized theories are precisely of this kind.

Let us now consider sentences of the form mentioned above, to wit, '(x) $A(x, \ldots)$' and '$(Ex) A(x, \ldots)$'. In Popper's view, the first sentence, though not verifiable, may well be falsifiable and in that sense '*one-sidedly decidable*'.[14] On the other hand, the second sentence is 'one-sidedly decidable' in that it may be verifiable, though not falsifiable. That is, if the former is false, it is logically possible to show that it is false; if the latter is true, it is logically possible to show that it is true.

Consider, then, a general factual sentence expressing some law of nature. If such a sentence is true, then, of course, it cannot be falsified; insofar as it is general, it cannot be verified. If we require that every factual sentence should be completely and not only 'one-sidedly' decidable, viz. that we in fact show it to be true or false, then a sentence of this kind is not a factual sentence. Some philosophers have in fact suggested such a concession. We may consider it evident, however, that this would be a desperate rescue attempt. The result shows that the original requirement is too extreme.

In fact, however, even this concession is not sufficient to save the situation. Closer inspection shows—and this point is commonly recognized among logical empiricists—that even a *singular f*-sentence is not verifiable in the strict sense of the word.[15] This means at the same time that a general sentence is not even falsifiable in the strict sense, for the falsification of the sentence '$(x) A(x)$' is carried out by verifying some instance '$\sim A(c)$'.

In what follows, we shall take special notice of some points raised by Hempel, another young advocate of logical empiricism.[16] Consider some sentence that reports experience. Following our assumption, this will be an *f*-sentence, say, "this piece is of chalk." A sentence of this kind in fact implies an unlimited number of facts, for example, "If this piece is of chalk, the microscope must disclose a certain structure in it, and not just a microscope in some one particular situation, but any microscope in any situation." Similarly, if this piece is of chalk, it must leave a white trail on any black board. It is clear that such sentences, which make assertions about an unlimited number of cases, cannot be verified.

13. H. Reichenbach, *Wahrscheinlichkeitslehre* (A.W. Sijthoff's Uitgeversmaatschappij N. V., 1935), §66. (English translation as H. Reichenbach, *Theory of Probability*. English translation by E.H. Hutten and M. Reichenbach. Second edition [Berkeley and Los Angeles: University of California Press. 1949].) Popper, *The Logic of Discovery*, 190.
14. Popper, *The Logic of Discovery*, 191.
15. See, for example, C. Hempel, *Beiträge zur logischen Analyse des Wahrscheinlichkeitsbegriffs* (Berlin: Friedrich-Wilhelms-Universität zu Berlin, 1934), 49; A.J. Ayer, *Language, Truth and Logic* (London: Victor Gollancz, 1936), 25.
16. See previous footnote as well as Hempel, "Über den Gehalt der Wahrscheinlichkeitsaussagen," *Erkenntnis* 5 (1935): 228-60. (English translation as "On the Content of Probability Statements," in Hempel, *Selected Philosophical Essays*.)

On the other hand, negative instances do not, in the strict sense, falsify them, either. Let us consider again our sentence "this piece is of chalk." When we test it for correctness, we may do so, for instance, by drawing on a black board. Let us imagine that the expected trail fails to appear on the black broad. The fault may of course be with the black board and not with the object that we used. Hence, a negative instance will not definitively falsify our statement. This is *always* the case in principle. When we test some *f*-sentence for its correctness, we always do so by observing whether such cases do occur that should occur, if the sentence is true. But this testing always takes place under certain determinate conditions and involves a number of assumptions. If the result is negative, this may be because the circumstances are not what we think they are.

The following, more general remark may be worthwhile here. From its very inception, the Galilean conception of knowledge involved the idea that general theories about reality cannot be proved to be correct; at most, they may receive repeated empirical confirmation under favorable circumstances. On the other hand, people used to think that the refutation of a general theory–by finding negative instances–would be possible in the strict sense. 'Experimentum crucis'–crucial experiment–was the term that people often used to refer to such singular instances that the took to be decisive. Strictly speaking, however, there are no such experiments. Suppose, for instance, that we have derived from some physical theory an empirical consequence and then come to see that experience does not correspond to the theory; in such a case we have always made a number of assumptions falling outside the sphere of the theory itself and concerning, say, the construction of the instruments we use in the experiment or the reliability of the observer himself. A negative test result can always be put down to such factors. We should note in particular that insofar as we can speak of experience refuting a theory, what gets refuted is the entire theory, and not just some particular statement belonging to it. Consider, for instance, Galileo's kinematics that involves three main assumptions. It follows from them that the path of a thrown stone is a parabola. If this were not the case, this would not yet show that one of the assumptions must be wrong, not to mention that in testing the theory one always makes a number of additional assumptions about, say, so-called disturbances. Even at the beginning of the century, Pierre Duhem, one of the earliest advocates of logical empiricism, showed convincingly that, strictly speaking, there can be no 'experimentum crucis'.[17]

Thus we come to the conclusion: Assuming our experiential sentences are *f*-sentences, *not even the requirement of 'one-sided decidability', verification or falsification, can be imposed upon factual sentences.* What we can require is testability.

So-Called Immediate Experience

Before considering the reasons underlying this requirement, however, we must look into the second of the two possibilities we mentioned above, viz. that experiential sentences are φ-sentences. Here we must address what is known as the 'problem of immediate experience'.

Before logical empiricism entered its present stage, it was commonly assumed among empiricists that 'immediate experience' would deliver absolute empirical truths whose validity could not, even in theory, be subjected to any kind of doubt. And it was precisely this feature that was used to define immediate experience. The idea was that insofar as one confined oneself to describing given phenomena, one could not err even in theory. Hence, at least in the case of singular observation sentences reporting experiences at a given moment, one could speak of incorrigible empirical truth. This view, however, is mistaken. Let us first take a concrete example, after which we may consider the issue from a more general perspective. Imagine a person smelling a scent, say, that of some perfume, and saying it is lilac. When, on some later occasion, he smells a lilac in blossom, he realizes he was mistaken and withdraws his earlier statement. This is possible because, as we have pointed out, even the most primitive φ-predicates are *general*, designating unlimited classes. A statement to the effect that such and such a φ-predicate applies to some x means that this x belongs in certain respect to the same class as certain y, z, . . . belonging to our past and future experience. To the extent that talk of immediate experience is at all legitimate, it must be confined to the present. But if all we do is give a name to something occurring now, this does not yet constitute knowledge because knowledge must contain some invariance; at the very least, it must contain the assertion that the x to which we have given a name belongs to some class whose members occupy different places in the stream of time. This statement, however, extends beyond the limit of present experience, and hence the possibility of error will always be there.[18]

Thus we arrive at the following principled conclusion: There is no empirical statement, not even a φ-sentence of the most primitive kind, which is not, in 'theory', subject to revision. Even when our experiential sentences are φ-sentences, we cannot impose the requirement of strict verifiability (or falsifiability) upon factual sentences; what applies is at most testability. We must now find reasons for this requirement.

17. Duhem, *La théorie physique son objet et sa structure*, second edition (Paris: Chevalier et Rivière, 1914), 285. (English translation as *The Aim and Structure of Physical Theory*, trans. P.B. Wiener [Princeton University Press, 1954], 188–90.)
18. See, for instance, C.I. Lewis, *Mind and the World Order* (New York: Charles Scribner's Sons. 1929), ch. V; Ayer, *Language, Truth and Logic*, 126.

Epistemological Conventionalism and Its Limitation

Given our previous results, one's first impression might well be that no such motivation for testability can possibly be found. After all, what are the real implications of our results? No factual sentence can be shown to be true (or false) in the strict sense. One might then conclude that the epistemological position known as 'conventionalism' is valid without restrictions. It holds that from a logical point of view, it is a *purely conventional decision which sentences are to be taken as true and which as false*. We can pick up any set of mutually consistent sentences and from them we can construct a theory that is successful in practice, using methods (in particular certain inductive procedures) that are themselves conventional in nature. This would be the only legitimate sense of 'truth'. This kind of view is also known as the 'coherence theory of knowledge'. We should mention that in Anglo-American 'pragmatism' such a view has been developed in its radical form. But it has found support even from some extremists among the logical empiricists.[19] What are we to think about such a view?

'Theory of knowledge' is first and foremost concerned with the construction of a logical structure which *describes formally*, and within limits such a description is at all possible, the *justification relations found within the sphere of our factual knowledge*.[20] Insofar as it turns out to be necessary to introduce some conventions here, this must be done in a way that agrees with the nature of human knowledge. We should, therefore, consider how the truth and falsity of sentences are conceived in empirical science and in our practical everyday knowledge.

Normally, and in the case of more general assertions, we judge their truth and falsity by their less general consequences and, ultimately, by the singular empirical sentences that follow from them. Considered from a purely logical point of view, though, an opposite procedure would be equally possible. And, we may add, this possibility is not always purely 'theoretical'. Let us consider a few examples from physics. We have seen that physical geometry can be given what we have called an 'analytic' interpretation, whereby one very general part of physics is promoted to the status of an analytic system that is independent of experience. In certain cases this procedure may be the appropriate one. For example, it is conceivable that the two main theses of the theory of heat, viz. the law of conservation of energy and the principle that a *perpetuum mobile* is

19. In particular, O. Neurath; see, e.g., his "Protokollsätze," *Erkenntnis* 3 (1932/33), 204-14. (English translation as "Protocol statements" in O. Neurath, *Philosophical Papers 1913–46*, ed. R.S. Cohen and M. Reichenbach [Dordrecht: Reidel], 91-99.)
20. Carnap, *Der logische Aufbau der Welt*, §54.

an impossibility, are given analytic interpretations; that is, we could lay down, once and for all, that no empirical fact shall undermine them, if we thought that the occurrence of such undermining facts was sufficiently improbable. Such a view has had its proponents. If, however, we found reasons to think that there exists after all a *perpetuum mobile*, we would consider it more appropriate to adopt what is always at least a logically possible hypothesis, namely, that the device exploited some unknown sources of energy. And yet, in fact, it is only in special cases that this kind of procedure, whereby very general theories are promoted to analytic and *a priori* systems, is at all appropriate. As a rule, we adopt a different strategy. The law of conservation of energy and the principle that a *perpetuum mobile* is an impossibility, for example, are construed as empirical laws, confirmed by all known, less general facts and, ultimately, by an indefinite number of singular empirical sentences. In this kind of case it may happen that even the most general of our theories become undermined by empirical sentences—if they are negative instances—that are concerned with very special circumstances but strike us as reliable. For example, Michelson's famous experiment, apparently showing that the speed of light was independent of the state of motion of the frame of reference, forced reconsideration in then prevalent conceptions of physical time and space.

The more general a statement is—that is, the greater its factual content—the more it asserts and the greater is the risk of error. It is therefore natural to regard less general statements as the 'criteria of truth' for the more general ones, to use this old phrase. We see, moreover, that even a simple f-sentence is in fact very rich in its factual content. If we compare it with a φ-sentence which is of the same logical type and degree, we see that the φ-sentence asserts a good deal less. A sentence like "this piece is of chalk" asserts much more than the sentence "this visual object is white." Hence, the 'risk of error' is much greater with the first sentence than it is with the second; we can see in fact that we frequently withdraw f-sentences we have asserted, that is, we frequently admit we have made a mistake. On the other hand, we only rarely withdraw a φ-sentence. The striped top of a washstand looks like it is made of marble; when we touch it, however, we realize it is wooden. A statement like "this is marble" is of the kind which we quite often have to withdraw, whereas those occasions where we renounce a statement like "this visual object is striped" are much rarer.

We must lay down a fundamental convention that will allow us to begin to consider epistemological problems—in particular the motivation of the principle of testability. We wish to lay down this convention in such a way that it agrees with the policy that we in fact apply when, under normal circumstances, we judge the validity of a factual statement. The convention is that *we regard as true some singular empirical statements* which may be either φ-statements or f-statements. In practice, this convention is so evident is immune to genuine doubt.

Using a formulation that is somewhat inexact but illuminating, we may ask, *Where do we find those things that our factual statements are about?* By no means do they exist in our thought. Thought is nothing but a representation of things, and it need not contain anything that is even remotely like these things. Insofar as there is any contact between us and things themselves, as opposed to the mere symbols occurring in our thought and talk, these things are to be found in our experience. Singular empirical statements representing our experiences are 'closer to things themselves' than general statements which are justified by distant empirical statements through labyrinthine logical relationships. Hence, only one sort of convention is possible in practice, namely, that singular statements decide the validity of general statements.

Hence we impose a rule on our quest for factual knowledge, a rule that we wish to follow consistently. Except where experience itself dictates that an alternative course of action is appropriate, we lay down that the *truth (and falsity) of our factual knowledge is to be decided by experiential statements only.*[21] If someone refuses to agree with us on this point, there is nothing more we can say to him, except that he himself in fact follows this rule, whether he is concerned with everyday or with scientific thinking.

Let us now imagine a subject, S, who has formulated to himself a scientific conception of the world. He is in possession of great many empirical statements; let them be φ-statements. Our convention now comes down to this: insofar as S's conception of the world is justified, this justification is to be found in his φ-statements. We may as well remark here that the majority of these statements are concerned with heard and seen word-tokens, namely, representations of other people's experiences.

A few matters of principle deserve a special mention. We saw above that even φ-statements are sometimes withdrawn; that is, that S sometimes admits he was mistaken even with respect to these statements. It is impossible to formulate an absolute rule helping us to reach a general decision here. All we can say is that such circumstances are quite rare and that *at every moment we regard a great many singular φ-statements as true.* For if this were not the case, there would be no testability. For instance, having left a room, I ask myself whether I closed the window. I return to the room, seeing that the window is closed. Thus, when I test whether something is as I remember it, the testing can only take place on the condition that my memory is reliable in certain other respects. The statement: "I closed the window of the room" can only be tested if I am correct in remembering that I was in the room a moment ago, and that there was an open window in the room, etc. When it happens, occasionally, that some singular empirical statement is withdrawn, this takes place on the condition that certain other statements reporting memories, even the great majority of such statements, remain valid.

---

21. Popper, *Logic of Scientific Discovery,* 108; Carnap, "Testability and Meaning."

Testability also presupposes past and future. S can speak of 'testing a statement' only if there are φ-statements available to him for testing in the future. This is important because it is doubtful whether there is anything past that we can 'point to'; it is doubtful, that is, whether the concept 'past' can be given a definition at all. And it is even more doubtful whether there is anything future that we can 'point to' (at the present moment, that is), and hence whether the concept 'future' can be given a definition. We must presuppose that we know them, for *otherwise we could not talk about testability in the first place.* For example, we could not ask whether there is something past or something future in the first place; we cannot ask such questions, that is, if there is to be testability at all.

We see, then, that we can address ourselves to epistemological problems only if we agree to a number of conventional stipulations, the validity of which is not open to discussion; unless we agree to these conventions, we must give up on our enterprise.

Justification of the Principle of Testability

We can now consider the question of how to justify the principle of testability (on the assumption that the conventions laid down above are valid). How can we show, given the above assumptions, that every factual statement must have determinate consequences with respect to experience?

This question may be answered in different ways depending on how the relevant factual statement has been formulated. Here we presuppose that the statement is not experiential. The first case we must consider is one in which the concepts contained in the statement have been formed by explicit definitions from primitive predicates occurring in experiential statements. In the case of explicit definitions, we can carry out a general elimination of defined expressions; or, as is the case with use-definitions, we can at least eliminate a statement in which a certain expression occurs, replacing it with another statement in which the expression does not occur.

We must emphasize that it is by no means self-evident that all empirical predicates have been formed in this simple way from the primitive predicates occurring in experiential statements. Nevertheless, we shall accept this simplifying assumption in order to consider the logical situation. It is then clear that if—as we assumed—experiential statements are φ-statements, every factual statement can be translated into an equivalent statement in a φ-language, either word-by-word, or at least statement-by-statement. In the simplest cases, all we have to do is replace the relevant expressions by the defining expressions, a procedure that eventually yields a φ-statement that is equivalent with the original statement and in which there occurs nothing but φ-predicates and logical constants. Having carried out a finite number of substitutions licensed by definitions, we must eventually come to a φ-statement of this kind; for we assumed that these substitutions were based on explicit definitions starting from φ-predicates, and the number of such substitutions that we have carried out is always finite. Let our statement be: "If this piece is of chalk, it leaves a white trail on a blackboard." Here we have a general implication. If the corresponding φ-statement, too, is a general implication, all its elements will be perceptual predicates. A rough and ready translation might be along the following lines: "If this perceptual object looks white and feels light and powdery, then there occurs, under certain conditions, a white trail on a certain black surface, which is of such and such kind."

This is an elementary case of the sort that logical empiricism was almost exclusively concerned with in its early, neopositivist phase. Here the principle of testability follows simply from the assumption that every factual statement is translatable into the language of experience. Once the translation is complete, the resulting statement makes an assertion about experience itself, for example, that if such and such perceptions occur, such and such other perceptions occur as well. Such a statement can of course be compared with experiential sentences which confirm or undermine it. But we must note that this translatability does not mean the same as verifiability or falsifiability. The φ-sentence resulting from a translation may of course be a general sentence (for instance a general implication), and such sentences can never be verified by singular experiential sentences; they can only be confirmed under favorable circumstances, or, if the instances are negative, they can be conditionally falsified.

Translatability of Factual Sentences into the Language of Experience

We have already mentioned the assumption that all predicates occurring in factual sentences, unless they are primitive predicates occurring in perceptual sentences, are formed by explicit definitions from such predicates. This assumption is far from self-evident. When on an earlier occasion we discussed definitions, we mentioned so-called recursive definitions. From a logical point of view, they are quite important particularly in the following respect: they allow the elimination of a given expression only under special circumstances, and not generally. Let us suppose that such definitions—to repeat, they are not explicit definitions—could also be found within our knowledge of reality, in definitions of empirical predicates. What would follow from this? In such cases there would be no general elimination of defined expressions. This would also mean that no translation into the language of experience—be it φ-language or f-language—would be possible, as this presupposes the said elimination. And since we saw in the simplest case above how testability was a consequence of translatability, we must now find a new justification for the principle of testability, assuming that such recursive definitions occur.

In fact, some advocates of contemporary logical empiricism–most notably Carnap–have indeed argued that there can be no general translatability of a factual sentence into the language of experience; in particular because explicit definitions are not the only kind of definition that we make use of in our knowledge of reality. Carnap has given arguments against the possibility of translatability. The first is as follows.[22]

Let us imagine a person, S_1, making an assertion to the effect that some physical sentence, '$P(t_n)$', is true; for instance, "at moment t_n, there is a table in my room." If we now try and translate this sentence into a φ-language, it seems that an implication, roughly along the following lines, will result: "If at moment t_n such and such perceptions occur (namely perceptions of my room), such and such other perceptions (perception of my table) also occur at t_n." We use '$V_1, V_2, \ldots$' to indicate the relevant visual perceptions, '$T_1, T_2, \ldots$' to indicate the relevant tactual perceptions and '$A_1, A_2, \ldots$' to indicate the relevant auditory perceptions. The translation would then be a certain conjunction of implications in a φ-language:

$$V_1(t_n) \to V_2(t_n), V_3(t_n) \to V_4(t_n), \ldots$$

$$T_1(t_n) \to T_2(t_n), ---$$

$$A_1(t_n) \to A_2(t_n), ---.$$

Here the question arises, to begin with, whether the number of these implications is finite.[23] For if it is not, they do not constitute a conjunction, and there can be no translation. To this we can only say that there are only a finite number of such implications, for we can never have more than a finite number of distinguishable singular visual, tactual, and other perceptions.

More problematic is the following issue. Suppose that at the relevant moment there is no table in my room and no perceiver, either. Sentence '$P(t_n)$' is now false. But then each of the above implications would be true, and hence their conjunction would be true as well. For if there occur no perceptions V_1, $V_2, \ldots, T_1, \ldots, A_1, \ldots$, each of the implications will be true, for an implication is true as soon as its antecedent is false. Our φ-translation would then be true, even though the original sentence that our φ-sentence was supposed to translate was false. Since a sentence and its translation must be equivalent, translation is not possible in this kind of case.

We can reply, however, that the translation here is mistaken on account the following fact. Every singular perception may be a 'hallucination', and even a conjunction of perceptions by different senses may be no more than a

22. Carnap, "Testability and Meaning."
23. Carnap, "Testability and Meaning," 464.

'hallucination', in which case a psychologist would speak of a 'systematic hallucination'. Now, what distinguishes such hallucinations from veridical perceptions? Leibniz has already answered this question. The difference between the two consists in the fact that veridical perceptions are law-like and, as such, can be used for predictions. We call a perceptual phenomenon a 'hallucination' when we are disappointed in the expectations to which it gives rise under customary conditions; and we call it 'veridical' when it turns out to be a reliable sign of other phenomena. What we call 'hallucination' and what we call 'veridical' may be phenomenally indistinguishable, like a fragment of a dream that may be quite indistinguishable from a state of wakefulness.

This must be taken into account when we translate into the language of experience a sentence like the '$P(t_n)$' that we considered above. The correct translation must be more than just a conjunction of singular implications as suggested above, for we get such a translation as soon as, and even if, all the relevant singular perceptions are hallucinatory. But our statement, '$P(t_n)$', was supposed to be about a real physical object. This is something that the translation must make evident, and it can do this by using a *general* implication in the translation. This can be made clear by assuming that the room was empty at moment t_n, that is, that none of the singular phenomena $V_1, V_2, \ldots, T_1, \ldots$ occurred at t_n. What reasons might S_1 then have for asserting the sentence? The reason might be that S_1 has seen the room and the object O at some earlier moment; or he may have seen someone carrying the object into the room but has not seen it being carried out; or he may have heard that someone else, S_2, has seen it, and so on. From all this he draws the conclusion–using the law of nature that objects are relatively permanent–that the object O was in the room at t_n, as well. Accordingly, if S_1 had at t_n perceptions $V_1, V_2, \ldots, T_1, \ldots$ and if he asserts on the basis of the perceptions that at t_n the object O was in the room, he asserts much more than those singular implications we mentioned above. For he asserts that there is a period of time such that these phenomena occur at each moment, t_i, of that period, whether or not any of the phenomena $V_1, V_2, \ldots,$ $T_1, \ldots$ occur at that moment; that is, he asserts certain general implications. In this case, the correct translation must be a conjunction of certain general implications of the form $(t) [V_1 (t) \rightarrow V_2 (t)]$; otherwise, as we said, we cannot exclude the possibility that the relevant phenomena might be hallucinations.

But here we remind ourselves of a point we made in our discussion of general implications, namely, that the formal representation of a general empirical sentence–for example, of a sentence expressing a law of nature–is an existential implication in which the antecedent is not empty. Applied to the present case, where S_1 asserts that there was an object O in the room at each moment in the period t, including moments when there occurred no perceptions, he asserts this on the basis of the law of nature that physical objects are relatively permanent, or some other such law. In logistic terms, this assertion must be an *existential* implication. In the simplest case, at some moment t, S_1 has had such perceptions, and now he generalizes a singular implication into a general one, an existential implication. Thus we have, for instance, '(Et) V_1 & (t) $[V_1(t) \rightarrow V_2(t)]$'. In a less simple case, when, for instance, S_1 has not had any perceptions of the room and objects in it and still makes an assertion '$P(t_n)$', this happens by deriving this assertion from some perceptions and other assertions, in which case the latter must, again, eventually be general implications. Let us take another example. When we assert that in all probability there must be on the other side of the Moon—on the side that is away from the Earth—mountains similar to those that are on the side facing the Earth, we derive this conclusion from certain observations and certain regularities in nature, regularities which must in the end be existential implications, for we only give the name 'law of nature' to those general implications that we consider true and whose antecedents are not empty. Taking this into account, the counterargument we have been considering falls through.

Carnap's second argument against the principle of translatability is as follows.[24] Let us suppose we have defined a so-called dispositional concept belonging to an f-language, a concept like 'solubility' or the property of 'electrical conductivity'. In such cases we attribute a property Q to an object x on the grounds that x behaves in a particular way, R, under certain circumstances P. Let 'Q' stand for 'electrical conductor'. This property is attributed to a thing x, if, for example, x, when connected in a closed circuit (= P), causes a magnetic needle to move (= R). It seems now—the reason for this will become clear in a moment—that a property of this kind, Q, cannot be defined explicitly. It can only be given what Carnap calls a 'conditional definition' in a way that is logically analogous to the recursive definitions that we considered earlier. In the simplest case, this conditional definition would be as follows:

(1) $P(x) \rightarrow [Q(x) \leftrightarrow R(x)]$,

that is, if x is P, then x is Q if and only if x is R. This kind of conditional definition of a property 'Q' is not an explicit definition. It does not allow of a general elimination of the expression 'Q'. For this to be possible, we ought to have at our disposal a defining equation $X = YZ$, in which the left-hand side is occupied by 'Q' and the right-hand side by a defining equation. In such a case general translatability will not be possible, either. Rather, the logical situation is as follows. In every singular case where '$P(x)$ & $R(x)$' holds, '$Q(x)$' holds as well by the above definition, in which case '$Q(x)$'can be replaced by the former conjunction. This implies that the principle of testability is valid also for those cases where such conditional definitions are in use. The statement that some x is an electrical conductor has determinate consequences with respect to experience, to wit, when $P(x)$ and $R(x)$ hold as well.

24. Carnap, "Testability and Meaning," 440.

Now we must address ourselves to the following question: Is it really impossible to find explicit definitions for such dispositional concepts as, for example, 'electrical conductor'. We consider first the simplest imaginable explicit definition

(2) '$Q(x)$' = '$[P(x) \rightarrow R(x)]$'.

Suppose that x is an object for which the experiment P has not been carried out, and cannot be carried out, say, because x no longer exists. In this case the implication on the right-hand side is true because its antecedent is false and, therefore, the left-hand side is true as well, that is, x is an 'electrical conductor' by this definition–no matter what object it is, as soon as the experiment P cannot be performed upon it. To avoid this result, we must make the defining implication existential, such as this definition, in which 'x' means any object of some particular class:

(3) '$Q(x)$' = '$(Ex)\, P(x)\, \& \,(x)\, [P(x) \rightarrow R(x)]$',

that is, x has the property Q if and only if, when an experiment P has been performed upon some x, it has yielded a result R, which holds for every x. But now we meet another undesirable consequence if, for some reason or other, the experiment P could not have been carried out for any x; for example, x might be some substance which spectroscopic measurement shows to occur in some other celestial body. In that case '$\sim(Ex)\, P(x)$' holds and the defining conjunction is false. By this definition, then, '$Q(x)$' is false as well. According to definition (3), then, any object x upon which we cannot perform the experiment P will be a 'non-electrical-conductor', unlike in the first case. This is an inappropriate definition, for if we put forth such a definition, it will render all unknown objects, upon which the experiment P has not been performed, 'non-electrical-conductors'. An appropriate definition is one that leaves it for future experience to decide whether some unknown object x is an electrical conductor or not. Such an explicit definition can, indeed, be given, but then we must introduce, in addition to an existential implication, one predicate variable:

(4) $Q(x) = (ES)\{S(x)\, \& \,(Ey)[S(y)\, \& \,P(y)]\, \& \,(y)[(S(x)\, \& \,P(y)) \rightarrow R(y)]\}$,

that is, x has a property Q if and only if, when x belongs to some class S, some member, y, which has been subjected to an experiment P, which has always yielded a result R; in addition to which it is assumed that this holds for every y which belongs to the class S and upon which the experiment P has been performed.

Let us convince ourselves that our definition (4) dispenses with the above difficulties and consider how the definition applies to some particular x. If C is some predicate constant and S a predicate variable, we infer in accordance with the rules of predicate calculus: $C(a) \rightarrow (ES)\, S(a)$. If we now have, as per our definition, '(ES) $S(a)$' = $Q(a)$', we get, by chain-inference, $C(a) \rightarrow Q(a)$. Let C, then, be a class of objects, say the class of all metals, some members of which have been subjected to the experiment P, which has always yielded the result R. We then infer in accordance with our definition (4): every a, whether or not the experiment P has been performed upon it, has the property Q, if only a belongs to some class C, of which the above holds. In this way we avoid the first difficulty. If, on the other hand, we do not know whether a belongs to any such class C, then we do not know whether '(ES) $S(a)$' is true or false, and we cannot draw the chain-inference as above. In this case we cannot at all use our definition (4). For this to be possible, a necessary and sufficient condition is that we know some class C to which a belongs and which fulfills the condition mentioned by the right-hand side of the definition. In this way we avoid the second difficulty. Definition (4) leaves for future experience to decide whether or not some object x when no object of its kind has been subjected the experiment P has the property Q.

Of course, we must note that when we use definition (4) to assert that some x is, say, an electrical conductor, our assertion is 'probable' only to the extent that the general implication occurring in the defining expression is 'probable'.

Thus we arrive at the following general result. Our question was whether the third, controversial main thesis of logical empiricism, namely the thesis of translatability, is correct. We have shown that the criticisms considered above are incorrect; it has not been shown that we would have to use, in our knowledge of reality and in the empirical definitions of concepts, definitions other than explicit definitions which would permit the general elimination of defined concepts. And as long as we use definitions of this kind, at least sentence-by-sentence translations will be available.

On the other hand, although we have shown that these criticisms fail, we have not, of course, thereby shown the thesis of translatability is correct. After all, we have not shown that we can make do with explicit definitions in our knowledge of reality. The possibility remains, then, that we cannot. Whether or not this is so is an unsettled issue at the current stage of development in theory of knowledge. To that extent the principle of translatability remains an open issue. Here we must emphasize in particular that the thesis of testability is independent of it.

Testability of Rationalized Systems

We recall now the assumptions on which we have based our previous investigations. First, there was a convention concerning the basics of epistemology, according to which some experiential basic sentences are accepted as true; these will then be able to decide the truth and falsity of all factual sentences, insofar as we can speak of decidability here. Second, we assumed that empirical concepts, excepting the primitive predicates of observation sentences, have been formed from them by explicit definitions. Given these assumptions, it will be possible to translate, either word-by-word or at least sentence-by-sentence, all factual sentences into the language of experience; and hence the idea of testability. Furthermore, we have seen that insofar as we make use of other than explicit definitions—although this has not yet been shown to be necessary—we no longer have general translatability, but testability will remain in force, because defined expressions can still be replaced by experiential predicates at least in singular instances.

We have in fact been working with one further presupposition, a tacit one that we must now make explicit. We have presupposed that general factual sentences are formed *by generalization from experience*, that is, by so-called induction. This implies that the operation we have called *rationalization*, which is essential in all human knowledge, has been ignored in our discussion of the principle of testability.

As we have pointed out earlier, rationalization takes place in prescientific thought, as well. After all, it is grounded in a law that governs all acts of human understanding. As we naturally understand them, spatial and temporal quantities in particular are continuous. As soon as it was born, Galilean science made decisive use of this rationalization, for example, when it assumed that the acceleration of a falling body is a continuous quantity. Through rationalization a regularity that experience has shown to be valid only within certain limits and sometimes with glaring exceptions becomes valid without restrictions and exceptions. Thus rationalization adds to the *regularity* of experience and not only generalizes it, as induction does. We must therefore address the remarkable problems that are involved in the testability of rationalized systems. We shall start with a special case to which epistemologists have probably devoted most of their attention.

The mathematical notion of probability is a typical result of rationalization. Suppose we are given a class of empirical cases—for example, dice throws or childbirths—where the relative frequency of some subclass—say the subclass of sixes or stillborn babies—fluctuates around a given value in such a way that its mean deviation from this value decreases as the number of cases increases; we then imagine the number of cases to increase to infinity and the mean deviation to continue to decrease. In this case the relative frequency of cases belonging to the relevant subclass converges towards a certain limit, p, which we call their mathematical probability. In this way we replace a constantly fluctuating empirical frequency with a constant number—for example, in the cases of sixes, with the number $1/6$.

The logical form of the sentence defining the relevant limit is $(x)\,(Ey)\,A(x, y, \ldots)$, which cannot be verified any more than it can be falsified.[25] For we say

25. Reichenbach, *Theory of Probability*, 342 (351 in the German original); Popper, *Logic of Scientific Discovery*, 192. G.H. von Wright, "Der Wahrscheinlichkeitsbegriff in der modernen

that the relevant limit exists when and only when, given a number δ which may be as small as we please, the fluctuation in the relative frequency remains within the interval $p \pm \delta$ as long as the number of cases, n, grows sufficiently large. Thus we say, for instance, that the relative frequency of sixes converges towards the limit 1/6 when and only when, no matter how small the deviation, δ, is from this value, there is some number of throws, n, after which the deviation will no longer exceed the said limit.

Let us now consider possibilities for testing the empirical validity of such sentences. When it is said that the probability of a six is 1/6, this means, again, that if only the number of throws becomes sufficiently large, the deviation in the relative frequency of sixes from the value 1/6 will become permanently smaller than any number, however small, we have decided upon in advance. Given any empirical series of throws, no matter how large their number is, that number will always remain a vanishingly small fragment, a mere initial segment of an imagined infinite series of throws. The first n throws may give us nothing but sixes, or not a single six, and yet the limit may be 1/6, for no matter how large n may be, it is vanishingly small in comparison to the number of all the imagined, infinitely many cases.

But this seems to show that the assertion "the relative frequency of sixes in an infinite series of throws is 1/6," that is, "the probability of a six is 1/6" is without empirical content. It seems to lack consequences with respect to experience. Not to say anything about verification or falsification, what facts of experience could we cite even to provide support for the statement or to undermine it? If we continue the series and always get a six, say, the limit of the relative frequency of sixes may still be 1/6.

One way to resolve this difficulty was first suggested by the probability-theoretician von Mises;[26] it has been further developed by Hempel.[27] This solution has won quite general acceptance among logical empiricists, although we should mention that a different solution has its advocates, too; among them Reichenbach is the most notable.

We may start by asking, How do we in fact judge the mathematical probability of empirical events? Imagine, again, a series of throws with a dice; if the dice turns up a six with a relative frequency that deviates significantly from 1/6, we shall soon become convinced that the dice is 'not fair' or that someone is using some gimmick to bring about the deviation. We then *renounce* the assumption that the probability is 1/6; that is, we give up the assumption that if we were to continue the series of throws, the relative frequency of sixes would converge towards this value. Instead, we adopt some other assumption, say, that the probability of a six is ¼. And this we do in spite of the fact that from

Erkenntnisphilosophie," *Theoria* 4 (1938): 3-20.
26. R. v. Mises, "Diskussion über Wahrscheinlichkeit," *Erkenntnis* 1 (1930): 279; R. v. Mises, *Wahrscheinlichkeit, Statistik und Wahrheit*, Second edition (Wien: Julius Springer, 1936).
27. C. Hempel, "Über den Gehalt von Wahrscheinlichkeitsaussagen," *Erkenntnis* 5 (1935): 228-60.

a logico-mathematical point of view our assumption is not only unproven but is, in fact, entirely without ground. To repeat, if among the first n throws the relative frequency of a six is 1/6, this proves absolutely nothing about what this relatively frequency will be as the number of throws increases without a limit. But what is shown by this policy that we in fact adopt? What is shown by the fact that we are willing to conclude, on the basis of a rather limited number of cases, that a given probability statement is, though not conclusively proved or refuted, nevertheless sufficiently warranted or disconfirmed? It shows that the mathematical concept of probability, when we apply it to our experience, is nothing but a shortening, simplifying, and idealizing, that is, a *rationalizing way of talking about these facts of experience.* Empirically, we never deal with more than finite sets like dice throws or childbirths. They exhibit certain relative frequencies, whose mean deviation from some determinate value decreases when the number of cases increases. Empirical relative frequencies, however, are values that fluctuate within certain limits. We pick up this indeterminate value and 'round it off' so as to get a determinate constant value that is easy to operate with when we have to decide questions about relative frequencies. If continued experience does not conform to our expectations, we are willing to reconsider this 'rounding off' so as to make it conform better to our experience. This shows that when the mathematical concept of probability is applied to experience, the factual content of the probability statement is nothing but the perceived empirical frequency, though we express this in a rationalized manner.

That this is the correct solution to our present problem is confirmed by the fact that other cases of rationalization–and these are frequent in our everyday thought but particularly abundant in science–can be given analogous interpretations. For instance, we have measured an object and we assert that it possesses a certain determinate length. And yet, if we repeat the measurement, trying to operate with precise values, our results will always exhibit some fluctuation. A fully determinate measured length is an expedient convention, that is, a fiction created through rationalization. Galileo experimented with acceleration, making use of an inclined plane, and concluded that there was no significant difference in the increments of speed per consecutive units of time. And yet such small fluctuations could be detected. We resort to rationalization, however, as we blame this fluctuation on some external 'interference', and talk of perfectly uniform acceleration. In principle, there is no difference between these two cases, on the one hand, and those concerning judgments of probability, on the other. Such differences as there may be concern matters of detail. In judgments of probability, when the number of cases becomes larger and larger, we observe a corresponding decrease in mean deviation. In the latter two cases the deviation may be there from the beginning and remain always within certain rather narrow limits. In the probability case experience speaks less clearly for the hypothesis or against it, supporting or undermining it, than in the latter cases, where hypotheses about the so-called real value are usually confined to a more narrow area; in the former case, by contrast, the choice may be made from a relatively wide range of hypotheses that are theoretically compatible with experience.

What deserves special emphasis here is that the kind of rationalization we have been illustrating with examples taken from scientific knowledge is quite common already in our pre-scientific thought. Even school children understand statements such as that between any two points there is always a third and, therefore, infinitely many points, that space is infinite, etc.–in spite of the fact that such statements do not precisely correspond to anything in experience. Anything actually infinite is a product of the rationalizing human mind which simplifies what are often quite rough, superficial, and very approximate regularities into precise laws that admit no exceptions. Our natural conception of space and time is thoroughly permeated by rationalization, that is, by that operation of the intellect which simplifies, unifies, and adds immensely to the invariances of perception.

It follows that an assumption we made above is valid only with severe limitations; the assumption, namely, that statements with factual content are always a result of mere generalization from experience, viz. are formed by induction. Hence, also, we must find new justifications for the principles of testability and translatability, taking into account the role that rationalization plays in theory formation.

With rationalized theories, the relationship to experience is a good deal more complex than it is with inductive theories that are formulated using nothing but generalizations from experience. True, rationalized theories are supported or undermined by experience no less than inductive theories, but this takes place in a way that is less clear-cut. If we take ourselves to have observed a certain negative case, we may conclude that a certain general, inductive sentence has thereby been refuted. If, on the other hand, experience fails to correspond to a rationalized theory, this does not yet refute the theory even under the most favorable conditions. For the theory is not a generalized description of experience as such but instead provides an idealized model of it. If experience deviates radically from the assumed model, we have good reason to replace it with another that better agrees with experience; but we cannot say that such a circumstance has shown the earlier theory to be false.

A further consequence is that there can be no general, formal rules for deciding when the deviation of a rationalizing theory from experience is sufficiently strong for us to be justified in giving up on it and replacing it with another one. Nor, when a theory complies well with experience, can such rules indicate when we can regard it as confirmed by experience and conclude that the assumption continues to be valid.[28] Logically, the resolution of these issues one way or another is a more conventional matter than is the case of inductive

28. Hempel, "Wahrscheinlichkeitsaussagen," 253.

generalization. Psychologically, resolving these issues will depend upon those rather obscure factors such as a scientist's 'sense of reality' or his 'scientific intuition'.

The implication for the theses of testability and translatability is that these continue to remain in force, but not in the relatively simple form they assume for inductive theories. When a rationalized theory is tested by experience, we think that certain experiences corroborate it while others undermine it. But *testability does not apply separately to each sentence of a rationalized theory*. It is *only as a whole* that an idealized theory represents some region of experience; its sentences do not have that relatively transparent relation to experience that we find in inductive theories. We cannot therefore require of such a theory that each of its sentences have some determinate consequences with respect to experience, but only that the whole theory stands to experience in such a relation that experience can corroborate or undermine it. We must, then, give the principle of testability a broad interpretation, so that a theory in its entirety can be regarded as 'one sentence'.

Earlier we justified testability through translatability. To the extent that translatability cannot be applied to rationalized theories in the same way as to inductive theories, but only in less stringent sense, testability, too, can only be required in this broader sense. Suppose, for example, we observe that the increment of speed for a falling body added in each observable, consecutive units of time is approximately the same. Through rationalization, we arrive at the concept of uniform acceleration, one which we apply, as is said, 'beyond the threshold of perception'; that is, we think that no matter how small some real number x is, there are equal intervals of time, whose measure is x, and that for a body falling in a vacuum the increment of speed added during each such interval is equal. Or, we observe a body swaying a few times in a second and hear a particular sound. Given our rationalized conception of space, we can think that a body may undergo small, invisible vibrations, for instance a thousand times in a second, and we establish a causal connection between the note we hear and the vibration we have conceived. Or we observe interference of water waves, and when we observe 'interference of light', we think that the latter is a similar phenomenon in which the wavelength of light ray may be, say, one thousandth of a millimeter. This was the line of thought that was followed by the founders of optics, Huygens and Newton, and this is the course that physics has continued to follow, in spite of the protests from philosophers of a radically empiricist bent. Berkeley, for instance, polemicized against Newton precisely on this issue, arguing that such theories are meaningless, because in perception 'there is no such thing as the ten thousandth part of an inch'.

When we try to translate such *micro-physical* sentences into the language of experience, we encounter a logical problem, one that does not concern *macro-physical* sentences. Earlier, when we considered the translation of a physical sentence, '$P(t_n)$', into a phenomenal language, we saw that even a singular f-sentence, when it is translated into φ-language, yields a general implication, indeed, an existential one. Let our sentence be "object O is vibrating." If the sentence is about some object and some motion observable in the f-sense, that is, if the sentence is macro-physical, we can express it in φ-language as a general implication concerning certain occurrences. In this case the antecedent of the implication is not empty: when we have observed this and this, there have also been such and such other observations. But suppose we are concerned with micro-physical sentences, that is, sentences like "this string vibrates, unobserved, a thousand times in a second" or "the light ray travelling through this hole has the wavelength of one thousandth of a millimeter"; now the translation into φ-language cannot be carried out in the same way as in the previous case. For the logical form of a general factual sentence is an existential implication. When, however, we assert, that a string vibrates a thousand times in a second, we do not have at our disposal observations concerning vibrating motion that we could use to translate this sentence into an existential implication in φ-language. And yet a physicist argues that his statements are based on experience. For example, he points out that if an invisibly vibrating string is tightened in front of an opening through which a beam of light passes, and if, on the other side, a telescope is set up so that a photographic plate can be moved through its ocular with a suitable speed, an enlarged picture of the vibrating motion we have conceived will emerge on the plate. An analogous situation holds, for example, for a light ray and its wavelength; a statement about it cannot as such be translated into φ-language, because there are no observations that would correspond directly to the statement. However, within the limits of optical theory we can nevertheless derive certain experiential consequences from a statement concerning interference trails or the distribution of light spots, for example. These examples show that the sentences of a rationalized theory cannot be translated separately into the language of experience. When we try to carry out such a translation, the result will be a *translation of the entire theory*. With respect to the principle of testability, a theory can be said to constitute a 'single sentence', and that is the only thing that can be tested against experience.

The Principle of Testability and Metaphysical Sentences

We addressed the question of how the principle of testability ought to be justified by considering some cases that were relatively simple and others less simple. When it comes to the formulation of the principle itself, our investigations reached the important conclusion that the term 'factual sentence' should be given a rather broad interpretation; it may mean an entire system of sentences, even an entire theory—as in the case of rationalized theories. We have argued that the principle of testability is analytic, that is, logically necessary; and also that sentences which are meant to be factual but which do not satisfy this principle are logically faulty. Moving now to general consideration, we say that the principle of testability in fact follows from the concept of factual sentence itself. The principle can be justified only after certain conventions have been laid down; but conventions are, logically speaking, definitions. What follows from definitions alone is analytic, that is, logically necessary. With the help of the conventions in question, therefore, we shall arrive at a definition of 'sentence concerning reality', that is, of the concept of factual sentence, in light of which the principle of testability is something logically necessary.

We say that a sentence is '*metaphysical*' when it is intended as a factual sentence but does not have any experiential consequences. Supposing that the conventions defining factual sentence have been fixed, metaphysical sentences must be logically faulty. This we now wish to establish by considering some typical classes of metaphysical sentences.[29]

Here we will assume the conventions that first define what a factual sentence is. Formally speaking, these conventions are a matter of stipulation; their content, however, is so evident that genuine doubt would seem to be excluded here. The first convention had to do with the concept of material or empirical truth. We say that a sentence, S, is true when and only when things are as the sentence say they are. Technical details aside, there is no doubt that this definition corresponds to the concept of empirical truth as this concept is in fact used and that, therefore, it will be accepted as soon as one sees clearly that there is a difference between material and formal truth. From this definition it follows that no factual sentence can be the '*criterion of its own truth*'. To put the point simply: the truth of a thought is instead decided only by the things that the thought represents. Rationalists say that reason itself decides the truth of a thought—that only thoughts that are clear and distinct are true; or that the truth of a sentence is established by its being psychologically apodictic (necessary). Such assertions, we say, neglect certain facts such as the difference between formal and material truth. The so-called clarity or distinctness of a sentence or its apodictic character is at best a derived or secondary criterion, whereas the original or primary criterion must be sought in the things that the thought represents. For it is about these things that a factual sentence makes an assertion, while a formal sentence remains within the realm of thought, so to speak.

When we advance a claim about 'reality', we do so with certain 'sufficient reasons', as Leibniz used to say. After all, a factual sentence is not just any fancy

---

29. Cf. here Carnap, "Überwindung der Metaphysik durch logische Analyse der Sprache," *Erkenntnis* 2 (1932): 219–41. (English translation as "The Elimination of Metaphysics through Logical Analysis of Language," trans. A. Pap in *Logical Positivism*, ed. A.J. Ayer [Glencoe, Ill.: Free Press], 60–81.)

or whim which we might care to mention and which satisfies the requirement of consistency. Where do we find these 'sufficient reasons'? That is, where do we find those things about which our factual sentences make assertions? Insofar as we find them, they are in our experience, and not in our thoughts. Thus we cannot avoid making another fundamental convention: To the extent that the truth (and falsity) of a factual sentence can be decided at all, it can only be decided by experiential sentences. It is only after these conventions have been laid down–conventions which are not only necessary but, practically speaking, immune to doubt as well–that we have a definition of a factual as opposed to a formal sentence.

Turning now to metaphysical sentences, that is, sentences which do not satisfy the requirement of testability, we see that they are, indeed, logically faulty. In the worst case these strings of words are not even sentences in the logical sense; they satisfy the requirements of grammar but not the rules of logical syntax (sentence formation). In many cases they rub against the theory of logical types; more commonly, they contain words whose meanings have not been even loosely determined. We shall briefly look at some typical cases.

The Aristotelian way of thinking, referring as it does to substances or essences, is an inexhaustible source of metaphysical sentences. As we know, it mistakenly assumes that all sentences are property-sentences, that is, that all predicates are unary predicates; this leads to the misconception that all change is an expression of the hidden essences of things. This kind of essentialism is still alive in the metaphysics of our time. Contemporary German metaphysics is largely dominated by so-called existentialism, which is preoccupied with 'essences' ('*Wesen*'). It is striking how completely this word is missing from our everyday knowledge and scientific thought, wherever these have reached even a modicum of logical precision. No tailor speaks of the essence of coat; no contemporary physicist speaks of the essence of electricity, or an economist of the essence of money. But an existentialist philosopher is preoccupied with statements like 'the essence of time is care', as says Heidegger, himself responsible for introducing this way of philosophizing. This string of words is either not a sentence in the logical sense, or if it is, it is false. If the word 'care' has its customary sense, 'care' cannot be the 'essence' of time, insofar as 'essence' means a property of some whole that is possessed by every part of that whole. Care can be the essence of time as little as pocket, say, can be the essence of coat. The metaphysician, no doubt, would reply that, as he uses it, 'care' has some deeper–some metaphysical–meaning. Yet as long as we have not been told what this meaning is or what meaning 'essence' has, this string of words remains something like a lyrical outburst. As such, it may be significant as it gives rise to some deeply felt thoughts. But such lyrical exclamations are a far cry from the 'prote philosophia' or first philosophy that Plato and Aristotle were concerned with. It is a far cry from the 'mathesis universalis' that Descartes and Leibniz were searching for. It is a far cry from the kind of research that seeks clarity in thought and which we have learned to respect as 'philosophy'.

Here a remark on the psychology of thought may be worthwhile. As long as our thought remains under some sort of control–as, for example, our everyday thought is controlled by practice and empirical scientific thought is subject above all to the requirement of testability–we tend to instinctively follow the logical presuppositions of factual thought. We require, for instance, familiarity with the meanings of the words that we hear. And we reject as sophistry strings of words that fail to comply with logical grammar, in particular, with the theory of logical types. But where this kind of control is lacking, the logical presuppositions of factual thought are often violated. According to the theory of types, only certain property- and relational predicates can be meaningfully applied to given things, that is, predicates that include these things within their value-range. No tailor would say that every coat desires "to be acknowledged"; and no physician would say that every quantity of electricity desires "to be acknowledged." But one contemporary metaphysician insists that fundamentally "Every thing demands to be acknowledged," where the word 'thing' is supposed to have so general a meaning that it can refer to coats as well as, say, numbers. As a result, this string of words is, logically speaking, not a sentence.

We earlier distinguished between the meaning-experience that a given word or string of words gives rise to and their factual meaning. This factual meaning is thus the state of things symbolized by the word or string of words, and it is the only one that matters in a logical respect, that is, with respect to validity, or truth. Metaphysics characteristically fails to draw this distinction. The reason why logical rationalism leads to metaphysics is precisely that in it certain meaning-experiences, or some psychological features thereof, have been raised to benchmarks of material truth. To illustrate this point, we consider one example from Descartes and another from Kant.

In a famous passage from his *Meditations*, Descartes asks us to consider a piece of wax.[30] It has certain visible properties, a determinate color, figure, hardness, and so on. But now it is placed near the fire; whereby all of these properties will change into something different. And yet we say it is still the same piece of wax. Does this not show, Descartes asks, that sense perception does not determine what "a thing remaining the same" really is; this is determined instead by the 'clear and distinct idea of a thing' that we apply to certain phenomena. But here we must ask: If sense perception does not decide when the question is about "a material thing remaining the same," how, then, do we know to which phenomena this idea may be applied? After all, it cannot be applied to just any. On the other hand, if experience does decide when the idea is to be applied, the factual content of the statement "x is a certain thing remaining the same" is nothing over and above the distinctive feature of a series

---

30. Descartes, *Meditations on First Philosophy*, Meditation II.

of phenomena on the basis of which the statement is applied. When we say that this particular quantity of a sticky liquid observed near the fire is the same piece of wax that was solid a moment ago, the factual content of this statement is nothing over and above the distinctive features of these phenomenal properties, connected to one another in space and time, and exhibiting a continuous transition.

While Descartes thought that the 'clarity and distinctness' of a thought are the criteria for its truth, the rationalist Kant held that these criteria lay in the psychologically apodictic character of thought. The characteristic feature of Kantian 'synthetic *a priori*' judgments was their 'necessity and strict universality'. For instance, when it comes to the principle of lawfulness or principle of causality, Kant says, Hume was right to hold that there can be no logical derivation of an effect from a given cause, and hence that the relationship between cause and effect was synthetic, rather than analytic.[31] And yet, Kant thinks, this relationship is *a priori*. Without consulting experience, he says, we cannot know the reason for a given change–say the melting of a piece of wax–but we do know independently of experience and apodictically that it must have some reason; we do know, that is, that it was preceded by some change from which it follows by some standing law. Like Descartes in his analogous situation, Kant has ignored the problem of application.[32] We do not apply the concept of a cause-effect relationship to just any series of consecutive changes, but only to those that fulfill certain empirical conditions. This being so, however, the factual content of the statement "*A* is the cause of *B*" is to be found precisely in that feature of empirical sequences that leads us to apply the concept of cause and effect to the case at hand. No matter how apodictic we find the judgment that every effect must have a cause, this postulate of our reason adds nothing to the degree of certainty that our experience attaches to a factual law of change. It makes us look for such laws, but cannot guarantee that we shall find any. If A and B stand in our experience in some cause-effect relationship, the additional assertion that A and B *also* bear some *a priori* relation to one another belongs to metaphysics because this assertion has no empirical consequences.

Such metaphysical claims, however, are not the exclusive prerogative of rationalists; they can also be found in empiricist philosophers. Their metaphysical claims are the most dangerous, so to speak, for they seem to flow from experience itself. Consider for example claims made concerning the debate–still ongoing even among the empiricist philosophers of our time–over the '*existence of external world independent of our consciousness*', or of 'transcendent' reality.[33]

---

31. See in particular Kant, *Prolegomena*, §27.
32. Reichenbach, *Theory of Probability*, 8–9.
33. Carnap, *Scheinprobleme in der Philosophie: Das Fremdpsychische und der Realismus-streit.*

To begin, the word 'real' has several meanings. In the most general sense, a subject S calls 'real' anything that is included in the temporal sequence of his experiences, hallucinations as much as veridical perceptions, dreams as much as the states of wakefulness. As Leibniz has already shown, we call something 'real' in the stricter sense, as opposed to illusion, if it is sufficiently lawful or invariant. A measured physical size and shape are 'real' as opposed to those merely observed because they vary less. From a logical point of view, 'physical reality' is a system of general implications containing certain experiential invariances. In this way we can give a satisfactory definition of the empirical concept of reality. Whether something is real or apparent, veridical or an illusion is decided by experience in this way.

But statements about reality are often accompanied with certain meaning-experiences. These lead us easily and against Leibniz's warning 'behind' phenomena, to look further, for "some reality over and above that which is contained in the invariant phenomena themselves," as he puts it.

Even in ancient Greece, philosophers fought a Platonic gigantomachia, a primordial battle–one that raged throughout the modern era and up to our day–over whether physical reality in particular exists only insofar as it is perceived, that is, whether the statement "esse est percipi" is valid or not. But what could such assertions mean, never mind whether we argue for or against them? Empirical reality can be defined–it is the invariance contained in phenomenal experience. If one asks whether such an invariance holds in perceptions only or whether it applies outside the 'sphere of perceptions' as well, that is, whether it is a description of a transcendent world behind phenomena or not, one must first explain what one means by 'outside', 'behind' and 'transcendent'. One then sees that these words have not been defined, and cannot be defined and that these questions, therefore, have no factual content whatsoever. For insofar as words possess some factual meaning, this can be traced back to experience. But we cannot by conjoining conceptual elements that are found in experience create a concept leading us 'outside', 'behind' or 'transcending' the realm of experience. Insofar as every factual sentence can be translated, at least in a broad sense, into the language of experience–and this is what gives the sentence its factual content–no statement about this so-called transcendent reality can have any factual content.

When we consider such metaphysical sentences in detail, we see that each contains some logical error: concepts left undefined, confusions of logical types, and so on. It is said, for instance, that things cannot cease to exist as soon as no one is there to perceive them; that things could have no effects

(Berlin-Schlachtensee: Weltkreis-Verlag), 1928. (English translation as *Pseudoproblems in Philosophy*, in R. Carnap: *The Logical Structure of the World* and *Pseudoproblems in Philosophy*.) Kaila, *Über das System der Wirklichkeitsbegriffe. Ein Beitrag zum logischen Empirismus*, (Helsinki: Acta Philosophica Fennica), vol. II (1936). (English translation as "On the System of Concepts of Reality. A contribution to logical empiricism," in E. Kaila, *Reality and Experience*, 59-125).

if they were not independent of perception; that the world must exist before and after all individual perceivers, and so on. But what is the meaning, say, of 'cease to exist' here, or of 'has effects'? As a visual object, a table ceases to exist, for example, when one closes one's eyes. As a physical object it ceases to exist, for example, when it is burned down. That a thing which is not perceived at this moment 'has some effects' means that there occur some phenomena according to some rules. That the world existed before human beings means that certain invariances are there, no matter what values, within certain limits, are assigned to a temporal variable, t. A sentence like "the Earth existed long before there were any perceivers" is logically of a kind with, for example, the statement that there is now behind my back an object that no one perceives. All these concepts, 'cease to exist', 'has an effect', etc. have certain empirical content; but when they are used in metaphysical sentences, they are not given meanings that we could trace back to experience. They are given instead some undefined, nonfactual meaning, no more than a felt meaning-experience. We cannot answer such metaphysical questions, because there is no way to tell what we have been asked.

Chapter 9

The Logic of Physical Theories

In the previous chapter we considered the logical principles underlying our factual knowledge. Now, in the final part of our investigations, we wish to apply these principles to some problems in the theory of knowledge. In the first place, we wish to establish—in more detail, and taking into account some contemporary theories of physics—the consequences for rationalized theories, their testability, and their translatability, of the fact that such theories cannot be translated into the language of experience sentence by sentence and cannot, therefore, be tested sentence by sentence, either. We must keep in mind that every theory of physics is in fact strongly rationalized and that similar rationalization pertains even to our prescientific, everyday notions of physical reality. The seed of the physico-scientific notion of reality is already sown in these prescientific conceptions of physical reality, in virtue of the fact that, among other things, 'real' determinations of size, shape, motion are nothing but measured relational determinations. First, then, a few words about this pre-scientific notion of physical reality.[1]

---

1. What follows is a summary of a more extended treatment that is found in my *On the System of the Concepts of Reality*.

Physical Space

We start with a few thought-experiments. Imagine a congenitally blind person who also lacks tactual experiences but is nevertheless able to move about and to distinguish kinesthetically that his various directions of movement are qualitatively different from one another. We imagine that this person lives in a room where each place on the floor, if stepped upon, will emit a certain tone. We may assume that the blind person will eventually form to himself a conception of acoustic space in the following sense. He distinguishes qualitatively different 'places' that lie in different 'directions' and at different 'distances'; and yet all these concepts–'place,' 'direction' and 'distance'–possess an acoustic-kinesthetic content for him. 'Place' means a certain tone in a certain tonal environment; 'direction' means a certain sequence of tones, which he can bring about at will, thanks to his ability to move about, and which he is able to distinguish kinesthetically from other sequences, even if these are acoustically identical. 'Distance' means a certain plenitude of tones, which occurs as he moves from one acoustically determined place A to another, B.

Once this acoustic-kinesthetic conception of space is developed, the blind person will speak, for example, of a place B lying at such and such a distance to his right, a place which he, however, being at another place A, cannot perceive right now; he says, for example, that a certain tone, the Middle C, is sounding now at place B, but he adds that it cannot be heard at place A because the nature of space allows one to perceive only the place where one happens to be.

Comparing the blind person's conception of space to our own, we notice that the two differ only in secondary way, that is, that the blind person's space is constituted by auditory-kinesthetic sequences while our own space consists of visual-tactual-kinesthetic sequences of perceptions. Visual and tactual, rather than auditory perceptions, are dominant in our conception of space. Just as our blind person means by a certain 'place' a position filled with a particular acoustic quality and determined by a certain acoustic-kinesthetic direction and distance, we, who can see, mean by a 'place' a certain position filled with visual and tactual qualities and determined by an acoustic-tactual direction and distance. Just as our blind person is inclined towards what we might call acoustic 'naïve realism', we are inclined towards optic-tactual 'naïve realism'. This means that just as the blind person might take it as self-evident that, for example, there is to his right and at a certain distance a place having the property 'Middle C', although he cannot hear it at the moment, we are inclined to take as self-evident that to our right, at a certain distance, there is a red, four-cornered object, although we cannot see it at the moment. We try to correct the naïve realism of the blind person, telling him that the factual content of his acoustic perception of space in fact consists in certain acoustic-kinesthetic sequences of perceptions, past and future, in which there occur certain regularities. With equal right, the blind person might set out to correct our optic-tactual naïve realism by telling us that the factual content of our optic-tactual conception of space is to be found in our optic-tactual sequences of perceptions in which there occur certain regularities.

The blind person's remark is a clue for how to translate f-sentences about the physical space and its places, distances and directions into a φ-language about sequences of our perceptions. To illustrate, we offer another thought experiment. Imagine a bird-man living in a cloud that constantly changes color. If the change is sufficiently rapid and thorough, the bird-man flying inside this cloud cannot ever know where he is or whether, after a certain time, he has returned to a place he has been before. He cannot distinguish the 'same' places from 'different' places, and supposing he possesses such concepts as 'direction' and 'distance', he cannot apply them to his experience. Statements about these concepts have no consequences with respect those sequences that constitute his experience. Talk about physical space has no real content for him; for him it is metaphysics.

Thus we can see that talk about physical space with its places, directions, and distances has certain real content for us, content that we must find in the sequences constituting our actual experiences. We use certain experiences of ours in the actual solution of such questions like, Is there now to our right, at such and such a distance, an object that we cannot see? Is some place B, at a certain distance and in a certain direction from the place A where we are now, the same place, or not, as another place, C, where we were a moment ago? As long as our conception of space does not contain any element of rationalization, but consists merely of inductive generalizations, and as long as we use nothing but explicit definitions, we must be able to translate every statement about physical space into the φ-language concerning sequences of our experiences.

Why can't the bird-man speak of place, direction, or distance, while we can? The respective sequences of perceptions must contain a difference in principle. What is it that allows our blind person to converse about physical determinations in the same way as we do? The sequences constituting his perceptions must possess, in principle, a structure that is similar to ours. What is this structure?

Suppose our conception of space did not involve any rationalization. Even in this elementary case the relevant structure remains somewhat complicated. The most important feature is the *reversibility* involved in optic-tactual sequences of perceptions.[2] In our sequences of perceptions, as well as in those of the blind person, there occur several segments with the form, $A, B, C, \ldots, M, N, M, \ldots, C, B, A$; a segment like this we may call a reversion. For example, we let our gaze wander in a kinesthetically determined direction, for example, to the right–here this experienced φ-direction must be carefully distinguished from an f-direction, which is merely thought–and then back to the left. What

2. Poincaré, *Science and Hypothesis*, ch. 4; *The Value of Science*, ch. 3 and 4.

happens is that the latter half of the perceptual segment is a mirror image of its first half. Such reversions also have the peculiar feature that they can, to a large extent, be brought about at will.

This means that such perceptual sequences involve certain relational invariances. These invariances, moreover, are rather stable, though not completely so. Let A be the present perceptual space; it is regularly accompanied by a sequence '$A° \to B$', as soon as A is modified by the visual or other kinesthetic impulse, $A°$, that we call 'looking to the right' and 'moving to the right', respectively. We generalize this into a general implication '$(t) [A°(t) \to B(t)]$', where the variable t indicates moments of time. If we now ask what is the real content of the statement that in physical space B occurs to the right of A, answers to this question will take this form of general implications.

The bird-man's perceptual sequences involve no such reversions; even less does it involve reversions that one may produce at will. Hence it would be pure metaphysics if he spoke about physical space. By contrast, the acoustic sequences of our blind person involve reversions which are similar to ours.

Starting now from these reversions occurring in our sequences of perceptions, we may move on, giving detailed definitions of such concepts as (physical) 'place', 'direction' and 'distance'. Exact definitions here are not entirely straightforward, and hence we must omit them. Instead, we shall consider a number of further issues. We draw a distinction between 'apparent' and 'real' changes and, among the latter, between 'changes of position' and 'changes of state'. Here is a brief explanation of what we mean by such distinctions when they are applied to our experience.

When—and here we are speaking in f-language—an irregular object is rotated around in front of one's eyes, its perceived shape will change eventually. When the object moves away from one's eyes, its visual size will diminish. On the other hand, an object may, as we say, 'really change' its shape and size. What does this difference consist in, when translated into the language of experience? Here, again, we come back to reversibility, namely, to a special case of it. For the sake of simplicity, we shall again speak in f-language and give the name 'optimal' to our perceptions of objects that are stationary relative to us, when we look at them from nearby, in good light, and with the direction of view perpendicular to their main surface. We call a change 'apparent' when it occurs under nonoptimal conditions but disappears as soon as perception becomes optimal again. Otherwise we call a change 'real'. These real shapes, sizes, etc. have higher invariance than 'apparent' shapes and sizes, and so on, insofar as nonoptimal perceptions of apparent change are less good for making predictions than optimal perceptions; for example, a spot seen from afar may be a horse as well as a car. In the same way we distinguish from one another 'changes of position' as well as 'changes of state'. First we define a physical object—a body—saying that it is a part of the physical space, namely a part delineated by tactual surfaces. A body is then a system of certain general implications. We say that a body changes its position–is in motion–when there occurs in a sequence of perceptions *partially reversible* changes fulfilling certain conditions. Speaking in *f*-language, we say that a body changes its position when we receive from it similar optimal perceptions as before but occurring in a new environment. On the other hand, a body is said to undergo a 'real change'–in particular a 'change of state'–when the change is not reversible in this way.

In this way, we can give a detailed translation of every *f*-sentence back into a φ-language, as long as the presuppositions indicated above and concerning the use of mere induction and explicit definitions remain in force; in other words, *physical reality*, as it is called, is definable in a way that reduces to perception.

Now, however, we must confront the rationalization that we find even in our prescientific notions of space and time. Its most conspicuous manifestation, again, is the fact that temporal and spatial quantities are conceived of as continuous. But rationalization shows itself in other respects, too.

The example of the bird-man showed that we could not develop or use a concept of physical space unless certain general invariances occurred in certain sequences of perceptions. Speaking in *f*-language, if the positions of all bodies as well as those of their parts were constantly changing in sufficiently radical ways, all talk of physical space in the factual sense would eventually lose its meaning and change into metaphysics. It is only because most objects– sea and land, forests and houses, streets and market squares, walls and windows, and so on–are relatively stable and retain their relative positions that we can speak of physical space. That is to say, *if there were no 'geography' in the most general sense of the word, there would be no physical space, either.*

However, the resulting 'geographical space', as we may call it, is not equivalent to the natural conception of space that is found at least in the civilized man. According to his way of thinking, space is different from the ordered multiplicity of objects and other physical things situated in it; all bodies may change their relative positions, in which case the geographical space is transformed into another one. The spatial placement and ordering of bodies, we think, is something accidental to space itself. No matter what changes it may undergo, and even if it should become quite empty of all bodies, it would still continue to exist *as this geographical space*. We fill this space with certain objects of thought, points, surfaces, and so on bearing to one another the topological and metric relations of Euclidean geometry, that is, relations of position and quantity. It is only with this geometrical 'perception' of space– what Kant described as the *a priori* form of sense perception–that we seem to have arrived at something corresponding to our natural conception of space.

It is easy to see that our geometric perception of 'space' cannot be an inductive generalization from regularities found in experience. Kant was correct, insofar as this is what he wished to argue. In making inductive generalizations we assume that certain properties or relations that we have found to hold without exception for the given members of a class of objects hold for all its members. But we only perceive some objects to change their relative positions, either in some regular way or, again, in some irregular fashion; we see the sun and its regular motion in the sky or snowflakes falling down haphazardly. We cannot generalize such experiences into the rule that *all* objects may change their places, because in that eventuality we could no longer speak about physical position, direction, distance, or even physical space itself.

The geometric space 'perception' is therefore not a result of inductive generalizations. It is a useful device for our thinking, formed through rationalization and compressing in an idealized form certain invariances pertaining to the more original, geographical space. As such, it has no experiential consequences. It receives a real content only through the fact that we set up, with the help of certain conventions, a correspondence between it and the geographical space in a way that we described above when we treated the applications of geometry.

The geometric space 'perception' is, logically speaking, a rationalized theory. Taken as a whole, such a theory constitutes an idealized representation of the structure of a certain region of experience, yet without being in a point-by-point correspondence to it. For this reason a theory of this kind cannot be translated sentence-by-sentence into the language of experience. This is of major importance when it comes to the logic of physical theories, for such theories are highly rationalized, making use of the sort of rationalization that is found already in our natural notion of physical reality.

Interpretation of Microphysical Theories

For over half a century, physicists have debated the question of how microphysical theories should be interpreted logically. At the turn of the century, this debate centered on the theory of the atom, in particular, with the radically empiricist or 'positivistic' physicists like Mach and the chemist Ostwald adopting for epistemological reasons a rather negative attitude towards it. Criticisms gradually waned, however, as it become more and more clear how exceedingly useful the theory was.

A similar debate has been going on in the past few decades in another region. Here the clash of opposing views may have been even more dramatic than debates over the atom. This debate concerns the foundations of modern *quantum physics.* Now that we have clarified the principles underlying the general logic of our knowledge of reality, we shall see in what follows what consequences these principles have for this current debate.

Since the time of Huygens and Newton, the so-called wave theory and the so-called emission theory of radiation have struggled for dominance. According to the wave theory, radiation–for example, radiation of light–is periodic motion of radiating energy in some medium (often called the ether). According to emission theory, radiation consists in particles emitted or flung away from a radiating object.

In explaining phenomena involving radiation, the former theory makes use of the *wave picture*, as it is called, while the latter uses the so-called *particle picture*. After Fresnel and others had shown at the beginning of the previous century how the wave picture could deliver excellent explanations for the interference and polarization of light, it came to occupy a dominating position for a long time, until, at the beginning of this century, phenomena were encountered which, it appeared, could only be explained by the particle picture. In these phenomena, light exhibits, in certain respects, corpuscular behavior like matter and electric current do. Radiant corpuscles are known as photons or light-quanta. It may be taken as established that these radiant corpuscles, when they move about separated in the so-called Wilson chamber, for example, in fact follow quite closely certain laws of mechanics. It turns out, furthermore, that 'material radiation', too–for example, electrons and so-called α-particles–possess, under certain circumstances, wavelike properties, giving rise to interference-phenomena, for instance.

The situation becomes problematic because of the following issue. Suppose we are detecting the motion of a radiating particle in a Wilson Chamber. Now it behaves like a minuscule body, following the laws of mechanics; in a sense, we can even photograph its trail. Let us suppose, further, that it ceases to move when it meets a grating with holes the sizes and placement of which have been suitably chosen. Now the radiation seems to lose its particle-like character and to behave like a wave, causing interference. These two explanations or 'pictures' are mutually exclusive. For example, every line in the interference figure of the radiation passing through the grating is dependent, as in the wave picture, on the *entire* grating; hence, the founders of modern quantum theory–Bohr,[3] Heisenberg[4] and Jordan[5]–were of the opinion that in this case it is logically impossible to derive the behavior of the bundle of rays from the behavior of separate radiant corpuscles. On the other hand, again, the same radiation in the Wilson chamber, for example, follows the particle picture. Thus radiation has these two 'complementary' sides, as the phrase goes; it has particle-like and wave-like properties visible at different times, but never simultaneously. Starting with the particle picture, the wave-laws

3. N. Bohr, *Atomtheorie und Naturbeschreibung* (Berlin: J. Springer, 1931).

4. W. Heisenberg, *Die physikalischen Prinzipien der Quantentheorie* (Leipzig: S. Hirzel, 1931); W. Heisenberg, *Wandlungen in den Grundlagen der Naturwissenschaft* (Leipzig: J. Hirzel, 1936).

5. P. Jordan, *Anschauliche Quantentheorie* (Berlin: J. Springer, 1936); see in particular 14, 116, 283.

governing interference phenomena, for instance, are probability laws which describe the mean behavior of a great number of particles; hence these laws are nothing but statistical probability rules just like the gas laws, for example. And it is not considered possible to derive these statistical laws from the laws describing the behavior of separate radiant corpuscles. In this way quantum theory ends up being *'indeterministic'*; that is, these microphysical laws are no more than statistical regularities, describing the mean behavior of some sample of cases.

But there is a further point. Suppose that we are trying to determine the position and velocity of some radiant corpuscle at some moment of time. It turns out that it is in principle impossible to determine both measures with arbitrary precision. The determination in question will of course presuppose the use of some physical device, in which case the measuring instrument and the object to be measured will be of the same order of size. Measurement is possible only if it does not interfere with the measured phenomenon to any great extent. Given a small drop of water, for example, its temperature cannot be measured with a big thermometer, but only vice versa. If we try to determine as precisely as possible the position of a radiant corpuscle, the measurement itself, for which we must use either radiation or some such device, will have an unpredictable effect on the state of motion of the corpuscle, so that its 'momentum' (= mass multiplied by velocity) will change, and vice versa. There even exists a certain threshold of precision, the so-called Heisenberg uncertainty relation, which is written $\Delta p \, \Delta x \geq h$, where the first factor indicates uncertainty of momentum (or velocity) and the second uncertainty of position on the x-axis. h is the so-called Planck constant.

It is precisely here, in Heisenberg's uncertainty relation, that we find the focus of the epistemological debate. Heisenberg himself has concluded that any use of the words 'position' and 'velocity' beyond the limit indicated by the equation–in subatomic dimensions, as the phrase goes–is without real content, and hence that all talk of a radiant corpuscle's simultaneously fully determinate position and velocity would be physically as erroneous as the use of any physically undefined concept.[6] Philosophers who are inclined towards radical empiricism or 'positivism' have eagerly adopted this interpretation and held that talk of the simultaneously fully determinate position and velocity of a radiant corpuscle is metaphysics that must be eliminated from physics.

It seems to follow from this, however, that talk of *deterministic regularities*–talk of regularities that can be determined with arbitrary precision–is equally metaphysical and without factual content; and that this applies not only to radiation phenomena, but to all natural events. To determine whether a particle follows some deterministic regularity, one must see how it behaves under certain circumstances. These circumstances include, of course, the

6. Heisenberg, *Die Physikalischen Prinzipien*, 11.

position and velocity of the particle at a particular moment. But if all talk of circumstances that are simultaneously fully determinate in these respects is metaphysics, we should conclude that this applies no less to talk of a particle's behavior as if it were capable of being determined with arbitrary precision. This seems to imply the collapse of the entire causal principle in its traditional form.

Other physicists and philosophers, those whose attitude is more 'realist', have argued that if there is no logical error in our talk about the fully determinate position of a particle—as in our talk about its position at two different moments of time—it must be equally admissible to talk of its velocity as well; for example, about its velocity when it moves from one position to another. What they say is this: the fact that the circumstances under which the motion of a corpuscle takes place can, for technical reasons, be determined with only limited precision does not mean that the circumstances themselves would be 'indeterminate'; hence it is logically equally admissible to continue to assume the deterministic causal principle.[7]

From the standpoint of logical criticism, this debate calls for comment. It seems that neither side has sufficiently appreciated the fact that physical theories—radiation theory, for example—are *highly rationalized*. Insofar as this is the case, one must not impose the requirement that every sentence of the theory should be translatable into the language of experience and in such a way that each such sentence would represent some physical experiences that are at least possible. Rationalized theories always involve elements having no consequences with respect to experience. And yet, such elements may be logically admissible; hence their admission need not involve metaphysics.

To illustrate, recall that we considered microphysical sentences like "the light beam passing through this hole has the wavelength of one thousandth of a millimeter." We may surmise that not even a physicist with a strongly 'positivistic' bent would consider this sentence logically faulty. Ernst Mach, an advocate of rather radical physical 'positivism', argued a quarter of a century ago that statements about the periodicity of a light ray or about the different properties of a beam of polarized light in different perpendicular directions "could scarcely be regarded by anyone [. . .] as otherwise than an expression of facts";[8] and thus he put such statements into a different category than, say, the particle or wave hypothesis. From a logical point of view, this separation is unjustified. From a perceived interference phenomenon, or some other such phenomenon involving light, there is a long way to highly rationalized talk about the wavelength of a light beam or its polarization, etc. There is no way to translate such statements directly into the language of experience. They have experiential consequences only against the background of the entire optical

7. Cf. Popper, *The Logic of Scientific Discovery*, 220-21.
8. E. Mach, *Die Prinzipien der physikalischen Optik* (Leipzig: J. A. Barth. 1921), 290. (English translation *The Principles of Physical Optics* [New York: Dover, 1953], 210.)

theory. Logically, there is nothing to be said against highly developed wave and particle theories if rationalization in general is allowed, provided only that the concepts used in these theories have been given physical definitions.

One of the starting points for modern quantum theory was the model of the atom that Bohr introduced a quarter of a century ago. According to this model, the atomic nucleus is encircled by wandering electrons; these determine the physical and chemical properties of the atom and can only travel in certain orbits, the radii of which bear certain integral relations to one another. Atoms emit energy and move from one energy state into another when an electron jumps from an outer orbit to an inner one. This is the last mechanical model for atom, and it soon turned out to be inadequate. When the founders of contemporary quantum theory, like Heisenberg and Bohr himself, gave up the model, they brought against it the epistemological point that the supposed orbital motions of electrons do not show up in any way in experience, for they have no effects outside an atom. It is only when an electron jumps from one orbit to another that there is an outward effect as the atom either emits or absorbs radiant energy. Taken by itself, this part of the theory, which deals with orbital motions, has no experiential consequences; hence, according to Heisenberg, it must be given up as a piece of metaphysics. Referring to Mach, he required that the theory must be confined to what can be 'directly perceived', that is, its oscillation rate and intensities. No mechanical model need be presented; it is replaced by a nonintuitive, mathematical theory providing a very accurate and economical description of the relevant radiation phenomena.

To this we must reply: as little as there can be translations of statements about the imagined orbital motions into the language of experience, just as little can there be translations of statements about, say, oscillation rates. If every physical statement for which there can be no sentence-by-sentence translation is metaphysics, then statements about oscillation rates, too, shall belong to metaphysics. In that case we must eliminate from a theory each and every one of its microphysical sentences; we must discard all rationalization and, indeed, confine ourselves to a generalizing description of interference and other such phenomena involving light. Not even the most 'positivistic' physicist, however, will go this far.

For it is precisely this rationalization, producing the mathematical theories of exact physics–among them, in particular, microphysical theories–that has turned out to be one of the mightiest weapons in this kind of research. In considering the development of physics, we observe again and again that some branch of physics develops after a discovery of some isomorphism between two different regions, a discovery that is made when the regularities governing these regions have been rationalized into mathematical formalisms that turn out to be isomorphic in this or that respect. For example, the starting-point

9. See, for example, A. Haas, *Materiewellen und Quantenmechanik* (Leipzig: Akademische Verlagsanstalt, 1928), 15.

for Schrödinger's so-called wave mechanics[9] was the isomorphism between geometrical optics and mechanics, which is grounded in the fact that in both regions their governing regularities can be condensed into general minimality principles: Fermat's principle, on the one hand, and the principle of least effect, on the other, which then receive similar mathematical formulations. This similarity led Schrödinger to the hypothesis that even so-called material radiation has wave-like properties under certain conditions. Experiment then showed, in way that is almost magical, that this hypothesis was correct. This kind of development would not have been possible at all but for the enormous rationalization that is involved in the mathematics of some physical phenomena. As far as the development of physics is concerned, we must therefore emphasize that physicists with a 'positivistic' attitude are prone to go too far and act inconsistently when they insist that all sentences of a physical theory that do not in themselves depict any experience must be eliminated as 'metaphysical'. If this requirement were upheld consistently, the result would be a rejection of all rationalization as metaphysics and we would lose the mighty weapon that we have in the mathematization of experience.

Physical Determinism and Indeterminism

On the other hand, however, we must take into account that the *epistemological* arguments by leading quantum physicists against such postulates of classical mechanics as the deterministic principle of causality, continuity of temporal and spatial quantities, and description of microphysical events through mechanical models are to some extent open to doubt. This does not mean, of course, that there could not still be *physical* reasons to doubt these postulates. After all, they are not *a priori* principles but results of rationalization, which means that their validity will be decided by empirical adequacy. They are justified to the extent, and only to the extent, that rationalized theories in general are justified, namely insofar as they facilitate a sufficiently precise and economical description of certain invariances in experience. From a logical point of view, there is nothing self-evident in the assumption, for example, that the rationalization of physical experience should have to make use of mechanical models or that it should presuppose our natural notion of time and space, assuming in particular that temporal and spatial quantities are continuous. We must keep in mind that even at the prescientific level such conceptions are rationalized theories, whose real content consists in certain invariances in macro-level experience. From a logical point of view, there is nothing to be said against the possibility that–as Schrödinger once said–these concepts

10. E. Schrödinger, *Über Indeterminismus in der Physik* (Leipzig: Verlag von Johann Ambrosius Barth, 1932).

appropriate to macro-level experience may turn out to be 'overstretched' when applied to the micro-experience addressed by quantum theory.[10] Our physical conception of space presupposes the 'geographical invariances' in our environment that we described above. It may well be that there is no reason to apply such 'geographical invariances' to micro-physical regions and that a more unified and economical description can be given by renouncing all 'spatio-temporal pictures', as Bohr is fond of saying,[11] and resting content with a nonintuitive mathematical formalism. According to Bohr, the wave picture and the particle picture, both of which presuppose our natural conception of space, are nothing but defective mechanical models facilitating an intuitive grasp of this or that aspect of a nonintuitive mathematical theory describing the relevant phenomena. From this point of view, one of the criticisms which we considered above, namely, that if there are circumstances under which it is legitimate to talk of the position of a radiant corpuscle, it must then be equally legitimate to talk of its velocity, is no longer valid inasmuch as the entire problem concerns a certain model and not the mathematical theory.[12]

We shall next apply the principles of logical empiricism to another question that is intensely debated in connection with quantum theory; this is the question concerning the causal principle, or the *deterministic or indeterministic nature of physical laws*. Our aim is to show that from a logical point of view there are other possibilities besides those that have led physicists to envision only two alternatives: either determinism or indeterminism.

Our experience exhibits different kinds of regularities: among others, there are 'geographical invariances' that constitute the real content of our concept of physical space and, on the other hand, a multiplicity of relational invariances between events, invariances that we rationalize into the mathematical laws of nature. The so-called causal principle says that all events are governed by laws, but in most cases the principle remains vague, particularly because it is far from easy to give an exact definition of 'law of nature'.

To see this, we shall call a lawfulness '*differential*' when the relevant dependence relation holds no matter how small the values assigned to the quantities standing in the relation. When one speaks of 'causality' in the stricter sense, that is, of *physical determinism*, what one is likely to have in mind is a differential lawfulness, as it appears, for instance, in the laws of classical mechanics. For instance, when it is said that in free fall, the distance travelled is proportional to the square of the time elapsed, it is supposed that the statement is valid no matter how small the relevant quantities may be; hence, the relevant dependence relations are represented by means of differential equations.

Setting aside the idea that such 'differential causality' might be an *a priori* assumption, we see at once that we cannot, strictly speaking, even ask whether

---

11. Bohr, *Atomtheorie*, 22.
12. M. Strauss, "Ungenauigkeit, Wahrscheinlichkeit und Unbestimmtheit," *Erkenntnis* 6 (1936): 90–113.

the assumption is empirically true or not, because it is an idealizing fiction. The only legitimate question about it is whether it is an appropriate way to describe certain invariances of experience, that is, whether it corresponds sufficiently closely to experience and whether it delivers a sufficiently unified and economical description.

A different conception of causation in nature is possible. It is conceivable that some lawfulness is valid only to a degree; in such a way, for example, that it holds even with great exactitude within ordinary 'macro-experience', concerned with sufficiently large regions, but that it is not valid in 'micro-experience' of very small regions. This is characteristic of the laws of gas theory, for instance. If we measure the pressure of a gas using an ordinary manometer, we will see that it is the same in all directions. This law, however, is not differential but a statistical law that is valid only within sufficiently large regions; for if we observe through a microscope a particle moving about in a liquid or gas, we see that the pressure on it is not the same in every direction at each instant because the particle moves in different directions in seemingly random ways. Within the kinetic theory of gases, this so-called Brownian motion is interpreted in terms of a random bombardment of the particle by individual molecules.

When the *kinetic theory of gases* was created, people reasoned that while individual molecules follow the differential laws of mechanics, their positional distribution and the distribution of their velocities are random processes. Since in ordinary macro-experience the number of molecules is always very high, it follows from this random distribution that macro-experience exhibits exact regularities when it comes to gas pressure, for instance.

Nevertheless, some scientists suggested long ago that another way of thinking would be simpler.[13] Let us put aside the assumption that individual molecules follow differential laws and rest content with what experience seems to show us, namely that certain laws of gas theory hold, and even with great exactitude, for sufficiently large regions. For taken together, the two assumptions–that individual molecules follow differential laws but their distribution is nevertheless random–yield the same result as the single assumption that sufficiently large collections of individual molecules are governed by statistical laws irrespective of the laws governing individual molecules. This indeterministic conception might be simpler, unless we had available to us experiences such as those we have already mentioned: Brownian motion or the behavior of particles in a Wilson chamber, for example. They seem to show that individual particles do follow differential laws under certain circumstances; whence we may conclude that statistical regularities governing multiplicities of these particles are no more than secondary mass phenomena and the fundamental laws of nature are deterministic, after all.

13. In particular, F. Exner, *Vorlesungen über die physikalischen Grundlagen der Naturwissenschaften*, Second edition (Wien: F. Deuticke, 1922).

By contrast, considering how *quantum theory* stands in this respect, it is logically impossible to interpret the probability laws governing the diffraction of radiation in a way analogous to this interpretation of gas laws. Jordan has used the following useful picture to describe the situation. Let us imagine two consecutive phases of radiation, the first exhibiting particle-like nature and the second exhibiting wave-like nature. First we investigate the first phase using, for example, a Wilson chamber in which radiation has particle-like properties. Let a bundle of rays meet a grating with appropriately sized and spaced slits. As we mentioned, radiation now assumes a wave-like nature. Behind the grating there occurs an interference pattern in exact agreement with the wave-theory–and the pattern occurs even with the lowest measurable intensities of light–provided, though, that the plane where the pattern occurs (for instance, a photographic plate) has been struck by a sufficient number of light quanta. Individual light quanta strike different spots on the plane with a probability that is proportional to the intensity calculated in accordance with the wave-picture; as soon as the number of strikes grows sufficiently high, their diffraction is in exact agreement with the wave-picture. In this way, according to the currently prevalent view, the distribution of light intensity in an interference pattern is a probability law that describes how a multiplicity of particles spreads out to form an interference pattern behind a grating. Here, the theory says, it is logically impossible think that this probability law could be derived from the behavior of individual particles following differential laws in the same way that the statistical laws of gases can be derived from differential laws of motion of individual molecules and some given, initial state of their positions and velocities. It is impossible because radiant corpuscles, when they pass through the grating, behave as if they are light-waves, that is, their interference "is a consequence of the nature of each individual light quantum."[14]

We shall now compare with one another, and in more detail than above, the diffraction of radiant energy, as this appears, for example, in a photographed pattern, and the diffraction of gaseous energy, as measured, for example, by manometer. In both cases certain regularities will be observed. In the case of gaseous energy, if we had at our disposal only macro-observations about micro-physically large temporal and spatial regions, we would be hard pressed to find good reasons to think that the observed regularities, which are actually quite precise, are no more than probability rules. Of course, these observations are not free from disturbing effects–measurement never is–but they are no more likely to occur here than in other cases. If, then, all our observations of gases were macro-observations, it might be advisable to rationalize observed regularities into differential laws, just as we rationalize, for example, ordinary regularities in kinematic phenomena into the differential laws of mechanics. In actual fact, however, we have reason to think of gases as collections of molecules in which individual molecules are randomly distributed

14. Jordan, *Anschauliche Quantentheorie*, 14.

independently of one another and with respect to position, velocity, and direction of motion. It's not until this assumption is in place that the conditions are fulfilled for there to be any talk at all of probability or of statistical laws. For, as we saw in discussing mathematical probability, we must have access to a sample of cases exhibiting certain relative frequencies, that is, we must be given a random distribution of cases into subclasses showing that when the number of cases is large, the distribution is, on average, constant. This kind of collection of cases, in which each individual case is irregular but which, when taken as a whole, is divided into subclasses according to some constant rule in the way indicated above, is also known as a *collective*.

If we now consider how radiant energy spreads out and forms an interference pattern, we can ask whether this presupposition is fulfilled so that a diffraction law in accordance with the wave theory could be given a natural interpretation as a statistical probability law? What in this case would be the collective that this probability rule is applied to? The interference pattern reveals a very exact empirical diffraction rule. Apart from usual disturbing effects, it admits no exceptions. *The diffraction law is not an average rule*, as it exhibits no increasing precision when the number of cases becomes larger, something that is typical of collectives and their relative frequencies. As soon as the amount of radiant energy is sufficient for an interference pattern to emerge, diffraction is quite exact. Where then do we find the collective–the sample of cases–that must be there in order that we may interpret the relevant diffraction to be a statistical rule? The fact that the interference pattern emerges quantum by quantum will not yet give us the collective we need. It would be there if with the increase of their number (their radiant energy) the diffraction of quanta *approximated, on average,* the wave picture. The theory tells us, however, that this is not the case; that a sufficiently large amount of radiation follows the wave picture *exactly*.

The prevalent view seems to be that no matter how low the intensity of the interference pattern is, the number of light quanta is always so large that the probability of deviation from a diffraction predicted by the wave theory is extremely low–much lower, in fact, than the probability that in measuring the pressure of a gas in a container we should find that it is different in different directions. But this interpretation, in which the distribution of gaseous energy and radiant energy are construed as comparable statistical phenomena, is faulty in an important respect. When it comes to the distribution of gaseous energy, we may resort to certain experiences–as in Brownian motion, for example–providing natural support for the interpretation that the macroscopic distribution of gaseous energy is a consequence of a random accumulation of certain *mutually independent* elementary cases. On the other hand, when we are concerned with the diffraction pattern of certain radiant energy, where do we find the *mutually independent* elementary cases whose random multiplication we could construe as resulting in this pattern? No such cases are known, and theory says there are no such cases; for diffraction takes place in accordance with the deterministic regularity of 'wave mechanics' that is represented in the form of differential equations typical of 'classical physics'. *In addition to* the fact that the diffraction pattern emerges quantum by quantum, we should find in our experience some reason to think that the elementary cases whose accumulation results in a diffraction pattern are in fact random, viz. *independent of one another*. But theory tells us this is not the case. Only if such reason could be given, would there be *experiential* support for interpreting the elementary cases whose accumulation results in a certain macroscopic distribution of radiant energy as a genuine collective in the sense of the mathematical theory of probability.

What, then, is the basis of the current interpretation? The idea seems to be this: Given, on the other hand, that we must regard light quanta as 'physical realities', so that, for example, diffraction patterns emerge quantum by quantum; and, on the other hand, that the diffraction of radiant energy, insofar as this takes place in accordance with the wave picture, cannot be derived from any differential laws of particles of light; it is then assumed that the said diffraction is a statistical mass phenomenon that can be treated as a genuine collective. This conclusion, however, is logically doubtful, because it presupposes that every law of nature has necessarily either a differential or else a statistical character. *These alternatives are not exhaustive*, however. As far as their logical character is concerned, we can conceive of laws that are somewhere between differential and statistical. From the fact that some macroscopic mass phenomena cannot be derived in any natural way from the laws governing some microscopic elementary cases together with their distribution, it does not yet follow that the mass phenomena to which a collection of these elementary cases gives rise must be taken as a collective governed only by statistical rules.

The difference between statistical and differential laws, we may conclude, has been given a satisfactory explication in contemporary epistemology. However, *there seems to be an inclination to think that this distinction is exhaustive in the sense that every natural law is supposed to be necessarily of the one sort or the other.*

Logically, there are other possibilities that can be put on a level with the above distinction. Imagine a bundle of rays meeting a suitable grating. What will happen to it? It will follow a certain lawfulness, the nature of which is different from the ordinary laws of classical physics, be they differential or statistical. This lawfulness, which governs the diffraction of radiant energy on the other side of the grating, differs from statistical rules in that it is, with certain qualifications, fully exact and not an average rule. In that respect it is like a differential law. On the other hand, however, it differs from differential laws since it describes the distribution of radiant energy in a region that is very large in comparison with the subatomic dimensions of the radiant corpuscles that compose the energetic distribution. In this respect the law resembles rules of statistical probability.

Result

Our investigations yield the following general result. Inasmuch as physical theories are strongly rationalized, translatability and hence testability are ruled out as a requirement on each separate sentence. This being so, a sentence of a physical theory cannot be ruled out as 'metaphysics' solely on the grounds that it fails to depict any specific phenomenon of experience. From a logical point of view, there is nothing wrong with developing a micro-physical theory as far beyond the 'threshold of observation' as one may wish, in which case the theory will of necessity contain many sentences that cannot be tested in experience, as long as they are considered in themselves.

And yet, on the other hand, such a theory is nothing but a rationalized and economic description of a certain region of experience. Its validity is decided by how well it meets this objective. From this it follows that nothing can be said *a priori* about what material principles one should follow in the formation of physical theories.

One important form of rationalization is found in the postulate of 'deterministic causality'. Strictly speaking, we cannot ask whether reality accords with this postulate or not; that is, insofar as it is not a generalization from experience but rather an idealizing formula. It is appropriate if there is sufficient agreement between it and reality and if it gives a sufficiently simple and unified description of experience. It may be that this is not the case and that it would be more appropriate to interpret the regularities of experience in terms of statistical probability laws, for instance.

This applies as well to the rationalization involved in our concepts of time and space. That distance, time, speed, and other kinematic quantities are continuous is, again, a mathematical postulate that may be judged only for its appropriateness. Furthermore, it may be that the two postulates mentioned above are inconsistent with one another to the extent that not both, but only one or the other, can be simultaneously satisfied by macro-physical events. This is the view of Bohr and his followers.[15]

It should be noted, as well, that 'deterministic causality' and statistical average regularity by no means exhaust all theoretical possibilities. As we have tried to show, we can imagine a lawfulness that is, in a sense, between these two. It is conceivable that in some cases the most appropriate interpretation of the behavior of some whole (in our example, a bundle of rays) would assume a

---

15. Bohr, *Atomtheorie*, 36.

lawfulness which we cannot in any natural way derive from the joint effect of its supposed parts–by 'natural' we mean a way that satisfies the requirement of relative simplicity; in which case the law is not along the lines of a statistical average law.

In Heisenberg we find the following remark–here he is thinking along lines we also find in Bohr.[16] People used to think that the theoretical edifice of science constituted a single unified system in the sense that the laws governing one part–mechanics, for example–applied to all other parts without any modification and even in such a way that the laws pertaining to these parts were just special cases of the first. In the light of recent quantum theory, such a unified description of experience is not possible. When we move from the laws of macro-physical mechanics to those of micro-physics, these laws change in their logical type. In particular, we must pay attention to this possibility when it comes to biological laws–a point that these physicists have often repeated.

The continuously progressive physicochemical analysis of organisms is a kind of micro-analysis. The question arises, to what extent it is plausible that this microanalysis, for all its progress, should one day yield a satisfactory description of the macro-behavior of organisms as well. This question is of principled importance for biological research, because an answer to it determines whether biological research will concentrate more on the micro-analysis of physico-chemical events or, instead, on macro-description of organisms and their behavior. Starting from the general conception of lawfulness and keeping an eye on the different possibilities that arise with respect to this concept, we come to the ideological battles currently taking place in biology, including psychology, as well. These issues, however, cannot be pursued further within the confines of our present investigations.

16. Heisenberg, *Wandlungen in den Grundlagen der Naturwissenschaft*, 25.

Chapter 10

Logical Behaviorism

Until now we have not considered the fourth basic thesis of logical empiricism, the so-called principle of logical behaviorism.[1] We are taking as our starting-point a question we left unanswered above.

The question depends on the distinction between φ-language and f-language; in particular, we distinguished between the experiential sentences of these languages. The experiential sentences of φ-language are singular sentences reporting perceptions (in the widest sense of the term) at a given moment. In f-language, experiential sentences are singular sentences relating to physical objects and events that appear to the speaker at a given moment. Yet the question remains open: Which of the two languages ought to be considered more basic?

Choosing φ-sentences as our experiential sentences and considering only the simplest cases—cases where nothing but induction and explicit definitions are used—f-sentences can be given sentence-by-sentence translations into φ-

---

1. Throughout the present chapter, our discussion is indebted to Carnap's seminal work: see Carnap, "Die physikalische Sprache als Universalsprache der Wissenschaft," *Erkenntnis* 2 (1932): 432-65. (Translated into English as *Unity of Science*, trans. Max Black [London: Kegan Paul, Trench, Truebner & Co. Ltd, 1934]); "Psychologie in physikalischer Sprache," *Erkenntnis* 3 (1933): 107-42. (Translated into English as "Psychology in Physical Language," in A.J. Ayer, ed., *Logical Positivism*, 165-98.). Good discussions of logical behaviorism can also be found in H. Feigl, "Logical Analysis of the Psychophysical Problem," *Philosophy of Science* 1 (1934): 420-45, and C.G. Hempel, "Analyse logique de la psychologie," *Revue de synthése* 10 (1935): 27-42. (English translation as "The Logical Analysis of Psychology,
" in Feigl and Sellars, eds., *Readings in Philosophical Analysis*, 373-84.)

language, in which case even a singular f-sentence yields a conjunction of general implications; this much we saw in considering how an f-sentence, '$F(t_n)$', is to be translated into φ-language. That such translations are available supports the view that we ought to choose φ-language as our basic language. Sentences concerned with physical events assert a good deal more than φ-sentences of the same logical type; which means that with the former type of sentence we run a much greater risk of error. Our choice of φ-sentences as our basic language is in line with the assumption that general sentences have their logical foundation in the singular sentences derivable from them; for even a singular f-sentence, once it has been translated into the φ-language, turns out to be a general sentence, the factual content of which consists of a certain class of φ-sentences. This is the position we shall now adopt, and we shall consider what consequences our choice has.

The Problem of 'Other Minds'

Imagine a dialogue between two subjects, S_1 and S_2. We assume that S_1 has explained to S_2 the course of our epistemological investigations. That is, S_1 has explained how he formulates to himself a scientific conception of the world, starting from the logical foundation of all these developments, that is, from the sequences constituted by his actual perceptions. And we suppose that S_1 has in this development arrived at the point where we are now. Another subject, S_2, now enters the dialogue; each of us can imagine himself in the position of S_2. To find out whether he has understood S_1's explanations, he tries to apply them to his own case. That is, starting from his own experiential sentences, he tries to carry through the same development that S_1 describes. Here, though, he encounters a remarkable problem: how is he to interpret those φ-sentences that S_1 uses to describe S_1's own experiences? Carnap, once he had fully appreciated the character of this problem, called it the problem of 'other minds'.[2] We must now consider this problem in detail.

S_1 and S_2 now discuss the question of what a person's talk about his own experiences and about φ-sentences depicting these experiences might mean to another person. Taking into account that the relevant φ-sentences describe what is going on in the two persons' minds, let us imagine that S_1 and S_2 first take up the question, Is it possible for a subject, S, to perceive what goes on in other persons' minds and, if not, how is one to know that there is something 'heteropsychological', that is, something pertaining to another person's mind?

Supposing S_1 and S_2 are familiar with descriptive psychology or 'phenomenology', they will first observe that two different meanings can be given to

2. Carnap, *The Logical Structure of the World* and *Pseudoproblems in Philosophy*; *The Logical Structure of the World*.

the expression 'another person's mind': a pre-scientific or Φ-meaning, or else a scientific or Ψ-meaning. We must first clarify what is involved in these terms, and here it helps to keep in mind that Ψ is the first letter of the Greek word 'psychologia'.

Suppose that in the course of their dialogue, S_2 notices that the other participant is irritated. S_2 notices that S_1's talk is fast and disorganized, that he moves about restlessly and is prone to outbursts. But such 'individual expressions of the affections of his mind' are not all that S_2 observes; in S_2's experience, the other participant's behavior as a whole–his talk, gestures, facial expressions, etc.–possess a certain 'complex quality', which may be so tangible that S_2 might well say to S_1: "I can clearly see you are agitated." For S_2, S_1's agitation may well be something that is included in S_2's so-called immediate perception. Here we are concerned with the Φ-concept of the 'heteropsychological'. S_2 is experiencing a heteropsychological occurrence, namely S_1's agitation. However, he does not experience it as an autopsychological but as a heteropsychological agitation, that is, as something that takes place in another person's mind, even though the experience belongs to his own phenomenal world. S_2's so-called immediate experience contains not only autopsychological occurrences experienced as belonging to one's own self, but heteropsychological occurrences such as feelings, thoughts, volitions and other such 'psychical' qualities that are experienced as belonging not to one's own self but to another person, namely S_1. In addition to these, immediate experience also contains the lived environment that lacks such 'psychical' qualities; for example, a desk as a visual object.

It should be pointed out that in the Φ-sense we are able to experience as heteropsychological not only agitations and other such feelings but, for example, thoughts and volitions, as well. Suppose, for example, that S_2 is listening to S_1's talking and hears utterances such as 'by no means' or 'exactly'; S_1's hearing will then be accompanied by meaning-experiences just as when he hears words that he himself utters. Listening to S_1, however, S_2 undergoes these experiences as something that belongs to S_1, and not to his own thoughts. In the same way, for instance, S_2 may experience S_1's growing irritation, even in the form of S_1's desire to attack S_2 himself.

These examples illustrate what is meant by heteropsychological in the Φ-sense. This is what we usually mean when we speak in our everyday, pre-scientific life about what goes on 'in other people's minds.' I once asked a painter, a man of considerable erudition, whose portraits were praised for their psychological perspicacity, where he actually perceives this 'other mind' that he describes by means of line drawing and hues. He replied: "I suppose it's mainly in the eyes of the model."

However, this heteropsychological in the Φ-sense is not what a scientific psychologist means when he speaks of what is going on 'in another person's mind.' When we create for ourselves our concept of reality, we move, logically speaking, from a φ-area to an f-area, which consists of nothing but the higher invariances involved in the φ-area; in the same way a scientific psychologist regards the immediately experienced Φ-heteropsychological as something that is 'apparent' and no more than an unreliable expression of the Ψ-heteropsychological, which is 'real'. The motive behind this change is the same as it was before, where we moved from the 'apparent' phenomenal world to the 'real' or physical world; in both cases we are concerned with the search for invariances.

There are two main categories of reasons that lead us, on continued reflection, to understand the Φ-heteropsychological as no more than an 'apparent' and unreliable expression of the 'real', Ψ-heteropsychological.

In the first place, we notice certain common mistakes relating to the Φ-heteropsychological. Suppose S_2 has an experience of something Φ-heteropsychological like S_1's irritation. He experiences this as a complex quality of S_1's behavior, and this then gives rise to certain expectations as to S_1's subsequent behavior. On occasion, however, one is let down in these expectations. One then says that S_1 was only feigning irritation, or that he was acting, or even that he was lying. S_2 concludes that what was really going on in S_1's mind is not directly observable to him and that what is so observable is nothing but an indirect reflection, as it were.

In the second place, S_2 concludes that the intellectual side of S_1's psychological life–S_1's observations, ideas, and thoughts–is not nearly as manifest as is S_1's temperament and his actions. It is often quite impossible for S_2 to find out what S_1 is thinking at a given instant, although later experience will suggest what S_1's thoughts were at the time.

Hence, S_2's general conclusion will be that S_1 has a 'secret inner life of his own'; this life he, S_2, will only learn about indirectly and in an incomplete way. Once S_2 has arrived at this stage, there will then occur the 'Cyrenaic problem' that we mentioned, that is, the problem of whether the sensory and other psychical qualities that other people experience are similar to ours.

Here S_2 introduces a new concept, the *concept of Ψ-heteropsychological*. Since every concept must be determined, S_1 and S_2 now take up the question of how this concept should be defined. We may suppose that they first engage in a brief conversation on what philosophers before logical empiricism have said about this question. We imagine them asking, "How can S_2 know that S_1 in fact has a 'secret inner life of his own'"? First, they come up with the following answer: S_2 knows it on the basis of analogical inference. In seeing that characteristics abc are regularly followed by another, d, one concludes that characteristics $a'b'c'$, which are similar to the former, will be followed by a characteristic d', which is similar to the latter. If, for example, the restless movements of my body are accompanied by an autopsychological agitation, I conclude that the perceived similar condition of another body is accompanied by a similar heteropsychological state. This kind of analogical inference is a special case of inductive reasoning, and inductive reasoning, no doubt, is used in science. And yet, strong objections can be brought against its specific application to the present case. We need not consider these objections here, for the present case fails to fulfill one of the necessary conditions for this kind of reasoning. When a new concept is introduced, there is an absolute requirement that it will be given a definition. No mention of 'analogical inferences' should be made here until we have defined the new concept of ' Ψ-heteropsychological'. We assume here and in what follows that only *explicit definitions* are legitimate. This simplifies the task at hand and will have no principled effect on the result. Thus, S_2's task becomes that of defining what he means by the phrase "what goes on in another person's mind" when he uses this phrase in this new or Ψ-sense. In this case, though, the Ψ-heteropsychological appears to be something that is in principle impossible for S_2 to perceive, and this despite the fact that it is assumed to be qualitatively similar to S_2's own experiences and to bear some sort of correspondence to things that S_2 can perceive in principle, such as S_1's body or his brain states, for example. Here it makes no difference whether we conceive of this correspondence in terms of 'interactionism' or 'parallelism', as they are called. Here we are concerned with an explicit definition of an empirical concept, one that will allow the defined expression to be replaced by the defining expression. If, then, S_2 offers this definition and repeatedly applies the substitution possibilities thereby created to any sentences describing S_1's psychic life, each such sentence will eventually be transformed into a sentence belonging to S_2's language of experience. But then it is a contradiction to assert that the original sentence represented something that is 'in principle' impossible for S_2 to experience. After all, the statement that something 'can in principle be experienced' by S_2 means nothing else than that this statement is transformed, via substitutions, into a statement belonging to S_2's language of experience. As soon as the relevant 'correspondence' has been defined, every Ψ-sentence about S_1 can be transformed into a sentence belonging to S_2's language of experience.

To illustrate, let us assume that this 'correspondence' between a state of S_1's body and a state of his mind has been defined in terms of a local correspondence; for instance, that it means *belonging to a same place*. In this case, each singular Ψ-sentence about S_1 would make an assertion to the effect that in S_1's body–for example, in his brain–there is such and such an occurrence at this moment. Given such a definition, the factual content of the relevant Ψ-sentence would then be constituted by certain things that S_2 could experience in S_1's body at particular moment of time. But what is perceived to exist and take place in some brain is physical. The Ψ-sentence would then depict something physical.

Let us imagine, on the other hand, that the correspondence has been defined in terms of 'temporal correspondence', say *simultaneity*, in such a way that each of S_1's states of mind bears a relation of simultaneity to a state of his body. 'Simultaneity' is a relationship that is 'observable in principle'. That is, it can be replaced by expressions that signify, in the last instance, something that is found in S_2's perceptual world.

How S_2 proposes to undertake the said definition is immaterial; every definition reduces, in a sense, to sentences belonging to his language of experience, in which case the original Ψ-sentence is transformed into a sentence describing S_2's perceptual world. If Ψ-sentences about S_1 are to have some factual content for S_2 in the first place, each and every concept occurring in them–in particular the 'correspondence' we have been discussing–must be given some definition; but as soon as this has been accomplished, the factual content turns out to be something that is 'in principle' observable by S_2.

What we have here said about the sentences describing S_1's psychic life and their meaning for S_2, applies, of course, to sentences about S_2's psychic life, when they are considered from S_1's point of view.

Intersubjective Interpretation of φ-Sentences

After these preliminary remarks we now return to where we began our discussion. This was the question of how S_2 should interpret φ-sentences representing S_1's experiences. For S_2 these sentences are a subclass of Ψ-sentences about S_1, namely, singular Ψ-sentences. In order for S_2 to know anything about them, they must be strings of symbols appearing to S_2. In this capacity, they can be given a formal characterization distinguishing them from f-sentences, for example. Without saying anything more about their having different meanings, they will be distinguished through the fact that their form is somewhat different, that different predicates occur in them, and so on.

The question of how φ-sentences are to be interpreted is a special case of the question of how Ψ-sentences in general should be interpreted.

S_1 and S_2 now set out to investigate how a psychological experiment, for example, would convince them that a creature either has or has not some particular kind of experience. We shall consider a few examples. An animal psychologist says that even a low animal like an ordinary house mouse apparently has at least such experiences as 'expectations'. What does such talk mean? It means, for example, that when the mouse that is running through a labyrinth from the place where it is kept to the place where the food is kept is left without a reward on a few occasions, the curve of its path will change; it will run at a slower pace and the path will include mistakes. This is taken to show that the mouse has expectations. For another example, consider a psychological test where a person is found to be red-green-blind. What does this mean? It means that the structure consisting of certain behavioral patterns–regularities in verbal and other such reactions–exhibit under specific conditions deviation from the normally-sighted person. This is taken to show that the person is 'color-blind'. Our third example is the case of a normal human child. For them, as is said, there develops a 'representing activity' or 'symbol function' during their second and third years. What does this mean? The answer to this question is found by observing certain changes occurring in a child's behavior during this stage of life.

Such examples testify that statements about a creature's mental life are in fact decided on the basis of what is found in other creatures' perceptions. For this to be possible–for S_2 to be able to judge the φ-sentences representing S_1's experiences, say–these must have some experiential consequences for S_2. For otherwise there is no way S_2 could decide upon their validity; and more strongly, *if they fail to fulfill this condition, they will not have any content whatsoever for S_2*. Assuming S_2 must be able to give explicit definitions for expressions occurring in them, φ-sentences must depict something that is 'in principle observable' for him. What, then, do they depict?

These sentences are concerned with S_1's perceptions and not with physical things or events in S_1's physical environment. A sentence like "I, S_1, am now seeing red" may be a 'hallucination' just like any other φ-sentence. Since this sentence depicts nothing in the physical environment of S_1's body, and since it must represent something that is 'in principle observable' for S_2, it cannot represent anything but a state in S_1's body, primarily a state of his brain.

To facilitate discussion, we shall first make the following simplifying assumption. We shall assume that S_2 is convinced, on the basis of a long-term acquaintanceship, that S_1 is a thoroughly reliable person. And we shall assume more strongly that not only are S_1's φ-sentences true, but also that whenever S_1 has felt that he was having an important experience, he has uttered a statement reporting that experience. S_1 and S_2 will then be able to specify a number of very simple use-definitions for determining the factual content that S_1's φ-sentences have for S_2:

φ-sentences:		f-sentences:
"I see red now."	=	"My body is now in a state of seeing red."
"I feel pain now."	=	"My body is now in a state of feeling pain."
. . .		. . .
. . .		. . .

Given the simplifying assumption above, the phrase 'body in a state of' occurring in sentences on the right hand side is defined in the following manner. Each of the relevant states occurs when, and only when, the string of words on the left hand side occurs. Through the equations (hence, equivalences) set up in this way, *φ-sentences have been interpreted as f-sentences*.

Consider now how the actual situation differs from this simplest imaginable case. Suppose that S_1 keeps his experiences to himself, that he pretends in his countenances and gestures, that he is untruthful in his speech; it will follow from all of this that his experiential sentences cannot be defined as *f*-sentences in this simplistic way, but turn out in many cases to be really quite complicated. And yet, we must always be in a position to give some such defining equivalence, insofar as S_1's experiences possess any degree of intersubjective significance, that is, insofar as they have any experiential consequences. For as soon as S_2 is convinced that S_1 has some specific experiences, he must be in possession of some experiential reasons for this conviction, and these are in the last instance based on S_2's behavior that is in the widest sense observable to S_1. *But the features of S_1's behavior that are necessary and sufficient for S_2 to be able to use them as a ground for judgments about specific experiences of S_1, will contain at the same time defining equivalences for sentences describing these experiences.* These equivalences are similar to but more complicated than the case we considered above.

In this way we arrive at the *fourth basic thesis of logical empiricism*, the principle of logical behaviorism. It holds that *φ-sentences describing the so-called immediate experiences of S_1 are intersubjectively equipollent with f-sentences describing certain states of S_1's body.* That a given *φ*-sentence and a given f-sentence are 'intersubjectively equipollent' means that the former sentence, insofar as it is meant to be understood by other people, agrees in its factual content with the latter.

Behavioristic Psychology

All sentences belonging to scientific psychology are *f*-sentences of this kind. After all, every psychologist speaks to other people and not only to himself. He presupposes that others will be able to understand him and check upon his statements. Hence, *the subject matter of scientific psychology consists of the behavior of living creatures*, where 'behavior' is taken in a wide sense that includes their doings and states reflected in these doings, together with their gestures, countenances and in the case of human beings especially, of course, their speech.

In public consciousness the term *'behaviorism'* is associated with certain views advocated by some contemporary psychologists, namely the American Watson and his colleagues. These scientists are fond of saying that there is no consciousness, or that an act of thinking is nothing but a weak whispering, or that all human action, including all representing action, consists of nothing but inherited, simple reflections, and so on. *Logical behaviorism* has very little to do with this sort of quite primitive, mechanistic and materialistic behaviorism. Logical behaviorism by no means wishes to claim that 'there is no consciousness'. It only asks, "What is the intersubjective factual content of the claim that there is consciousness?" and replies that this factual content consists in a specific kind of physical behavior. Logical behaviorism by no means claims that laws governing the behavior of creatures—human beings in particular—could be derived from reflex-like units of behavior. How these questions are to be answered is for future experience to decide.

That the sentences of psychology are interpreted as f-sentences in this way means that all intersubjective knowledge of reality speaks one and the same language everywhere; this language is f-language, the language whose expressions refer to things, their properties, and relations in 'physical reality'.

Three Objections

The dialogue between S_1 and S_2 comes to an end as S_1 raises three objections to which S_2 replies. The first objection goes like this:

> As you know, I have carried out the logical construction of physical reality in such a way that even singular f-sentences, once they are translated into φ-language, will turn out to be conjunctions of general implications in that language. In this way, for instance, an f-statement that my body is in such and such a state, once it is translated into φ-language, will be a conjunction of certain implications. What you are claiming, though, is that each of my singular φ-sentences must be equivalent with a statement about the state of my body. But how could this be so, when statements about the state of my body are f-statements and, as such, conjunctions of certain implications between φ-sentences?

S_2 replies,

> The principle that f-statements like 'here is a red apple' or 'this is my hand' are conjunctions of implications between certain φ-statements will remain valid, but with an important proviso. Insofar as you experience your own body through sense perceptions, like visual, tactual and other such perceptions, the situation with respect to your body will be exactly the same as with any other object. The φ-statement 'I now see a red apple' has an entirely different content from the f-statement 'here there is now—namely as a physical object—a red apple'. The former sentence may depict a 'hallucination'. Imagine a war veteran

who is an invalid, having lost an arm. As is well known, for some time after the loss he will continue to feel his arm in the form of tactual hallucinations. Hence, an f-statement like 'this is my hand, namely as a physical object', is equivalent, not with some singular φ-statement, but with an entire system of φ-sentences.

Here, though, comes the proviso. Your φ-sentences depict the state of your body, but if your body is analogous to other physical objects, they do not depict it as a thing experienced through so-called sense-perceptions but only insofar as your body, among all physical objects, possesses a privileged position for you. You may lose a leg or an arm, but at least your brain must remain, together with some organ that enables you to communicate your own states to others by means of some system of symbols. Your φ-sentences are such strings of expressions. Their intersubjective meaning is to be found in what they say about the state of your body and, in the last instance, about the state of your brain. Descartes said: 'Cogito, ergo sum.' We must say: 'Cogito, ergo est cerebrum meum', 'I think, therefore I am my brain'. Even your brain can be an ordinary, physical object, observable through some system of mirrors, say. On the other hand, however, the brain produces φ-sentences as strings of signs and its state is depicted through these φ-sentences.

> For me to be able to know that you are 'real,' your expressions must possess a sufficient degree of invariance. This means, however, that you must be something physical, because a series of occurrences constitute a 'physical thing' or event when and only when they possess a sufficient degree of invariance.

S_1 now states his second objection:

> You are in the habit of talking about φ-sentences depicting something or possessing such and such intersubjective meaning. We have agreed, however, that these sentences are to be construed formally, as certain strings of sound or of other such physical occurrences. If we 'physicalize' everything and speak nothing but physical language, we will speak only of things, their physical states and other such physical matters. How, then, can you speak of 'representing' or 'meaning'? After all, physical things, even when they are living human bodies that make gestures and utter sounds, cannot as such represent or mean anything.

S_2 replies as follows.

> But there you are mistaken. Imagine a child whom you are observing and who is beginning to use a representing language. This observation is based on the child's behavior. But then it is exactly this behav-

ior that will define 'representing activity'. If certain physical things, namely living human bodies, did not represent anything through their signs, our talk of 'representing' and 'meaning' would not have any factual content. There is a very important behavioral difference between animals, which produce mere signals or reaction-signs, and human beings, who also produce symbols or representing signs. It is precisely this difference that defines the so-called symbol function. The importance of logical behaviorism for psychological research lies in the fact, for example, that it requires a precise statement of what this difference consists in; for this is something that no one has accomplished yet. So far we possess nothing but a very primitive concept of symbol function. Insofar as we have it, however, it is a behavioristic concept. Logical behaviorism by no means implies that all psychological concepts ought to be redefined and transformed into behavioral concepts. Insofar as they have been given any definitions, these have been behavioral throughout. Those behavioral features that we use to decide whether a person is, for example, color-blind or has eidetic memory, involve, at the same time, scientific-psychological—that is, behavioristic—definitions for those concepts. This being the case, I can, as a behaviorist, continue to use psychological expressions like 'represent' or 'mean'. When I say that your φ-sentences mean the same as certain f-sentences about your body, the word 'mean' must here, as everywhere, be understood along the lines suggested by behaviorism.

Let us consider the following case. Let us suppose I explain to you some axiomatic system like a system of sentential calculus, with its rules of inference. Naturally, I will state these rules in a natural language, presupposing that you understand what the rules thus introduced 'mean'. But suppose a doubt arises in me as to whether you have understood them correctly. How do I discover this?—Naturally, by observing your behavior when you carry out a formal inference, that is, when you write down formulae in accordance with agreed 'game rules'. That you do understand what the rules of inference mean is something that has been defined through the behavior you exhibit when you carry out a formal inference.

Finally, S_1 comes up with the following objection.

I do understand that the principle of logical behaviorism is a necessary consequence of the requirement of intersubjectivity, that is, the postulate that my sentences describing my own experiences must have some factual content for other people. Since they may have such consequences for other people only on the condition that they represent states of my body, I do admit that my φ-sentences must be interpreted as f-sentences, as we have done. But I do not see that this *postulate itself of intersubjectivity* has been given any justification. It seems to me that I am free to deny it. In that case, what would you do? What would you do, if I now tell you that I want to talk to myself, in a monologue, and not to you, in a dialogue? In which case I would refuse to accept your equivalences between my φ-sentences and certain f-sentences. In fact, I now announce that I hold the postulate of intersubjectivity to be arbitrary; hence, I will renounce it.

To this S_2 gives the following reply:

What you renounce in your words, that you accept in your deeds. I may learn about your theoretical rejection of the principle of intersubjectivity only if you execute it in practice. You can renounce this principle in one way only, by remaining silent. At most you can say, with Prince Hamlet: 'The rest is silence'.

Index

53/.42